KV-428-658

Good Business

BISHOP BURTON LRC
WITHDRAWN

ACCESSION No. T047838

CLASS No. 658·401

Good Business

Your World Needs You

Steve Hilton & Giles Gibbons

Good Business
Steve Hilton and Giles Gibbons

Copyright © 2002 and 2004 Good Business Ltd. Published by TEXERE, an imprint of Thomson Business and Professional Publishing, a part of the Thomson Corporation. Thomson, the Star logo, TEXERE, and Thomson Business and Professional Publishing are trademarks used herein under license.

Printed and bound in the United States by JD Edwards Brothers.
ISBN 1-58799-161-6

1 2 3 4 5 6 7 8 9 07 06 05 04

For more information, contact Texere at Thomson Higher Education, 5191 Natorp Boulevard, Mason, OH 45040 USA. Or you can visit our website at www.thomson.com/learning/texere.

ALL RIGHTS RESERVED. No part of this work covered by the copyright hereon may be reproduced or used in any form or by any means—graphic, electronic, or mechanical, including photocopying, recording, taping, Web distribution or information storage and retrieval systems—without the written permission of the author.

For permission to use material from this text or product, submit a request online at http://www.thomsonrights.com. Any additional questions about permissions can be submitted by email to thomsonrights@thomson.com.

This publication is designed to provide accurate and authoritative information in regard to the subject matter covered. It is sold with the understanding that the publisher is not engaged in rendering legal, accounting, or other professional services. If legal advice or other expert assistance is required, the services of a competent professional person should be sought.

Composed by: Macfarlane Production Services, Markyate, Hertfordshire, England.

The names of all companies or products mentioned herein are used for identification purposes only and may be trademarks or registered trademarks of their respective owners. Texere disclaims any affiliation, association, connection with, sponsorship, or endorsements by such owners.

This book is printed on acid-free paper.

"From virtue comes all wealth"
Socrates

"I want to discuss *why* a company exists in the first place. In other words, why are we here? I think many people assume, wrongly, that a company exists simply to make money. While this is an important result of a company's existence, we have to go deeper and find the real reasons for our being. As we investigate this, we inevitably come to the conclusion that a group of people get together and exist as an institution that we call a company so they are able to accomplish something collectively that they could not accomplish separately – they make a contribution to society, a phrase which sounds trite, but is fundamental."

David Packard, co-founder of Hewlett-Packard, speech to employees, 1960

Contents

Contents

Introduction

The Israelis and the Palestinians were shouting abuse. Feelings were running high, tempers getting frayed. Any minute now, one side would defeat the other. But who would be the victor; who would be the vanquished?

The result should come as a big surprise.

For in the event, neither of these traditional foes was beaten. Because the Israelis and the Palestinians were not fighting each other – they were fighting the United States.

This is not some ghastly and perverse doomsday scenario, with the international coalition against terror unravelling in ways that even the most conspiratorial Pentagon planner could never have imagined. This is the scene at the University of Vermont in a snowy February in 2002. Not a war game, but a basketball game. Israelis and Palestinians shooting hoops instead of each other. Playing on the same side. Co-operating. Yes, even hugging one another. As Iris Goren, an Israeli basketball coach put it: "we became a group, and a team, and we got to know each other, and now we'll take that back to the Middle East and try to carry this spirit of peace and unity with us in our lives."

A month later, a few blocks from Ground Zero, Ed Moses and Boris Becker led a team of international sports celebrities up to the seventh floor of an office building in Cooper Square, Lower Manhattan. Inside, groups of young people affected by the atrocities of September 11th were learning to rebuild their lives. Through structured programs of gymnastics, grief counselling and life skills training, they showed that out of tragedy could arise hope. They were an inspiration, even to the legendary sporting heroes that came to be with them that day.

About the same time, a curious mood could be detected in corporate America. The latest annual reports of blue-chip behemoths like General Electric and IBM did not look like the usual deluge of narcissistic spin. They'd all but dried up, those perennial rivers of rose-tinted verbiage pouring from companies' headquarters suites. In their place, that rarest of flowers in the corporate jungle: humility. Some observers suggested that reading this new breed of annual reports was rather like attending a meeting of Alcoholics Anonymous, or a church confessional. "Forgive us America, for we have sinned." And what prompted this bout of ego-downsizing? Here's a clue: it's the name of the business that's notched up the rather remarkable achievement of single-handedly undermining people's faith in corporations, capitalism and globalization more effectively than millions of passionate street protestors have been able to over the last few years.

Enron; 9/11; a basketball game. These things are intimately connected, and it's those connections that we'd like to explain to you in this book.

In 1994, while working at the ad agency Saatchi & Saatchi, we helped launch an anti-racism campaign. It was the moment when something crystallized in our minds, an idea which had been nagging away at us throughout the time we'd spent putting the campaign together. You see, we thought we'd found something: a new way of tackling social problems, and a positive response to people's concerns about an over-commercialized, over-branded, over-globalized capitalist world. No honestly, we did.

We got there in a roundabout way. We'd needed to raise money to make the anti-racism campaign happen – our non-profit client barely had enough to pay for lunch, never mind a big budget media blitz. So we had optimistically toured the well-appointed offices of our Saatchi & Saatchi clients with what we thought was an enticing begging bowl, asking the marketing directors of big brands if they'd support the campaign. This was a tried and tested path for public service advertising: work out your message, get a corporate sponsor, then hope it has an effect on public attitudes and behavior. Anti-racism, anti-smoking, anti-drugs, anti-leaving the lights on in a room you're not in. It always seemed to be the government, or non-profits, or quasi-government bodies telling people not to do something for the sake of a cleaner, greener, safer, better world. All well and good, except that many social problems appeared to be getting worse. It struck us that the traditional levers of social change were getting a little rusty. We started to think more deeply about the anti-racism message. How could we make sure it really had an effect? How could we stop it turning into yet another here today, gone tomorrow, good cause campaign?

We thought about some of the other marketing campaigns we'd been involved with. Not just for big global brands, but for Presidents and Prime Ministers, for political parties, for pressure groups. We'd done this all over the world, from Russia to Colombia, from Hong Kong to Norway, from Australia to the UK and the USA. And what was striking in all those countries was the degree to which citizens felt disengaged from their politicians, losing their faith in the ability of conventional politics to make their lives better. Even in new democracies like Poland and Hungary, people often saw politics as nothing but a managerial and technocratic function, and worse, one that was poorly managed and technically inept. But oddly, while they had little faith in politics, they placed considerable trust in those big global brands. Consumer brands didn't break their promises like the politicians did: when people saw an ad for a consumer product, and then went and bought that product, it usually delivered exactly what it promised. And especially in newly-capitalist economies, it was interesting to see that people actually admired business: corporations provided jobs and created wealth, they gave people a sense of direction, they provided purpose and meaning to their lives.

But like the Force in *Star Wars*, business had a dark side. We observed in our political work around the globe a gnawing concern that increasingly, the world was being run for commercial interests, with human interests coming a distant second. There was a feeling that consumerism was driving out values that were, well, valuable: like community, and morality. Market capitalism may be a dependable source of creature comforts, but was the resulting society the good society, or just a society of goods?

So as we prepared to reveal our anti-racism campaign one sunny day in the mid 1990s, we felt the satisfying clunk-click of two arguments slotting together ...

Few people would disagree that despite the best efforts of politicians, we're not making as much progress as we'd like in tackling social problems. Equally, few people would disagree that business is a powerful force in society. Sometimes good, sometimes bad, but always powerful. So why couldn't that power be harnessed to help tackle social problems? And wouldn't it be in a corporation's commercial interests to play a more active social role, helping to show that consumerism needn't always be a shallow and destructive religion? Wouldn't it be good business for business to do good?

We tried to persuade our Saatchi & Saatchi clients to give us more than their money. We wanted to tap in to their expertise in changing consumer behavior, and harness this as a way of changing social behavior. We wanted them to incorporate the messages of the anti-racism campaign in their own advertising; we wanted to use their commercial skills and resources for a social purpose. But our begging bowl remained as empty as the streets on Superbowl night. The corporations we spoke to almost invariably supported our aims, and in many instances were willing to help in a practical way: they could give us some money from their philanthropy budgets, they said. They could give us some free airtime, or a few billboard sites or newspaper ads from the campaigns they'd already booked for themselves. But they didn't really understand what we were going on about when we tried to explain that they could have a potentially dramatic social role, that they could actually use their business to change the world. Not just through the products and services they made, not just through the wealth they created – but through harnessing their unique and powerful position in the public consciousness for social, as well as commercial ends.

Looking back on it now, it's hardly surprising they didn't understand. This is a pretty fraught argument. Companies are understandably nervous about taking on new and unfamiliar responsibilities. And people are understandably nervous about corporations taking on a still greater influence over the state of the world. But we had got it into our heads that uniting social and commercial objectives could help solve two problems simultaneously: the problem faced by corporations – how to deal with the growing anti-capitalist, anti-globalization clamor, and the problem faced by governments: how to deliver social change in an age where public faith in politics is at an all-time low.

So we left our jobs at Saatchi & Saatchi in order to make it happen. We set up a company called Good Business, and this book is the story of what's gone on since then. (Those of you who have eaten there will be pleased to know that we've left out the story of the Good Cook, the community restaurants that we set up and ran for a while.) Our idea is one that still baffles many people, which is why we've tried to explain it in this book. It's also an idea that horrifies many people, for different reasons. Some, who are fiercely critical of business and the capitalist system, see corporations as the source of most of our problems. The idea that these corporations could help make the world a better place comes across as a bit of a sick joke: "Yeah right, let's put Enron in charge of tackling social problems, and while we're at it, let's put the pedophiles in charge of our kindergartens". Others think that business is just fine thank you very much, and that the last thing we should be doing is adding global salvation to its in-tray. But bear with us: why not think about it with an open mind, at least while you're reading this book? You could consider the possibility that not everything that business does is bad, and that it might be possible to change business so that it does more good. You might also be prepared to accept that it could be in corporations' commercial interests to behave like this. In other words, boringly enough, the anti-capitalists and the pro-capitalists could actually reach a consensus. By the end of this book, we hope you'll all agree that it seems pretty insane to waste the huge resources of corporations by rejecting the possibility that they could use those resources to help society.

Since you're very busy, we thought it might be useful if we told you the bits you can skip, depending on what you already know and what you already think. Chapter 1 can be avoided if you're not particularly interested in what all this anti-capitalist, anti-globalization fuss is about, and why it might not be as simple as some of the critics make out. If you're completely sure that every-thing about business and capitalism is inherently bad, you can probably skip Chapter 2 as well, because all it does is try to put the other side of the story, challenging some of the myths that are out there about the role of corporations and brands in our world today.

Since we first had the idea that corporations could benefit commercially from taking a more active role in society, and that this would benefit society as well, the business case for such an approach has become infinitely stronger. As we'll explain in Chapter 3, it's no longer a commercially viable option for com-panies to ignore what has become known as corporate social responsibility – but if you're up to speed with all the ins and outs of this strange new phenomenon, you can probably move straight to Chapter 4, where we explain why social responsibility isn't really enough. That if companies really want to see commercial returns from their social impact, and if we really want to see companies make the most of their potential to help society, they'll need to do more than what's necessary to cover all their bases and avoid criticism. It won't be enough simply to be "responsible" on issues like corporate governance, environmental protection and child labor. Corporations will have to follow a new doctrine: corporate social leadership.

If, like us, you find it tiring to get your head round airy-fairy concepts and prefer to deal in practical matters, then you'll enjoy Chapter 5, where we describe some examples of corporate social leadership by looking at the anatomy of corporations, and how various companies have used different bits of their anatomy for a dual purpose, social as well as commercial. It would be a shame to miss out on this part, as it includes some surprising tales. This is where the basketball game comes in, the one where Israelis and Palestinians were playing on the same team. Because that game is part of the work of a global car company that's teamed up with sports stars like Boris Becker, Pele and Ed Moses to tackle social problems all over the world. And this chapter is where we show you what a soft drinks brand is doing about the AIDS crisis in Africa. And how one of the most demonized brands on the planet is helping to reduce bullying, racism and anti-social behavior amongst young children. But if you prefer fiction to fact, you might want to jump to Chapter 6, where we try to imagine some of the possibilities in the future: whether or not, for example, a corporation could get young people re-engaged in politics, or help the poorest people on earth achieve economic independence, or tackle the growing problems connected with mental health, or help bring about world peace – you know, nothing too ambitious. If you're really busy, or know already that you agree with us, then all you will want to read is Chapter 7. It's very short, and it describes in eminently practical detail what you can do to help change the world – as a consumer, an employee, a charity worker, a politician, a shareholder, or a Chief Executive.

The point of this book is to get you thinking, and then hopefully, to get you to act. It's not supposed to be some comprehensive survey of every social issue in the world, or of every aspect of business and capitalism. We're bound to have got lots of things wrong, and we know we've left lots of things out. Having said that, please try not to pick holes. The big picture is what matters, and the big picture looks like this.

We're pretty fed up with the idea that caring about people, that a belief in social justice and a desire for social progress, is something worthy, dowdy, dull and depressing; while vacuous celebrity-drenched consumerism is seen as glamorous and aspirational. This is obviously the wrong way round, but we reckon the answer lies in uniting these things, in bringing social values to consumerism and capitalism, not destroying one in favor of the other.

So the thing is, we're on a bit of a mission here. We want everyone to realize that they can help change the world. If you're worried about globalization, if you're concerned about social justice, there *is* something practical you can do. If you think it's an obscenity that one corner of the world lives in lavish wealth while most of it struggles in degrading poverty, there *is* something practical you can do about it. If you think it's an obscenity that much of your city lives in lavish wealth while certain corners of it struggle in degrading poverty, there *is* something you can do about it.

You don't have to wait, despairingly, for the politicians to sort things out. While they carry on thinking about the big things, we can all help do something about the small things. Add up all the small things, and something big will happen. The power is in your hands: you just need to know how to use it. That power is the power of business, something that we all have access to, whatever our station in life.

Shopping, working, trading, investing. We're all in business. Let's make sure it's good business.

Orthodoxy

Did capitalism save your life?

Without the drugs produced by pharmaceutical companies like GlaxoSmithKline, or the medical equipment produced by engineering companies like General Electric, there's a fair chance you would have been a victim of one of the myriad afflictions that we take in our stride today but which just a hundred years ago used to claim lives with dreadful regularity. Even if you take the view that government spending on medical research, training and healthcare is your true saviour rather than big business, you have to ask yourself what paid for that government spending. Taxes? Sure, but where do they come from? From companies, that's where. Whether it's a company that employs you, or a company that you own and run, it's companies and the people who work for them that are the source of nearly all the taxes we so lazily describe as "government money." If you work for the state or for a charity, you may think you have no immediate relationship with the business of capitalism, but it's the activities of capitalists that generate the money to pay your wages.

So what do people think of capitalism? What are they like, these curious individuals called capitalists who so ruthlessly dominate our lives? Ask that question in a focus group, and you'll get a strangely uniform answer. (A focus group, for those uninitiated in this modern form of tribal witch-doctoring, is a collection of around eight or ten "ordinary people" specially selected to sit in a room for a couple of hours so that they can be paid around $30 to eat plastic food, drink cheap wine, and give their opinions on some topic or other to a researcher working for whoever is interested in finding out the opinions of said "ordinary people." The subjects under discussion could range from the urgently vital: "Would you prefer Froot Loops if they had an extra layer of sugar frosting and we gave away a free make-your-own Homer Simpson horror belly with each packet?" to the spectacularly trivial: "Do you think the President should bomb Saddam Hussein or should he, you know, give the guy a chance to show he can play a constructive role in the fellowship of nations?" You may not think focus groups are that important – unless you're one of those canny people who make their living, and indeed get their daily meal, from attending these séances on a regular basis – but Britain's Prime Minister Tony Blair has gone on record as saying that the most powerful people in the world are members of focus groups. So now you know.)

These focus group members, when asked to depict "capitalists", unerringly draw pictures of stout men in bulging waistcoats and top hats chomping on big cigars. The same is true if you ask them to draw pictures of "business people", only in this scenario, the cigar and the top hat tend to be replaced by briefcases and cell phones. But the one picture that is never drawn by focus group members in such situations is the one that would be most accurate: a picture of themselves. Yes that's right, we're all capitalists now. We all keep those wheels spinning, from the charge-card shopaholic who can't let a day pass without a new pair of shoes, to the strait-jacketed lunatic whose daily dose of sedatives keeps the profits rolling in for some drug company or other. Capitalism, like illicit sexual fantasizing, is one of those things that we all do but not all of us admit to. Which is a shame, because capitalism is rather a good thing, and we should pat ourselves on the back for helping to keep it going.

Reliable collective social welfare provision on a mass scale is impossible without capitalism. New technologies and strategies to protect the environment are impossible without capitalism. Improving the quality of life for the poorest people on our planet is impossible without capitalism. And capitalism is impossible without profit-making companies, or to use the faintly more sinister-sounding term employed by their critics, corporations.

It may seem unnecessary, even patronizing, to be making such stupefyingly obvious points. What next, you're thinking? Are they going to be informing me that there are seven days in a week or that Michael Jackson has looked a bit peculiar since *Thriller*?

The reason for stating the obvious in this way is, frankly, that it's rarely stated these days. The fact that thanks to capitalism life expectancy is up, infant mortality is down, people's opportunities are transformed, their lives are easier, education is better, horizons are broader, self-expression is richer, environmental awareness is deeper, social concern is greater, global understanding and co-operation are possible: the fact that it's capitalism that has enabled all these good things to happen is just accepted, never acknowledged. But it's time we woke up and smelt the Starbucks coffee. Popular support for capitalism shouldn't be taken for granted, because there's a rising tide of opposition to it that we would be foolish to underestimate.

To be fair, capitalism has never exactly been popular. Because it's based on harsh and unpleasant sounding concepts like "return on investment," "profits," and "market forces," it's tended to attract pretty negative portrayals in popular culture. Think of recent movies like *The Insider* or *Erin Brockovich*; look at what the evil Mr Burns gets up to in *The Simpsons*. It's hardly surprising that focus groups see capitalists as manipulative, greedy scumbags when that is how capitalists are generally presented to the world. But in recent years, the mood has changed. No longer is it just a question of a latent hostility to capitalism occasionally surfacing in the media and entertainment worlds. Increasingly, we're being presented with a well-organized and reasoned critique of global capitalism. The *Financial Times* has taken this backlash so seriously that in the summer of 2001 it assigned one of its senior journalists to spend months with the leaders of the "anti-capitalist movement;" to assess its significance in a series of in-depth reports under the banner

BISHOP BURTON COLLEGE
LIBRARY

"Capitalism Under Siege – how anti-globalization activists are rattling the world's biggest companies and governments."[1]

The *FT* concluded – by a strange coincidence on September 11th 2001 – that "people in business and politics are right to take [the anti-capitalists] seriously. [There are] tens of thousands of committed activists at the nexus of a global political movement embracing tens of millions of people. Just over a decade after the fall of the Berlin Wall and the 'end of history' promised by Francis Fukuyama, who argued free market liberalism had triumphed forever, there is a growing sense that global capitalism is once again fighting to win the argument. In the last 18 months, a million people have taken to the streets in what has become a rolling globalization ... Taken together, the string of protests since Seattle in 1999, which have torn through Washington, Melbourne, Prague, Seoul, Nice, Barcelona, Washington DC, Quebec City, Gothenburg and Genoa have cost more than $250 million in security precautions, damage and lost business ... Voter turnout may be plummeting in Europe and the US, but political activism is enjoying a resurgence not seen since the Vietnam War ... It turns out to be a formidable movement. Or, to be precise, a movement of movements. Anti-globalization activism is diverse and inchoate, without a unified agenda or a traditional leadership. It is, however, well co-ordinated. It is well-informed. It is increasingly well-funded."

A movement of movements ... diverse and inchoate ... well-co-ordinated ... well-funded: the report's author, James Harding, could just as easily be President Bush talking about his "war" on global terrorism and Osama bin Laden's Al-Quaida network. There's a crucial difference though, and it's the reason why the anti-capitalist argument actually represents more of a long-term threat to the creation of a peaceful and prosperous world order than the terrorists do. In Harding's words, "most alarming for elected politicians and corporate leaders, a growing number of people think [the anti-capitalist movement] has mainstream values and mass appeal." Since September 11th, there may be fewer anti-capitalist protestors on the streets; but who thinks their arguments have just melted away?

As a result of the growing appeal of the anti-capitalist message, we're in danger of forgetting exactly why it is that the last century saw the most extraordinary advances in human progress. More importantly, we're in danger of believing some pernicious myths that are starting to gain popular currency – myths that challenge the very system we need to protect and improve if we want to advance social progress. So the aim of this first chapter is to examine and challenge this new orthodoxy, this idea that capitalism is a bad thing.

We're going to look directly at what the leading anti-capitalists have been saying. Why have they got big business and global capitalism in their sights? Why do they hate brands so much, and why is it mainly American brands that they hate? And what of the response to the anti-capitalists? We'll see if the main arguments that have been presented so far actually stack up. We'll show that although the points the anti-capitalists make may sometimes be unbalanced and extreme, they shouldn't just be ignored. At the same time, we'll highlight the fundamental mistake that anti-capitalists make, which is to see corporations as the "problem." We will introduce the notion that they could actually be part of the solution; that it's futile to think we can somehow tackle global poverty and inequality, deal with debilitating social issues, improve the quality of life for every citizen, and protect the environment for ourselves and future generations without harnessing the most powerful force for good at our disposal. What is this mysterious and munificent power? That unlikely hero, global capitalism, brought to you by profit-making corporations.

You may think that all this goes without saying. That basically – even if sometimes reluctantly – everyone agrees capitalism is a good thing (or at least, as Winston Churchill said about democracy, the worst possible system apart from all the others). Really? If you work for a major corporation today, you'd be forgiven for feeling a little beleaguered. You realize that you're a part of the capitalist system, so what are you to make of the growing appeal of the anti-capitalist movement? You know that your job and your family's future depend on your company making profits, so what are you supposed to think when you turn on the radio and hear the word profit spat out like a dirty word? You see the courts kept busy by lawsuits against corporations; you see your bosses on the defensive, fighting off critics from every quarter. When was the last time anyone had a good word to say about you and what your company does? When was the last time anyone told you that you and your company could help solve society's problems, rather than being the cause of them? When was the last time you felt proud of being part of the "business community"?

There seems to be an assumption on the part of many anti-corporate critics that not only is business a bad thing, but that it's a deliberately bad thing. That the motivation behind capitalist activity is inherently pernicious. Apart from the fact that the collective social impact of capitalism is overwhelmingly positive, as we will show, this is a pretty insulting and shabby way to describe the billions of people who go to work every day in the capitalist system wanting nothing more malevolent than to be successful in what they do.

Many readers who are instinctively (if perhaps vaguely) in sympathy with the anti-globalization argument will already be feeling their stomachs turn at this "poor little me" interpretation of the corporate psyche. Not only do corporations rape and pillage the environment, rip off their customers, exploit their workers and pay their top executives obscene salaries, but now we're supposed to feel sorry for them too because we don't all put the flags out every day and sing their praises? Not quite. The point is not to pretend that corporations never do anything bad; the point is to acknowledge that most of what they do is good, and that it's in all our interests for them to be successful. If we can agree on that, then we can have a sensible discussion about how to encourage more of the good things business does while discouraging the bad things. Because corporations are run by people, and because some people are rapacious, incompetent and dishonest, there will always be the risk of corporations staggering, Enronly, from greedy peak to sleazy trough. We need constant vigilance, and frankly more vigilant vigilance, to stop this happening. But it would be madness to allow such corporate criminality to prevent an open debate about the potential of business to help our world.

The problem is, most of the current popular debate about business is so one-sided that it's stretching things even to call it a debate. Of course, it's always easier to criticize than to discuss, but still ... If you look at the recent crop of books about business and society that have made the jump from the business pages to the news and features pages, the ones that have gained a momentum in popular culture; the ones that have become the sacred texts of the counter-capitalists on the streets – they're almost all unremittingly hostile to business and the principles of the capitalist system.

These books are well-researched and well-argued. Their authors' criticisms of corporations and of the relationship between business, government and society deserve to be taken seriously. Their part in changing corporate behavior for the better, with potentially far-reaching benefits, should not be underestimated. But look what happens when valid criticism turns into absolutist dogma. When Friedrich Engels toured the industrial heartlands of Great Britain in the mid-nineteenth century in order to draw attention to the appalling working and living conditions of the people he and Karl Marx described as the proletariat, he provided a crucial public service and undoubtedly contributed to a better life for millions of people. However, he also contributed to the development of an economic, social, and political order that caused indescribable cruelty and hardship for decades to come in those countries that were forced to turn away from capitalism. And so today, it's essential that we distinguish between those anti-capitalist arguments that are accurate and legitimate, and those that are alarmist and potentially destructive.

The black and white picture that is increasingly presented: capitalists black, everyone else white – is simplistic and wrong. The motives ascribed to business leaders: world domination and screw anyone or anything that stands in my way – is a false caricature.

And the remedy proposed for most of our social ills: destroy the power of the corporations – would amount to a tragic missed opportunity if it were ever to be implemented.

Here are some things that we all want to see: social cohesion, environmental protection, the elimination of absolute poverty, the reduction of crime, world peace, individual freedom, opportunity for all. You could sum it up by combining into one phrase two of the most famous constitutional slogans on earth: life, liberty, fraternity, equality and the pursuit of happiness. The critics of capitalism seem to believe that business is an enemy of these objectives, and that in order to achieve them, capitalism must be fundamentally changed.

But there's another way of looking at it. Rather than separating business from our objectives for society, putting capitalism on trial while politicians, state employees, charity workers, activists, campaigners, writers and journalists figure out how to make the world a better place – why don't we involve the corporate sector in that quest? Wouldn't it be a better idea to stop the blanket denunciations of capitalism, recognize the good that it's already done, and develop its potential to do more good in the future? Sadly, this kind of engagement is anathema to the opponents of business. They close the door on any kind of inclusive approach, since it compromises the purity of their critique. Their binary world view allows for no rapprochement.

In order to sustain the faith of their followers, the intellectual prophets of the anti-globalization movement make the dubious claim that salvation depends on the current world order being decisively overthrown. They talk in revolutionary terms about smashing the system, changing the rules. In her hugely influential book *No Logo*, the Canadian writer Naomi Klein talks about the need to "subvert" multinational corporations, and demands "a citizen-centered alternative to the international rule of the brands."[2] The fighting talk is echoed by George Monbiot, a British environmental and anti-capitalist campaigner. Monbiot has developed a reputation as the leading critic of Tony Blair's policy of involving private companies in the financing and management of schools and hospitals in the UK. His book *Captive State – The Corporate Takeover of Britain* is a brilliant and rigorous attack on big business, but like most polemics, lurches every now and again into assertions and rallying cries that are preposterously unbalanced and over the top: "The struggle between people and corporations will be the defining battle of the twenty-first century. If the corporations win, liberal democracy will come to an end."[3] No less breathlessly nightmarish is the vision outlined by Cambridge academic Noreena Hertz in the concluding passage of her book *The Silent Takeover – Global Capitalism and the Death of Democracy.* Her phrase "Silent Takeover" refers to the alleged replacement of democratically elected government by global corporations wielding unrestrained economic power. It could mean, she argues, that "the world we live in will be one in which corporations rule, markets are above the law, and voting becomes a thing of the past."[4]

This type of apocalyptic doom-mongering is not confined to authors on the liberal left of the political spectrum. Stuart Reid, deputy editor of the right-wing *Spectator* magazine in the UK has attacked British Prime Minister Tony Blair for "removing power from democratically elected governments and handing it to large corporations."[5] To round off this brief survey of radical chic polemic, let's bring on the American social critic Thomas Frank. Tucked away in *One Market Under God*, his exhilaratingly violent and coruscating dissection of what he calls "market populism," is his argument that what society "desperately requires in order to restore a sense of justice and fairness is not some final triumph of the corporation over the body and soul of humanity, but some sort of power that confronts business … "[6]

Frank's use of the word "confronts" is revealing, and symbolic of the polarization that's taking shape. Black and white. Business versus society. Capitalism or social justice. Corporations are granted no role whatever in dealing with social and environmental challenges: they're defined as the problem; incapable of helping, excluded from civilized debate. It's us against them: you can forget about international terrorism or murderous religious fundamentalism, just get ready to choose which side you're on in George Monbiot's "defining battle of the twenty-first century," the one between democracy and capitalism.

In a nutshell, the charge-sheet reads like this. Big global brands exploit those of us in the rich parts of the world by using manipulative techniques to create in us the previously non-existent desire for junk with a logo sold at extortionate prices to feed the insatiable demands of rapacious shareholders for ever higher profits. They peddle the myth of a lifestyle that we can never achieve and by using their economic muscle to elbow out of the way traditional and wholesome institutions like family, local community, religion, and culture, they've turned us into miserable, craven, overworked, greedy consumption addicts who've lost sight of the basic principles of humanity. They've degraded all sense of public space by smearing their garish marketing materials over every available surface, including our schools, and they've turned our cherished pastimes like sport and music into commercial transactions through the cynical device of bribing those who run such activities with irresistible amounts of sponsorship money. Their expansionist mania forces smaller companies out of business, wipes out craft skills built up over centuries, and turns the countryside from the food basket of the nation into a playground for braying super-rich yuppies. This process has been aided and abetted by a ruling class of unprincipled political cowards from all parties who, desperate for cash to finance their increasingly tawdry election campaigns, terrified of raising taxes lest they be flung out of office, and prepared to do whatever it takes to encourage businesses to invest in their country, lie prostrate at the feet of each passing corporation, giving them everything they want in secret deals that turn the bosses into our rulers and our rulers into corporate stooges. As a result, the global corporations career unchecked down a path of unthinking environmental destruction, immoral scientific experimentation, and stony-faced human exploitation. Blimey. And that's just at home! Are you still standing? Look what's going on in the developing world ...

Here, big business leaves people twice enslaved – first to the sick and decadent dream of the brands, so that indigenous cultures are wiped out in favour of homogenized western pap; and second to the factory owners who on the corporations' behalf snatch twelve-year-olds from sunny fields to work unceasingly in dingy sweatshops that make the factories Friedrich Engels described in his *The Condition of the Working Class in England* look like the trendy Manhattan lofts of dot-com start-ups before the bubble burst, complete with ping-pong tables and bowls of organic fruit.

Can it really be so simple? When so many billions of people depend for their personal and family well-being on successful capitalist enterprises, it seems bizarre to simply condemn those businesses out of hand. When so many of the innovations that improve the quality of life for individuals and communities around the world are produced by capitalist corporations, it just doesn't ring true to label them all as part of an enemy that needs to be confronted, resisted, beaten. Given the energy, brainpower and creativity that reside in the corporate sector, isn't it wasteful to push it aside in the angry belief that business is inherently bad? What about the possibility that the very things that are easiest to dislike about big business – the cultural dominance, the economic clout – could actually be turned into positive forces for good in society? To an impartial observer, the rigid certainties of the anti-capitalists seem too extreme to be taken as read. But there's no denying that their arguments have struck a chord; and there can be no questioning of their motives, which are rooted in a sense of social justice. So what is it exactly that so enrages these people?

The immediate answer can be found in the historical (and sometimes current) behavior of corporations themselves. For many years, companies both large and small have done things that fully deserve the strongest condemnation. Unencumbered by the scrutiny to which they're increasingly subject today, many businesses in the past would think nothing of despoiling the environment, damaging local communities, covering up health risks associated with their products, exploiting their workers, misleading their customers. While still making a positive *economic* contribution (for example by creating jobs, paying taxes, developing socially beneficial new products and services and so on), their *social* impact was often negative, and substantially so. It is these negative social impacts that are the starting point for today's anti-globalization activists. They apply considerable effort and forensic skill to the task of highlighting the bad things that corporations do. In this, they should be supported and applauded, and in Chapter 3, we show how businesses should react to this type of scrutiny, which quite rightly is bound to increase.

But is it really rational to denounce the entire capitalist system on the basis of such corporate transgressions? Most businesses are mostly good, most of the time. When they step out of line, by all means cry foul. But that's no reason to argue that the overall structure is flawed, any more than we should send the concept of romantic love to the scrapheap just because many relationships don't work out. There's a strong flavor of conspiracy theory to the anti-capitalist philosophy, and a hint of it is revealed in this extract from *No Logo*: "Corporations are increasingly serving as the common thread by which labor, environmental and human rights violations can be stitched together into a single political ideology."[7] Think about the meaning of that sentence. Naomi Klein, if we take her words literally, is arguing that corporations, in conscious acts of political ideology, deliberately set out to violate basic rights along the lines she describes. Anyone who's spent any time at all working in business will be scratching their head in amazement at the idea that business leaders have the time or the inclination to construct and implement any type of political ideology – they've got enough on their plate simply doing their job. Even if Klein's intention is simply to describe the combined consequence of disparate business decisions, her use of the word "ideology" feels like the over-egging of a pudding that's hardly lacking in rich ingredients. Another writer, Benjamin R. Barber, has gone even further and set up the choice facing the planet as *Jihad vs McWorld*, where capitalism and globalization represent an ideology of "sterile cultural monism."[8] You can't help feeling that alongside the legitimate criticisms of corporate behavior, there's a recurring whiff of plain prejudice.

Diane Coyle, in her book *Paradoxes of Prosperity*, captures this feeling neatly, describing Naomi Klein's world view as being "in the slightly patronizing tradition of critiques of consumerism, dating back at least to Aldous Huxley's *Brave New World*, which usually imply that the masses have rather doubtful taste and don't really know what's good for them. It sneers at the lack of originality and exaggerates the passivity of consumers, who in reality choose a brand for its signal of quality and consistency as well as the lifestyle image it encourages them to aspire to. Whatever you think about McDonald's, eating at the sign of the golden arches will give you a reliable and cheap meal above a certain minimum standard. Some people even like the food."[9]

McDonald's, alongside other (usually American) global brands like Nike and Coca-Cola, provides an easy outlet for a real sense of disquiet about the intrusion of the market into every nook and cranny of our lives. But let's get a sense of proportion: McDonald's at least provides a service for everyone, unlike the painfully hip, over-priced and exclusive cafés that are the favored watering holes of those who plot the downfall of big business. With its global presence, consistent quality, good value, friendly service, and welcoming atmosphere, McDonald's is one of the most democratic institutions on the planet. This doesn't mean every right-thinking person should go out and buy a Big Mac Meal as an act of global solidarity; nor does it mean we should overlook any lapses it may make from acceptable standards of corporate behavior. But surely it's reasonable to acknowledge what's good about McDonald's as well as what's bad? What's wrong with noting that in countless neighborhoods around the world, McDonald's provides a useful community service, a meeting point for people with nowhere else to go? You don't even have to dress it up with social meaning: isn't it enough that billions of people actually like McDonald's? Are these people all wrong?

It's also worth pointing out that a sophisticated and well-resourced global company like McDonald's, with the McSpotlight ready to illuminate even the slightest wrong-doing wherever it may occur, pays far more detailed attention to its social responsibilities than, say, a small local restaurant. Prompted by their numerous and vocal critics, big global businesses like McDonald's are pioneering ways to monitor and improve their environmental and social impact while profitably meeting our needs as consumers. And because, for business efficiency reasons, such companies need to apply the same standards everywhere they operate, they are often a force for improving social and environmental conditions when they enter less developed markets. Indeed it's precisely because such corporations are big, global, rich and powerful that they can make a positive contribution to social progress – this is a central theme of this book, and is explored in more detail in subsequent chapters. But we'll never make the most of these potential benefits as long as we shut business out of the discussion, as long as we characterize capitalism as part of the problem rather than the solution.

It's easy to see why people get steamed up about the dominance of big global brands. It goes with the territory of being successful, and it applies not just to companies but to countries. In the immediate aftermath of the terrorist attacks on the World Trade Center and the Pentagon in September 2001, many Americans took to the airwaves in displays of mystified angst: "why do so many people hate us?" they wondered, "what have we done?" The answer is not hard to find. It starts with the cumulative impact of US foreign policy since the Second World War, which looks to many – and in particular to Muslim – eyes like a combination of oppression and hypocrisy, with the promotion of American strategic interests overriding all other concerns and exposing as the most ludicrous cant the United States' claims to be universal and consistent champions of democracy. Organizing a military coup to depose the democratic government of Iran in 1956; helping to overturn the general election results in Algeria in 1992, and consistently backing the repressive religious extremism of the feudal regime in Saudi Arabia are not the best ways to convince Muslim citizens that you're on their side. But these are not the most important reasons for suspicion of the US. The rise in some people's blood pressure when the word America is mentioned is mainly because America is top country, and that's that. Everyone hated Britain when the British Empire ruled the world; for a short period in the late twentieth century, it was Japan that took on the role of the world's favorite whipping-boy, as mass media panic broke out on the grounds that we'd all be going to work in overalls and eating sushi. Of course, now that Japan's economic dominance has receded, we *are* all eating sushi, which just goes to show that you don't have to have your cake in order for others to eat it. Or something.

The same type of psychology is at work in the anti-globalization culture. There are many specific, detailed and valid criticisms that could be made of a company like McDonald's. But then, those same criticisms could be applied to nearly all fast food suppliers – it's just that McDonald's takes the rap, which goes with the territory of being the world leader in the market. The consequence of this perhaps inevitable character assassination is that it's almost impossible to get a hearing for the positive characteristics of big businesses like these. Many people express concern about the wages and employment conditions of McDonald's employees, the infamous McJob victims. But do they feel as bad about the local deli or corner shop, where wages are almost certainly lower, working hours are longer, and where any staff member that dares to raise the thorny subject of training programs or career development opportunities of the type that are standard practice in corporations like McDonald's would soon find themselves out on their ear? No, you don't see many liberal activists picketing Hank's 24/7 grocery store.

The real reason for so many people's readiness to bite the hand that (much to their consternation) feeds their children is often just as much emotional as it is rational. A generation that has benefited to an unprecedented degree from the capitalist system has somehow developed a deep distaste for business. You can add to that a healthy dose of anti-American feeling, for which globally dominant US brands are such a convenient cipher. And so it's a natural step for people with genuine and legitimate social concerns to feel that they're doing their bit by professing a dislike for the big brands. These prejudices are powerful, and significant. Superficially, it may not seem to particularly matter that business, capitalism, even America, are not universally loved. Isn't it enough that we buy their crappy products: do we really have to like them as well? The answer is of course no we don't, but it would be helpful not to hate them, since by hating them, we turn a blind eye to their potential to help us. That's why it's important to remind ourselves of the huge and positive contribution that capitalism has made, and is making, to our world.

But it would be a mistake to overdo the emphasis on élite anti-business and anti-American prejudice in shaping the anti-globalization movement. Such prejudice may be there on the part of some anti-capitalists, but a mistrust of big business is certainly not just an élite preoccupation, and even if it was, this doesn't mean that concrete arguments about business behavior aren't valid. When confronting the anti-globalization phenomenon, many business leaders, commentators and politicians tend to fall back on the limp line of attack that the protestors are just a bunch of spoilt rich kids, bellyaching pointlessly about things they don't understand, looking down their noses at the consuming masses, with no substantive arguments worth considering. However true it may sometimes be, all that this type of attack does is give the protesting classes an easy riposte. Here's Thomas Frank again, talking about the reaction of centre-left politicians like Bill Clinton and Tony Blair when accused of selling out to corporate interests under the guise of free-market populism: " ... when they are called to task over the collection of privatization, deregulation and sweetheart deals that make up their industrial policy, they fall back mechanically on the criticism-as-élitism patter that they can only have learned from the American right."[10] Frank then quotes a British journalist, Nick Cohen, a columnist for *The Observer* newspaper: "When you attack them, you are accused by the élite movers and Third Way shakers of being a 'liberal élitist' even though you have no chance of getting near power because you suffer from the crushing disability of not being a businessman."[11]

While it's an interesting development for a journalist to describe himself as being nowhere near power – in our media-obsessed information age, it seems like quite an influential place to be – Cohen's got a point. The reason that the anti-business mood has caught on so strongly is precisely because it's not just an élite preoccupation, and precisely because it's not just about prejudice. There are real issues of social and environmental performance, ethics, accountability, and justice that concern citizens in societies right across the globe; in the developing world as well as in the richer countries. It's not good enough to dismiss these concerns with an airy and glib insult. That's just as patronizing as the attitude of many anti-capitalists to popular culture and to consumers who worship big brands.

There's another lame criticism that's sometimes wheeled out, particularly by politicians, on those increasingly rare occasions when the anti-capitalists are challenged rather than indulged. When discussing this issue, politicians like to focus on the easy and predictable target of the violence that has tended to accompany anti-capitalist demonstrations. World leaders, rather than bothering actually to address the anti-globalization arguments on an intellectual level, are happy to take the simplistic route of describing those who believe in the arguments as mindless thugs, vandals, hooligans, a travelling circus of social misfits and drop-outs … you know the kind of stuff. Again, while some of this may be true, it's a complete cop-out. Simply attacking the anti-globalization movement for the violent activities of the relatively tiny number of young criminals who misappropriate its banner is actually rather infantile and reveals a lack of confidence, like having a go at the Ku Klux Klan on the grounds of inadequate fire safety procedures at their public rallies. Politicians should fight the anti-capitalist philosophy with reasoned arguments, as well as fighting the anti-capitalist demonstrators with riot police. To be fair, there is one politician who seems to get this point: Tony Blair. Here's what he had to say on this subject in October 2001, in his keynote speech to the annual conference of the British Labour party: "I realize why people protest about globalization. We feel powerless, as if we were now pushed to and fro by forces beyond our control. But there's a risk that political leaders, faced with street demonstrations, pander to the argument rather than answer it. The demonstrators are right to say there's injustice, poverty, environmental degradation. But globalization is a fact ... the issue is how we use the power of community to combine it with justice. If globalization works only for the benefit of the few, then it will fail and will deserve to fail. But if we follow the principles that have served us so well at home – that power, wealth and opportunity must be in the hands of the many not the few – if we make that our guiding light for the global economy, then it will be a force for good ... "[12] Blair is consistently straightforward in backing globalization as the best tool available for the reduction of world poverty, and more recently, he's been promoting an exciting and inspirational vision of a new, globalized world community that can be mobilized to tackle pressing issues wherever they occur. But Blair is rare in this regard.

Another argument that's been used to try and fight back against the anti-globalization brigade is to mock their lack of a coherent policy platform. "We all know what they're against," the wise pundits opine, "but what are they actually for?" Well, if you want to know, read *The Other Davos*, edited by François Houtard and François Polet. It's a book that summarizes the proceedings of the World Social Forum, an event organized to coincide with the World Economic Forum in Davos, Switzerland, the annual meeting of what anti-capitalists would call the faceless plutocrats who run the world in the interests of corporations rather than citizens. The

World Social Forum, by contrast, is a meeting of colorful idealists who, in the words of Houtard, "know that there are alternatives to a system that privatizes the world, exhausts nature, and destroys life in the name of profit for a minority."[13] Here you will find all manner of very specific proposals for a new world order. Some of them are reasonable and sensible, while some of them are quite wrong-headed, based as they are on the notion that what we all really want is a return to some kind of medieval peasant lifestyle with local artisans and farmers meeting the needs of local populations, without recourse to the debilitating framework of capitalist exploitation that has snatched some mythical golden age away from us. But it's simply not true to say that there are no concrete alternatives being presented.

The peasant lifestyle schtick is the final refuge of the defenders of the status quo. "How can we take these anti-capitalists seriously?" they cry. "The consequence of their arguments would be to turn our modern industrial economies into Marxist states, or rural poverty traps." (Or even both at the same time – as has been the case in much of sub-Saharan Africa over the last fifty years or so.) This line of criticism points out, accurately enough, that most of the people who have actually been subjected to the Marxist or pre-capitalist model of economic organization are so enamored of the simple, old-fashioned, egalitarian way of life that they can't wait to abandon it in favor of the superior healthcare, education, hygiene, choice, opportunities, and sheer ease of living in the richer parts of the world – benefits that the anti-capitalists would allegedly throw away. Of course, the idea that life was better before capitalism came along to ruin everything is about as stupid as you can get, ranking alongside belief in the tooth fairy and the conviction that if only we'd been nicer to Hitler he wouldn't have tried to occupy most of Europe, as examples of some people's seemingly limitless capacity to put heart before head. The philosopher Thomas Hobbes described life in the "state of nature," before mankind organized himself into the structures of civil society, as "nasty, brutish, and short." He could equally well have been talking about life without capitalism, but try telling that to an anti-globalization street protestor.

On a stressful afternoon in the office, or stuck in a seemingly endless traffic jam, or plagued by hundreds of e-mails, or looking for work on meager social security benefits, or terrified by young hoodlums that hang out on the street, or choking on polluted air, or toiling away in an airless factory, you can see how the romanticized pre-capitalist lifestyle would hold some appeal for a few minutes. But why should it be a choice between bad capitalism and no capitalism? Surely the sensible approach is to accept capitalism but try to make the office less stressful, the traffic less jammed, the e-mails less frequent, the job opportunities greater, the hoodlums more positively motivated, the factory more pleasant? The vast majority of the anti-capitalist movement, and certainly its leading writers and thinkers, accept this more moderate view, so it's an unhelpful caricature to describe them all as latter day Lenins bent on returning us to the Middle Ages. But let's be honest: they do ask for it, as evidenced by some of the more colorful rhetoric quoted earlier. And if they're not actually against capitalism per se, then why are they content to be described as anti-capitalists? OK, OK, perhaps that's not a fair question either: after all, Arnold Schwarzenegger never used to object when he was described as an actor.

The reason for reviewing the various objections that have so far been made to the anti-globalization critique is to show how weak they are. Those who express concerns about the values and consequences of globalization and modern capitalism are either dismissed as élitists, condemned as hooligans, denounced for having no positive proposals, or ridiculed as hippies. None of these criticisms really stack up. It's just as myopic to ignore the merit in some of the anti-capitalists' arguments as it is for the anti-capitalists themselves to ignore the many good things about capitalism. The tendency to indulge in high-octane grandstanding, on both sides, has created an unhealthy state of affairs – a media and popular culture increasingly dominated by anti-business sentiment, and established political and social leaders uncertain about how to respond – and therefore just lashing out at any challenge to the status quo. Interestingly enough, the one area where you might find people responding constructively and creatively to the ever-growing number of assaults on the legitimacy of business is business itself. This is in many ways to be expected, since the best businesses are always far more closely in touch with social trends than politicians are, and tend to be nimble in responding to those trends – otherwise they lose out financially. That's not to say, however, that their responses are always the right ones, as we'll see later.

The real problem with the lack of a coherent and reasoned answer to the questions raised in books like *No Logo*, *Captive State* and *The Silent Takeover* is that the emerging camps – anti-business and pro-business – will move further and further apart through lack of engagement. So both sides should relax. There's plenty to agree on, and it's important that agreement is reached. Otherwise, there will be a danger that policy-makers and business leaders retreat into defensive positions where they do the bare minimum required to buy off protest, rather than embracing the opportunity that now exists to take on board the criticism, and to make capitalism the most powerful force for good in the twenty-first century world.

This book describes just some of those possibilities, and we hope it will inspire many others. But this won't happen if more and more people accept the current orthodoxy, and get it into their heads that business is a bad thing. Think of all the myths that are out there: you'd have to have cloth ears and a heart of stone not to have absorbed some of them. The next chapter looks at the top six, and presents what in some quarters will be seen as dangerously heretical views.

2

Heresy

Put yourself in the position of the cute donkey in the movie
Shrek. (You don't have to start talking like Eddie Murphy, but it
helps.) You're walking through the woods one day, and you're
captured by the evil king's men. But amazingly, you're saved from
a miserable fate by ... no, not a ruggedly handsome hero/
pneumatically sexy heroine, but by a truly hideous green ogre.
What a sight he is! Most normal people treat this ogre with the
utmost contempt – after all, he's hideous, and green. The ogre is
shunned by all right-thinking folk, banished to the fringes of
society, destined to live out his days in a disgusting swamp, with
nothing but maggots, parasites, and vermin for company. But you,
being a cute – and surprisingly open-minded – donkey, can see
beyond the superficial. You're grateful that the ogre has saved your
life, and now you want to hang out with the ogre, to work with
him. You're not put off by conventional wisdom; you can see the
good inside this foul, green creature. And so you embark upon a
series of exciting adventures, and amongst other things end up
ridding the world of the evil king. Hooray!

Guess what? Business is the ogre. You, of course, are the cute –
and open-minded – donkey. And so naturally, you want to look
beyond conventional wisdom to find the beauty that's inside the
ogre. But first, you have to steel yourself. You have to remember
that being hideous is no barrier to being good. Like it or not, that
means dealing with some of the misconceptions that exist about
business and globalization. Some of these myths are so well-

established that they're no longer presented as opinions about business; they're assumed to be fact. These myths are the building blocks of the anti-capitalist orthodoxy.

In this chapter, we'll look at six. Yes, it's the top six misconceptions about global capitalism. Perhaps not the most glamorous hit parade you've ever seen, but stay with us. Number One is "poverty and inequality," a tune you must have heard by now. Hot on its heels at Number Two is "human rights," followed at Number Three by the emotive "sweatshops and child labor." Fourth on the list, that old favorite: "cultural imperialism," followed by an equally well-worn classic, "profit is bad." Finally, at Number Six, a new entry in this rather odd rundown. Let's call it "every company wants to rule the world" – the idea that corporations are more powerful than governments.

Not one of these popular hits is quite what it seems. By looking in some detail at the facts behind the headlines, we hope to show that not only are globalization and capitalism not as bad as some might think; they're actually rather good things. It may seem like heresy to admit it, but so what? There was a time when you'd be sent to the swamp as a dangerous heretic for arguing that women should have the vote. With any luck, the ogre that is big business and global capitalism might start to look a little more attractive. And we come to a surprising conclusion about the anti-capitalists and anti-globalizers too.

Here we go then.

There is poverty in the world. There is globalization in the world. So it's obvious, isn't it, that globalization causes poverty? Well not really, any more than it's obvious that Friday causes Tuesday, or that *Seinfeld* causes *Friends*. Of course these things are not *un*related, and neither are poverty and globalization unrelated. But the incorrect assumption, taken as axiomatic in many quarters these days, that the former is the direct result of the latter, is extraordinarily difficult for some people to shake off. But it must be shaken off, otherwise it's impossible to have an open mind when looking at what's actually going on in the world.

How many times have you heard it said that globalization makes a few people richer (the guys with the top hats, cigars, etc.) at the expense of making many more people poorer (the twelve-year-olds snatched from the sunny fields, etc.). This has become so accepted as fact that it slips unchallenged into almost every discussion involving global business, global brands and the plight of the Third World. You'll hear this "fact" repeated around sophisticated dinner tables, in the columns of newspapers, in media reports on overseas events, in corporate meeting rooms, and amongst friends chatting about the state of the world. It's one of the most powerful forces driving support for the anti-capitalist movement, because it creates in people a sense of guilt: how can we reconcile our comfortable lives, replete with every conceivable creature comfort that consumerism can provide, with the knowledge that those comforts are bought at the price of poverty elsewhere on the planet? If this were true, it would absolutely be right to feel guilty.

But it isn't true.

How can we prove this? We'll try with some arguments, and we'll throw in some statistics. You may not believe the statistics, since they point to the opposite conclusion from the one reached by anti-globalization writers like Noreena Hertz, even though the sources of the statistics are in many cases the same.* You could look at this in a number of ways. You might just ignore them all, believing statistics to be the last refuge of didactic scoundrels. On the other hand, you may believe one set of statistics and reject the other, dismissing it as "selective." But the use of statistics is always selective. They're selected to back up an argument. So to be honest, whether or not you believe the ones that we've used will depend more than anything on where your initial sympathies lie. The purpose of using them is therefore not necessarily to convince,

---

* We have relied heavily in this section on Johan Norberg's *In Defence of Global Capitalism*, a comprehensive compendium of information and argument on the positive side of the globalization story. Page references are given in the Notes on pages 242–3.

merely to demonstrate that there *is* another way of looking at the globalized world, one in which the glass is half full rather than half empty. In this, more positive analysis, even bad things can be good if they're better than they were. Anyway …

The central proposition in this first anti-capitalist myth is that thanks to global capitalism, the rich have got richer while the poor have got poorer. Let's start with the first part. There isn't really any dispute that the rich have got richer, but just in case you're worried about it: in today's money, the average American income per head in 1900 was about $4,800; by 1998 it had risen to $32,000[1] – and the average income of a middle class family in the USA has more than doubled since 1950.[2] There's a huge mass of indicators describing the social benefits of this increase in wealth, but perhaps the most telling is that the average US life expectancy in 1900 was 47 years; in 1998 it was 77.[3] Yes there's inequality in western countries, yes there are people living on the streets, yes there are social problems. But who thinks these things didn't exist before global capitalism? Would you rather be alive in 1900 or 2000? In the developed countries of the world, life has got better, the rich have got richer, and so have the poor. There's no need to bore you with any more figures, because there's really only one key question to ask: how did it all happen?

It's important to be crystal clear about the process, because it's central to an understanding of the developing world's situation today. Forgive the simplistic nature of the following description, leaving out as it does the role of politics, trade unions and other social forces, but basically, it went like this. Capitalism, powered by the Industrial Revolution, enabled western societies to produce more goods. Workers became more productive, and because there were enough different customers around who wanted to buy the goods they made, the workers became more valuable, and were therefore paid more. This in turn made more money available to pay for the increased supply of goods produced, and so on. At the same time, global trade meant that goods could be bought from and sold to people in other countries, and raw materials could be imported in order to turn them into higher priced goods that other people wanted to buy. This upward spiral – actually nothing more complicated than people making, buying, and selling more of the things they wanted – made possible a huge growth in tax revenues that could be spent on tackling social problems like disease, hunger, and illiteracy. This was the first great leap forward in global prosperity and living standards – but it was pretty much limited to North America and Europe.

So much for the rich countries. What about the rest?

A second advance in prosperity began after the Second World War, and this time, it included developing countries, especially some in Asia. Because these newly industrializing countries didn't have to invent from scratch the technology that could help them to be more productive (like the western countries originally had to), they could move up the prosperity spiral more quickly. They rapidly developed their own businesses and began to specialize in what they were good at and what they could sell for a profit. Their workers became more valuable and were paid more, this led to higher consumer demand, and this in turn generated more production, profit, and investment. Taxes on all of this enabled higher government spending on infrastructure, education, and welfare services. So, for example, in twenty-five years, Taiwan achieved the sort of economic development that took a European country nearer a hundred years. Taiwan is one of the famous "Asian Tigers" who collectively performed the "Asian miracle." And it *was* pretty miraculous: in the 1960s, South Korea was as poor as Bangladesh, and half as rich as Zambia. Today, South Korea is twenty-seven times as rich as Zambia and one of the world's top ten economies, having doubled its wealth in eleven years[4] (while its Communist neighbor, North Korea, is collapsing in mass starvation). The number of Asian people living in extreme poverty (defined as less than a dollar of income a day) fell from six out of ten in 1975 to two out of ten today.[5] Japan, Taiwan, Korea, Singapore, Malaysia, Indonesia: how did these countries, one by one, make themselves richer? What about Vietnam – why has poverty fallen there but not in nearby Myanmar (Burma)?

The answer, just as for the rich West, lies in capitalism, business, and global trade. Those developing countries that got richer were the ones that opened their borders to foreign investment, cut the tariffs they charged on imports, and made sure they had in place the basics that would make a capitalist economy work: the right for people to own property and use it to make money, a properly enforced legal system, and so on. The two biggest countries in the region, China and India, were initially resistant, but followed these policies eventually – and it seemed to make things better for their people. In China, after Deng Xiaoping unleashed the capitalist economic experiment in the late 1970s, the numbers of people in extreme poverty fell by around half a billion.[6] Similarly in India, since the liberalizing economic reforms of the early 1990s, three hundred million people have been lifted out of poverty, whereas the numbers in poverty had been static or growing in previous decades.[7]

Just as in the West, these increases in wealth have brought real social benefits, with infant mortality in developing countries falling from a truly horrendous 18 percent in 1950 to 6 percent in 1995,[8] and the rate of illiteracy in those countries falling from 70 percent of the population in the 1950s to 30 percent today.[9] That still leaves 900 million adults who can't read and write,[10] but still, it's progress. Villages that once had only mud huts now have solid brick houses and electricity; more girls are going to school; new opportunities are opening up; people have greater personal freedom and independence.

These developing countries are a lot poorer than the rich western countries. But they're also a lot richer than they once were. And yet it is the very policies that China, India, and the Asian Tigers have benefited from over the past fifty years that the anti-capitalists so vigorously attack. They say they want it to stop. But why would anyone want to stop this process when in the fifty or so years it's been going on, according to the United Nations Development Programme, world poverty has fallen faster than in the previous five hundred?[11] When in the 1990s, the number of people on less than a dollar a day fell from 1.3 billion to 1.2 billion?[12] OK, it's still 1.2 billion too many, but surely we must be doing something right if the numbers of people in poverty are falling so rapidly, in historical terms?

So perhaps the more serious objection to global capitalism is not that it makes people poorer, but that it makes people more unequal. The anti-capitalists often claim that hidden amongst the overall income statistics is a widening gap between rich and poor: that the economies of developing countries may indeed have grown, but that this growth has benefited the rich élites at the expense of the poor peasants.

This inequality argument is always a divisive one, at home just as much as on the global front. Many people can't see the problem with inequality: as long as everyone's getting richer, who cares? But in this instance, your philosophical and moral standpoint on the equality debate doesn't really matter, since the "widening gap," though easy enough to believe in, doesn't actually exist. A study of forty years' worth of income statistics in eighty countries showed that economic growth benefits the poor just as much as it benefits the rich.[13] Globalization and capitalism are associated with greater equality, not greater inequality. Other figures show that overall, between 1965 and 1998, while the average world income nearly doubled from $2,497 to $4,839, the poor actually saw their incomes rise by more than the rich. The per capita income of the richest 20 percent of people in the world rose from $8,315 to $14,623, up by 75 percent; but for the poorest 20 percent it went up from $551 to $1,137, an increase of more than 100 percent.[14] Neither is it the case that inequalities *between* countries have grown over the past few decades, as many of us would suppose. Researchers in Norway have shown that inequality between countries has actually been consistently declining since the beginning of the 1970s, falling most sharply between 1993 and 1998.[15] Another sign that the gap between rich and poor countries is getting narrower rather than wider is the fact that since 1975, the share of the world economy accounted for by the group of rich

BISHOP BURTON COLLEGE
LIBRARY

nations, the OECD, has fallen from 80 percent to 70 percent.[16] Images of starving street children huddling in the doorways of Asian skyscrapers shouldn't lead us away from the facts. Desperate as such individuals' plight may be, it's nothing new. There have always been starving street children: before, they'd just huddle at the gates of a different type of rich man's palace. Things are getting better, not worse – the last fifty years have made everyone richer, and in the most open economies made income gaps narrower.

There *is* an exception to all this. If you look not at the poorest 20 percent in the world, but at the poorest 10 percent, you'll see a group of countries that has comprehensively failed to get richer over the past fifty years, and where inequalities have generally widened. These are the only countries where living standards have actually fallen: where hunger, disease, and illiteracy have got worse. These countries did not follow the Asian Tigers or the other developing countries down the globalization route. Determined to cast off colonial shackles and demonstrate their independence, they refused to join the emerging global trading system and they shut out foreign investment as it would threaten local power. They didn't produce what they were good at, they tried to produce everything – and not very well. As a result, the workers did not become more valuable, they did not earn more, there was not enough consumer spending, not enough profits, too little investment, barely any tax revenue to pay for public services. To protect what little they had, these countries imposed high tariffs on foreign goods, and they prevented businesses from operating on capitalist lines, preferring state control. But instead of self-sufficiency, they ended up with poverty, oppression, corruption, and despair. These are the nations of Africa, especially south of the Sahara, some of the poorest countries in the world.

There's no doubt that these countries were severely hampered by the legacy of colonial exploitation: an over-dependence on commodities, a lack of education and infrastructure, and rule by corrupt elites rather than democratic institutions. That's why the rich countries of the world have a moral obligation to do all they can to help Africa. Effective development aid and genuine debt relief are the essential starting points. But then what? Can anyone seriously believe that that's enough to provide a long-term solution to the immense social and economic problems faced by many African countries?

In Nigeria, in just four years between 1992 and 1996, the numbers of people living on less than a dollar a day rose from 43 percent of the population to 66 percent.[17] In Zimbabwe, the figure rose by 10 percent during the 1990s – that's around 3 million extra desperately poor people – as its crazed President, Robert Mugabe, imposed more and more anti-capitalist and anti-globalizing controls.[18] Why are these African countries still so poor? Is it just because rich countries are mean and don't give them any aid? Hardly – the sub-Saharan region has received more development assistance per head than anywhere else in the world, and in some countries, the foreign aid they receive is more than twice the size of their domestic income.[19] Is it because they've suffered more than their fair share of conflict? It clearly doesn't help, but you could equally argue that globalizing, capitalist democracies don't tend to fight wars in the first place; that African countries suffer conflict *because* they're poor. Or are they just poor because African countries are bound to be poor, given their climate? Not if Botswana, Uganda, and Ghana are anything to go by. Botswana for many years, and Uganda and Ghana more recently, are achieving impressive economic growth rates and poverty reduction.[20] This happens to have coincided in each case with the introduction of policies favoring greater trade and business freedom.

The truth is, the poorest countries in the world are poor today because their rulers have refused to learn the lesson that has been learnt comprehensively by billions of people and their governments all over the world. The more you encourage private business, the more you welcome foreign investment, and the more you trade, the more wealthy you will become and the higher living standards you will have. There is simply no other consistent and plausible explanation for the current state of the world.

The research publication *Economic Freedom of the World* compares global living standards over the period 1975–1995. Again, its conclusions show beyond question that the more a country exhibits the characteristics of a free enterprise, capitalist system, the less poor its people are. Between 1975 and 1990, the countries that had the greatest increases in economic freedom were Chile, Jamaica, Iceland, Malaysia, and Turkey. Each of these showed increases in per capita GDP over the period – their citizens got richer. The five countries with the greatest decreases in economic freedom, through closing their borders to trade, investment and so on, were Nicaragua, Somalia, Iran, Honduras, and Venezuela. In every case, their per capita GDP fell – the people were made poorer.[21] The causal connection between free-market capitalism, globalization and rising living standards is staring us in the face.

It's such a clear-cut case, such an obvious interpretation of the facts, that it is genuinely astonishing how widely the poverty/inequality myth of global capitalism is accepted. It can only have one basis: the original, erroneous belief we started off with, that because globalization and poverty co-exist, that because globalization and social injustice co-exist, one must inevitably cause the other. It is our moral duty to campaign against global poverty and to work for its reduction. But because anti-capitalists misunderstand the causes of poverty, their proposed remedies would simply increase it. Anti-capitalists attack multinational corporations that invest in developing countries. But in the last ten years, such investment amounted to 1 trillion dollars, ten times as much as in previous decades, and more than the sum total of all the foreign aid in the entire world over the past fifty years.[22] How would they replace that investment? Where would the money come from? Anti-capitalists want to limit world trade and "protect" developing countries with higher tariffs and restrictions on imports from richer countries. But "protection" of this kind just means that domestic production would have no competition, it would have no reason to improve, its value would therefore not increase, and people's wages would not rise. Which is exactly what happened in some countries in Africa. It's been estimated that a 50 percent cut in trade tariffs would give developing countries an extra $150 billion of income a year, three times the world's aid budget, and that liberalizing trade barriers could result in lifting 900 million people out of poverty by 2015.[23] Why deny that to some of the poorest nations on earth? Anti-capitalists attack the World Trade Organization for allowing the "exploitation" of poor nations by multinational corporations. Why aren't they attacking the shameful behavior of the farmers in their own countries, whose insistence on shutting out competitive agricultural products from developing countries is estimated to cost the poorest in the world at least $20 billion every year, twice the GDP of Kenya?[24]

The anti-globalization movement is entirely justified in pointing to the many and severe problems that exist in the developing world. But not one of those problems – poverty, hunger, disease, illiteracy, the availability of life-saving drugs – can be tackled successfully and sustainably without more globalization and more capitalism. The world has tried everything else: Communism, protectionism, self-sufficiency. None of it worked. It took the rich West hundreds of years to move from subsistence to affluence. Thanks to technological innovation, to capitalism, and to globaliza-tion, there's every chance that today's developing countries could make far more rapid progress. How sad and selfish it would be for us to slam on the brakes.

Number Two on the myth list is human rights. Look at what Shell did in Nigeria. Look at … well, that's usually as far as most people get. But anyway, it's common knowledge that corporations violate human rights in the developing world. Which is another reason to believe that globalization and capitalism are negative forces.

Of course it's true that sometimes they are. Without a shadow of a doubt, corporations have been and probably still are involved in human rights abuses around the globe. This is not the right way to do business, and companies with any business sense, never mind any sense of morality, will do everything they can to stop it happening – as we will argue more fully in the next chapter. But here, while we're correcting some negative misconceptions, it's worth pointing out that the process of globalization does not automatically entail human rights abuses, and that if anything, the overall impact of capitalism and globalization is to improve human rights.

This is because of the part that capitalism and globalization play in promoting democracy, which is itself the most powerful bulwark against human rights abuse. It would be wrong to overstate the case: the factors that cause a country to become or remain a democracy are many and complex. But one of them, without doubt, is the civic culture inside a nation. And if people are free to control their economic destiny, it's more likely that they will demand democratic control in the political sphere too. Of course, the most powerful counter-argument against this is China: not much sign of democracy there despite years of vigorous capitalist enterprise. But equally, look at Indonesia, or Latin America, or the former Communist regimes, where economic freedom was followed rapidly by political freedom. And look at the countries where human rights abuses have been most widespread: Afghanistan under the Taliban, Burma, North Korea, Sudan. These are among the least capitalist and least globalized countries anywhere. One hundred years ago, there was not a single country on earth with universal suffrage. Over the last fifty years, as globalization has gathered pace, the proportion of countries which are democracies has risen from just over 14 percent to over 60 percent, and the percentage of the world's population living in a democracy has gone up from 31 percent to 58 percent.[25]

This is positive and uplifting. Globalization and business enterprise not only help raise living standards, but give people a stake in society, therefore making them more interested in seeing that it is well – and democratically – run. An excellent specific example of the beneficial political effects of globalization can be found in Mexico. In her essay, "First, Open Markets," Mary Anastasia O'Grady celebrates the role of the 1994 North American Free Trade Agreement (NAFTA) – condemned by anti-globalization activists as symbolizing America's exploitation of her poorer neighbor – in helping to bring about political change as well as economic growth: "Last summer, a few days after Mexico's elections turned the ruling

Institutional Revolutionary Party (PRI) out of office after 71 years of uninterrupted power, an incredulous young friend e-mailed me from the capital: 'It was a great party in the city and we look forward to the near future with hope and amazement' … the surprise that characterized most observers' reaction to the PRI's defeat, both inside and outside Mexico, was driven in large part by the failure to appreciate the extent of the damage inflicted on the PRI's notorious machine by NAFTA … NAFTA's most important effect on Mexico was not more choice for consumers or a larger market for producers – although these are certainly significant – but rather a change in the ownership and control of the political economy … here is just one example: in February 1999 I interviewed Eugenio Clariond, CEO of the Mexican conglomerate Grupo IMSA, based in Monterrey. Mr Clariond told me that NAFTA had changed his company into a multinational organization – an importer and exporter – that would benefit from a dollarized economy … it demonstrated how NAFTA weakened the old statist model, and thus the PRI's near-monopoly control of the economy."[26]

Anti-globalizers would take issue with the selection of Mexico as an example of a country where globalization has brought benefits to local people. But on what grounds? Not economic ones: since NAFTA began, Mexico has enjoyed over 5 percent annual growth, and has moved up from being the world's 28th largest exporter to being the 6th.[27] (And the exports are more likely to be high-value manufactured goods, rather than basic raw materials which sell for less.) Instead, the anti-capitalists point to the strong support for the Zapatista movement, which opposes NAFTA, and uses this to argue that the Mexican people themselves – as opposed to the neoliberal bankers, economists, and businessmen that allegedly control their fate – are against globalization.

But the main issue on which Zapatista support is based is nothing to do with globalization or capitalism – it's the demand for self-determination for the Chiapas state in southeastern Mexico. This highlights a classic technique of the anti-capitalist approach. Local rebellions against local authority – whether it's the Zapatistas in Mexico, labor unions in the US, or gay rights campaigners in

Malaysia, all find their localized struggles hijacked by the umbrella "resistance" movement and described as human rights violations to be blamed on globalization. Thanks, ironically, to the globalization of communication, what were once local and often quite parochial arguments are now wrapped up into one big global grumble. Since the enemy in each case is "authority" in some form or another, and since in the eyes of the protestors, authority is synonymous with globalization and capitalism, it stands to reason that practically every conflict and dispute in the world is in some way a protest against multinational corporations and the world order that indulges them in their systematic abuse of human rights.

Where corporations *have* been involved in human rights abuses, it has often been only thanks to the courage and determination of anti-globalization activists that the incidents have come to light. But as with so many of their arguments, they undermine their force when they overstate the case and fail to recognize that corporations could possibly play any kind of positive role in society.

This applies with equal force to misconception Number Three: "sweatshops and child labor." The misconception concerns the best way to get rid of sweatshops and banish child labor to the history books. The image of the hot and dingy factory with children toiling away in Dickensian conditions to churn out western consumer goods has become firmly established in popular culture. So it's quite understandable to view the relocation of manufacturing from the developed world to the Third World as somehow a bad thing, to be resisted. Undoubtedly, there exist factories and workplaces where conditions are appalling – people are over-worked, there is no air-conditioning, the lighting is poor, accidents and unsafe equipment are overlooked, and so on. If you look hard enough, you'll probably be able to find such places anywhere – not just in Thailand, but in Texas too. That doesn't mean that all factories in the developing world are like that, and the appropriate response to such conditions is to try and ensure proper health and safety practices are observed, not to try and remove the factories (and the jobs that go with them).

The indiscriminate use of the word sweatshop to describe just about any workplace in a Third World country obscures the reality that manufacturing investment is precisely what's needed in order to raise incomes and improve standards of living in those countries. We may feel a sense of guilt about less well-paid people in factories on the other side of the globe producing consumer products on our behalf, but the truth is that working for a multinational corporation will almost certainly provide better pay and conditions than any other type of work that's available. Diane Coyle, in *Paradoxes of Prosperity*, points out that: "the work is often – excepting the factories run by unscrupulous exploiters – better paid and more skilled than the alternatives available in poorer countries. A job in a factory with a contract to supply a multinational is often the only escape from grinding rural poverty and traditional oppressive attitudes for young women from villages in countries like China or Thailand, and certainly better than prostitution in the sleazy bars of Bangkok. Even in middle-income countries like Mexico, such transplant jobs are giving women new freedoms. Like so many arrangements in the global economy, it is genuinely a win-win pattern. Less directly, developing countries also gain technical know-how and management expertise from foreign investors. Somebody who works as a foreman in one of their plants is soon equipped to set up his own business instead."[28]

The Harvard economist Jeffrey Sachs, well known for his work with U2's lead singer Bono on the Jubilee 2000 debt relief campaign, put the point even more brutally when he said: "my concern is not that there are too many sweatshops but that there are too few … those are precisely the jobs that were the stepping stones for Singapore and Hong Kong and those are the jobs that have to come to Africa to get them out of back-breaking rural poverty."[29] In Chapter 5, you will find specific information about independent investigations of Nike's factories in various parts of the developing world, but our aim here is simply to make the general point that we can't get rid of sweatshops and child labor by simply wishing them away. Of course we must get rid of them; the question is, how?

Every decent person wants to see an end to child labor: children should be in school, not at work. And while it's easy to get caught up in technical niceties about the precise age at which a child stops being a child – we say 16, they say 14 – it's not a bad rule of thumb to argue that we shouldn't expect people in other countries to make things for us under conditions that we wouldn't accept here. But the problem isn't as straightforward as that. First of all, it's worth remembering that the vast majority of child labor in the developing world takes place in the rural agricultural sector, where education opportunities are few and far between and where globalization and capitalism are a distant dream. Secondly, the reason that parents send their children to work is not because they're bad parents, or because western companies malevolently seduce them away. The reason parents do it is that they're poor, and they need the money. So the long-term, sustainable solution to the problem of child labor is not to try and instantly ban it, which would make families even poorer, but to help families get richer so that children don't have to work.

The problems that can arise from well-intentioned bans and boycotts of factories using child labor have been well documented. In 1992, following the revelation that certain Wal-Mart garments were manufactured by child labor in Bangladesh, the textile industry sacked around 50,000 child workers in order to placate the US Congress, which was threatening a trade ban. International organizations investigated what happened to them: many took on even worse – and worse-paid – jobs, and some became prosti-tutes.[30] A similar story was uncovered by UNICEF, which found that 5,000 girls from a Nepalese carpet factory were forced into prostitution as a result of a boycott. Such stories should not be used as a reason to relax effective pressure to end child labor, but as warning that hasty action can be counterproductive.[31] As Baron Mitri, a leading Indian campaigner and writer has put it: "Clearly, a focus on particular export sectors may lead to an effective political campaign, but does very little to address the real issue … Good intentions are never a sufficient condition for improving social and economic realities. It will be a tragedy, if as a result of well-meaning but hurried policies aimed at prohibiting child labor, children are further victimized because the policies fail to take into account context-specific situations of the developing countries."[32]

The sweatshops and child labor arguments have sometimes been used in a pernicious way by rich countries to protect their own workers at the cost of jobs in the developing world. This point has not escaped people in those countries: "the question is why industrialized countries are suddenly bothering about Third World workers now that we have shown we can compete with them," mused Youssef Boutros-Ghali, Egyptian trade minister in 1998.[33] The Seattle world trade talks broke down not because poor countries thought the rich were doing too little to improve social conditions in their countries, but because they were trying to do too much. The nations of the developing world interpreted Bill Clinton's desire to impose the same labor standards on Bangladesh as those that operate in Baltimore as nothing more than a sop to US trades unions desperate to protect the jobs of their Baltimore members (whose concern for the economic development of Bangladesh is unsurprisingly subordinate to their desire to keep the paychecks coming in). The claims of well-meaning people in rich countries to want to "protect" low-earning people in poor countries are often highly dubious, and frequently lurch into selfishness and hypocrisy.

Western countries grew rich through their own sweatshops and child labor. Thankfully, social campaigns, as well as technology and productivity advances, meant that they were eliminated around the early twentieth century. Today, developing countries are trying to increase their living standards in exactly the same way. Surely our aim should be to help poor countries minimize the period of time during which *they* tolerate Dickensian working conditions? And surely the best method would be to help the poor countries develop more quickly? That means investing in their countries, sharing know-how and new technology, exporting higher health and safety standards, and helping their domestic producers to increase their productivity. Globalization speeds that process up, and is therefore the single most practical and long-term solution; the best way of ending sweatshop working conditions and child labor without causing local people in developing countries pain of a different, and often much worse kind. Anti-globalization policies would reduce the need, and the means, for developing countries to improve working conditions.

This is not an easy message to deliver, so it's no wonder that it's rarely heard. But for every foreign aid charity's communications director that attacks multinationals and globalization, you'll find indigenous local campaigners calling for free trade and more investment. It's just that they don't have the benefit of a well-resourced press office to get them on the media, since they are after all poor and live in the Third World, unlike the charity executives who are rich, live in New York or London (or both) and can afford to invest money in "marketing initiatives" to promote their wrong-headed views in line with their new "strategy" of transforming themselves into "campaigning" organizations, secure in the knowledge that the actual alleviation of global poverty can safely be left in the hands of others while they get on with the real business of becoming media stars and commissioning controversial ad campaigns that pick up creative awards earning them plaudits for being "brave" clients, despite the fact that they singularly failed to make the tiniest alteration to the ideas presented to them by their advertising agency, who know a safe bet when they see one, and understand that a pro bono charity client is not going to look a gift horse in the mouth. This is clearly quite a cynical inter-pretation – did you notice? – and of course the usual caveats apply: there *are* many honest and sincere charity workers out there; they're not all selfish self-righteous self-publicists, etc., etc. But you get the point: a pinch of salt every time you hear someone speaking on behalf of the poor in developing countries.

Number Four on our list of misconceptions is "cultural imperialism", the belief that the global advance of western brands is a corrupting force, ruining local cultures by spreading the polluting effects of consumer desire and turning the entire planet into a homogenized, lowest-common denominator replica of the Mall of America. Again, this is an argument that intuitively rings true. Western tourists, anxious to visit parts of the world that afford them a different cultural experience to the one back home, throw their hands up in horror when they see the famous and ubiquitous Coca-Cola logo dogging their every footstep as they press on optimistically in search of the unspoiled ancient civilization/ desert/temple/jungle/beach, etc. (Although, with the promise of elephants bathing in the local river the following day, there is a surprising lack of revulsion at the ubiquitous yellow of the Kodak film boxes that fill the local shops.) Whatever the inconsistencies, however, there's a genuinely felt sense of sadness, even anger – "I can't believe they're getting the same treatment from the brands that we have to put up with" – and it's too trite to dismiss this as just another example of patronizing cultural relativism, an attempt by smug westerners to deny to the poor of the world the benefits of the consumer goodies they enjoy, simply to ensure the preservation of a suitably exotic vacation aesthetic. There are no easy answers to this one, but try these two.

First, is it really the case, even in the rich West, that the spread of global brands corrupts local cultures? Japan has McDonald's, but is it any less Japanese? Have they stopped eating sushi? Britain has Starbucks, but is it any less British? Have people stopped going to the local pub? France has the Gap, but is it any less French? Have they stopped wearing berets, stripey T-shirts and strings of onions. … OK, better stop there. But the point is a serious one: local cultures are strong. They've evolved over hundreds, sometimes thousands of years. The idea that they can be undermined by a foreign product or service – albeit one with a striking and omnipresent visual identity – is a bit far-fetched. We've had global trade for centuries, think of the spread of French wine from the sixteenth century onwards – did that undermine local cultures? And in any case, the same brands often mean different things in different countries. Their ability to chime with people's emotions and values is what makes them successful, and it's hard to see how that can be a bad thing.

If you wanted to really push the boat out on this line of argument, you could even raise the thorny subject of racism. When it comes to individual people from another culture entering a country, any opposition to their presence would be characterized as racist and no doubt condemned by the anti-corporate critics. Transform the invading army into a commercial, branded one, however, and it's perfectly acceptable to let rip with the "we don't want your sort in our country thank you very much" form of parochialism. While it's totally understandable that some people may not like their neighborhoods invaded by alien brand names that are the same ones as can be found everywhere else on the planet, aren't there bigger issues to worry about? And aren't local planning authorities and architects more appropriate targets of venom when the conversation turns to the quality of public space and the local environment?

The second argument against the idea that global brands undermine local cultures is to be found amongst the local people on whose behalf the anti-globalizers express such concern. Guess what? Those people, who aren't yet sick of it, actually want the stuff. Eastern Europe is a classic case. It's difficult to explain to someone who's unfamiliar with life in those countries during the Communist era just how important the arrival of western brands turned out to be. The ability to buy a Big Mac, to shop at Tesco, to buy real Levis rather than fake ones, was not just a welcome extension of consumer choice, but the most tangible possible symbol of individual and political freedom – a daily reminder of the right to choose. Globalization is giving more people the choices that in the past were available only to a privileged few. It's a clear extension of pluralism, something which anti-globalizers, of all people, should applaud.

Since September 11th 2001, an anti-capitalist theme has crept into the prevailing left-of-centre discourse in an unmistakable way.

Many commentators have tried to blacken the name of western brands by suggesting that they're the vanguard of a new form of brutal and crass colonialism. For example, while arguing for cultural tolerance and diversity in the West, many anti-capitalists seem to suspend judgment when it comes to the Middle East. Some have even suggested that it's no wonder New York is attacked when people in Muslim countries see McDonald's restaurants opening up. But cultural tolerance and diversity are indivisible. If you think that people should be free to practice whatever religion they choose, then how can you object to them shopping where they choose without contradicting the very principles you wish to uphold? Umberto Eco explains the dilemma for the left neatly: "We are a pluralistic civilization because we allow mosques to be built in our countries, and we are not going to stop simply because Christian missionaries are thrown into prison in Kabul. If we did so, we too would become Taliban. The parameter of tolerating diversity is certainly one of the strongest and least open to argument. We consider our culture mature because it can tolerate diversity; and those who share our culture but reject diversity are considered to be uncivilized, period. We hope that, if we allow mosques in our country, one day there will be Christian churches in their countries, or at least Buddhas won't get blown up there ... It seems that defending western values has become a rightwing prerogative, while the Left, as ever, is pro-Islamic ... this ignores a historical phenomenon which is there for all to see. The defence of scientific values, of technological development, and modern western culture in general, has always been characteristic of secular and progressive political circles."[34] Seen in this light, the objection to western brands in eastern lands is nothing more than a blinkered prejudice. Support for free-market capitalism, based as it is on the principle of individual choice, is no different in a cultural context from support for religious tolerance. To adapt Eco's formulation, if we allow halal butchers over here, what's wrong with McDonald's over there? Isn't the spread of brands a great symbol of cultural diversity? That's certainly how it's been seen in many other parts of the world.

In Eastern Europe, in Asia, in Africa, in South America: everywhere there is poverty, there is a demand for consumer products and branded goods – just as there is in North America and Europe, where there is also poverty, just less of it. Indeed, you could argue that it's the poorest people in societies everywhere who want branded goods, because having branded goods shows you're not as poor as you once were. And what's wrong with that? Rather than agonizing in a concerned and tortured manner about this reality, we could do worse than accept it for what it is. Wouldn't it be more constructive to think of ways in which to harness the brands' global cultural dominance, and use this dominance as a force for good? Later on, we'll describe how this could be done.

Number Five in the hit parade of myths about business is the idea that there's something wrong with profit. The word profit is sprinkled liberally throughout the writings of the anti-capitalists, and rarely is it used, either by them or in popular culture generally, in anything other than a pejorative context. This is no surprise, since profit is the absolute core of the capitalist system, the very lifeblood without which none of the benefits of capitalism would ever occur. The distaste many people feel when they hear the word profit is wrapped up in their distaste for capitalism generally. "Profits" conjure up those stout gentlemen in waistcoats and top hats again, counting their money while lighting their cigars with rolled up $100 bills – or increasingly perhaps, rolling up the bills for an altogether different purpose. Despite the comprehensive humiliation of Marxism as a serious economic doctrine, there's still a feeling out there that capitalists exploit the labor of decent working people, and that profit is the yardstick by which to measure the degree of exploitation.

One of the chief evils of profit, in the eyes of its detractors, is the fact that we don't all share in it – only shareholders do. How outrageous! If workers help create the profits, shouldn't they get some too? Of course they should, and they do – sometimes in straightforward and direct ways, where workers are also shareholders (a category which includes over half of all US workers, incidentally),[35] but mostly it's in less obvious ways. This has allowed a degree of ignorance to develop, and it's this lack of under-standing of the basic functions of business and the capitalist system that lies behind much of the negative feeling associated with profit. It's astonishingly poorly understood that a large proportion of the nefarious shareholders who "cream off" profits from the workers are actually pension funds and insurance companies. In other words, profits don't just disappear into the coffers of rich people – they're recycled in order to provide *all* people with a living income in their retirement, or compensation if they suffer loss. There's another way in which profits are recycled on behalf of the many, not the few: through the tax that companies pay on their profits, taxes which contribute to the funding of public services, social welfare and so on. And finally, without profits, how are corpora-tions to invest in new products and services, new technologies to protect the environment – all the things we say we want?

It's increasingly common to hear the argument made that companies should be run in the interests of "wider society," not just shareholders. But what does this mean? Surely through their contribution to pensions, insurance and tax revenues, companies *are* acting in the interests of wider society if they maximize their profits? This is of course not to say that profits are the *only* thing corporations should think about, but frankly, corporations are not much use to anyone if they don't make profits, since they go out of business and people lose their jobs. It would be such a joy if we could all just agree that profits are a good thing and that the key question is not *whether* companies should make profits, or how much profit they should make, but *how* they make those profits. A key argument of anti-capitalists is that the profit motive leads to bad outcomes for society. This denies the possibility, which is the central contention of this book, that not only is it possible to combine profit-making with socially beneficial outcomes, but that we should all work towards a situation in which helping society becomes the single best way to make profits.

And so, it's the last on the list: Number Six in the countdown of anti-capitalist myths. This is the "fact" that corporations have turned into all-conquering Leviathans: their power is beyond the reach of democratically elected governments; no-one and nothing can stand in their way. The favorite slogan used to justify this charge is the observation that 51 of the world's largest 100 economies are actually corporations, not countries.[36] This specter of corporate power is another key element in creating hostile or wary attitudes towards business: the feeling that anonymous global corporations are in charge, rather than the politicians on your doorstep, leaves people feeling buffeted around by uncontrollable forces. It's obvious how this feeling can arise – if a company is big and rich, if its turnover is greater than the GDP of many smaller countries, if it operates in every corner of the globe – well, it's more powerful than some puny little government, isn't it? The logical answer must therefore be, in the name of democracy, to limit its power. This is the central thesis of Noreena Hertz in *The Silent Takeover*.

The main problem with this analysis is that it misses the real target. Yes, corporations are immensely powerful – but not in the way their critics claim. The critics claim that corporations are institutionally and economically powerful – their economic muscle gives them the ability to shape public policy, to decide how our lives are run – and that this power is dangerous, because it is unaccountable. So the corporations' power should be limited, even destroyed, and the best way of doing this is to restrict their ability to make profits and to operate as they decide. In reality, corporations are far more powerful in a cultural sense, and in their grass-roots impact, than they are as big, anonymous institutions. But most of this power is untapped: they don't actively use it for any social ends, good or bad. In this analysis, it's possible to imagine that corporations' cultural and grass-roots power is a good thing, because it can be used for positive social ends while helping the corporations make greater profits – which is also good and should be encouraged. In Chapter 5, we'll look at the anatomy of corporations, and show how they can use the genuine power that they do have, positively. But it's worth knocking on the head those arguments that imbue corporations with power that they don't actually have.

First of all, the size of the state sector relative to the size of the private sector has grown hugely during the twentieth century, and at around 50 percent in most European countries is running at an all-time high. It's just not true that companies in general are taking over more and more of the economy. Individual companies may be getting bigger, but this doesn't count for very much when the biggest corporations' market share is getting smaller (as it is), and when their share of employment is also shrinking (as it is).[37]

Second, remember all the things that governments still control: defence, foreign policy, economic policy, constitutional arrangements, the electoral system and voting rights, residence, citizenship, the legal system, cultural concerns, education, public provision for health, pensions and welfare … the list goes on. The image of the State as David, cowering before the corporate Goliath, was given a resounding jolt by the events of September 11th. Even Madeleine Bunting, a trenchant critic of consumerism and corporate power, has pointed out that: "September 11th and its aftermath have starkly exposed what was the glaring weakness of the [anti-capitalist] movement all along. Its analysis focused on the dwindling power of the state and overweening corporate power. Its disregard for the state was such that it had no strategy for achieving the political power necessary to deliver its aims, and fell back on subverting the state by declaring it impotent. All that looks a bit threadbare now in the midst of war, as the state re-emerges as hugely important in delivering that most basic of its functions – security."[38]

But it doesn't require September 11th to bring home this reality: it's always been the case that coercive power lies in the hands of governments, not companies: who employs and gives orders to the armed forces and the police; who makes laws and levies taxes? The idea that globalization or privatization has changed the basic set-up is just melodramatic foolishness. And if you actually look at how the State has been using its coercive power in respect of companies, you could argue that the last ten years or so have seen a reduction in corporations' freedom of action. In most developed economies, there's now far greater regulation of businesses in areas such as competition policy, the environment, health and safety, and employment. The trend towards liberalization of trade and investment, and the stricter enforcement of anti-trust rules and cartel-busting provisions has further eroded corporations' ability to behave exactly as they please. In the old days, giant companies, many of them state-owned and most of them protected from international competition, could do almost what they wanted. That's not the case any more. And the final point to bear in mind is the response of companies to the last few years of sustained criticism from pressure groups and activists. As we'll see in the next chapter, this has contributed to a dramatic new trend in business, with corporations taking a far more active and structured approach to their social and environmental impact. The alacrity with which huge corporations are making often revolutionary changes to the way they operate gives the lie to the idea that they're above the law or any other section of society.

Ultimate power always rests with the politicians. They can choose to make life easier for corporations, or they can choose to make life harder – but they are in charge, and businesses are at their mercy. You only have to visit a couple of smart-but-not-lavish restaurants within walking distance of every Congress, Parliament or National Assembly building in the world to see which side the bread is buttered. At practically every table, the same scene will be played out: corporate interests pleading their case as the politicians sip on their Pouilly Fume. Does anyone suppose that corporations pay exorbitant fees to armies of lobbyists for the sheer hell of it, or because they like wasting money, or because they want to keep these restaurants in business? Or is it because they know where power truly lies: with elected governments, precisely where it should.

But what if the wining and dining works, argue the critics. Doesn't that show that the democratic system is undermined? Writers like George Monbiot, observing the tendency for policies to be introduced which favor business interests, immediately cite this as evidence that the corporations have "taken over." Such criticism doesn't even consider the possibility that what's in a company's interest might also be in the public interest. In other words, that the politicians have decided that the best way of meeting their public policy objectives is to listen to the arguments of private companies. Of course it's possible that the politicians get it wrong, and that in a few – or even in many – cases, the public interest would have been better served by denying the corporate interest. But politicians get all sorts of things wrong, on a regular basis, and that's a completely different argument. What it doesn't mean is that corporations have wrested power from our elected representatives in some kind of disturbing new trend. Again, Madeleine Bunting makes the point from the left: "The anti-corporate movement can no longer convincingly bemoan that the governments of western democracies are simply puppets of corporate interests. It has to revise its analysis of political power and develop its own understanding of how to achieve it."[39] We'd add to that by saying that the movement needs to develop a more sophisticated analysis of the different ways in which corporations are powerful. Some of them could prove useful by serving a social, as well as a commercial purpose, as we'll see in Chapter 5.

Take another look at that hideous green ogre called business. At first glance, because of the co-existence of globalization and shocking poverty, it may seem as if one causes the other, that free-market capitalism impoverishes the developing world. But the evidence points in the other direction: business is the way to make everyone richer, everywhere. At first glance, it's easy to read into well-publicized violations an assumption that companies are the enemy of human rights. But most of the time, capitalism is if anything a positive force for freedom and democracy. At first glance, sweatshops and child labor are unqualified evils that are inextricably linked with multinational companies. But capitalism and globalization turn out to be the best ways of getting rid of bad working conditions. At first glance, the global dominance of western brands is a blot on local cultures around the world. But actually, local cultures seem to be thriving – and people who in the past have been "spared" the impact of those brands actually welcome them with open arms. At first glance, profit is a bad thing, siphoning off resources to favor the rich. But in reality, profits pay for pensions, insurance, welfare, public services, investment – and make sure that people have a job to go to. At first glance, corporations rule the world: but they know, and the politicians know, that lawmakers are still in charge.

When you look in detail at the arguments of the anti-capitalists and anti-globalizers, one thing becomes utterly clear. They're not really against globalization; nor are they really opposed to capitalism. They're actually just good old-fashioned campaigners for social justice and environmental concern who have found a new set of clothes to wear. The fact that the clothes don't fit hardly matters when they get you so much attention.

And here lies the opportunity. Our reason for analyzing the anti-capitalist arguments and for telling the other, heretical, side of the story is to try and create a more constructive environment for debate, one in which business can be brought into the fold of those working for social progress, rather than being banished like Shrek to the swamp with the maggots, parasites, and vermin. Capitalism is here to stay. Globalization is here to stay. As Clare Short, Britain's Secretary of State for International Development put it: "Globalization is a set of economic and technological developments in the world which are a fact of history. The job is to manage history, not to oppose it."[40] So for those of us interested in improving social conditions, in making the world a better place – in what ways should we manage globalization? How exactly should we work with business and capitalism? What steps should we take to improve it?

We should identify the specific ways in which business could do more to help society. We'll need to inspire business leaders to do things differently, to help them see that they don't have to make a choice between making money and making the world a better place. We'll want to shake them up a bit, to show them that the traditional social role they've played is out of date, and indeed is no longer commercially sensible, let alone socially responsible. We should praise examples of companies that have found a new way of working that makes the most of their power to do good, and we'll have to fire the imagination of everyone connected with companies, whether they're owners, managers, employees or customers. We must encourage politicians to think more creatively about the ways in which they could harness the resources of business to tackle social issues. We'll want employees to take pride in the role that they play in their business, and the role that their business plays in society. We'll want people to care about business, not be ashamed of it. And we'll want to make sure that all the things we propose end up improving business success and profitability, because we recognize that without these things, everyone will be worse off.

This is the defining battle of the twenty-first century: not between people and corporations, as George Monbiot argues: corporations are comprised of people – they're on the same side. The battle will be between those who see nothing but a negative social role for business, and those who want to promote the positive. The green ogre is not as hideous as many people currently think. And the good news is that the ogre itself is looking at ways of becoming less hideous. Over the last few years, a big change has been taking place in the business world. We referred to it earlier; it's called corporate social responsibility, and it's worth knowing about.

3

Responsibility

In the 1790s, a woman called Elizabeth Hayrick whipped up the housewives of Leicester, England, into a passionate protest against capitalist exploitation. Leaflets were distributed outside local shops, proudly announcing that "we, the people, can overthrow slavery!" The target of this pioneering anti-globalizer? It was that "blood-stained luxury": sugar. In those days, sugar was brought into Britain from plantations in the Caribbean, harvested and produced by slaves – hence the Hayrick campaign, one of the first recorded examples of a consumer boycott. What's more, it seemed to work: within thirty years, the East India Company was satisfying the sweet tooth of British households with free-grown sugar from Bengal, and by mobilizing public opinion behind anti-slavery, Hayrick helped pave the way for the abolition of slavery by William Wilberforce a few years later.

Was this the first notch on the anti-capitalists' belt, or an early example of the phrase on a growing number of executive lips: corporate social responsibility? A bit of both, really, since the story captures many of the dilemmas that companies are going to face in the twenty-first century, as well as making the point that targeted protest against business can quickly deliver results – a striking lesson in the power of consumer choice. The anatomy of the Hayrick sugar boycott is simple enough: a strong-willed critic of business behavior provides consumers with information about the alleged unacceptable practices of a company; said company gets in a panic about the potential negative impact on its sales, and then changes its behavior in an attempt to pacify its critics and maintain its commercial position. Call it corporate social responsibility, or call it robber-baron capitalists dragged kicking and screaming to the altar of decent values by the only language they understand (money); but either way, the overall outcome is better for society and better for business. Since that first outing in the eighteenth century, consumer boycotts have popped up in economies all over the world to throw an intermittent spanner in the well-oiled works of industry. You can probably remember the most recent – wine from South Africa anyone? How about some Chilean Chardonnay, or Pinochet Grigio? Nike trainers? Shell petrol? Nestlé baby milk? The latest corporation to find itself in a well-organized firing line is ExxonMobil, or Esso. As Anita Roddick puts it in her book *Take it Personally*, "the worst nightmare of companies like Esso's [sic] is a customer revolt. Help make their nightmare come true."[1] (You can see what the boycotters are on about by visiting the campaign website, stopesso.com). For a hardcore group of concerned citizens, products from companies targeted for a boycott instantly change into badges of shame. The emotional intensity of such campaigns is illustrated by a Doonesbury cartoon describing the advent of a new Wal-Mart store in a US town. A Wal-Mart executive had agreed to attend a town meeting to address local residents' concerns about the ethics of the superstore giant. In the end, he resorts to the tried and trusted formula: "But we'll have the lowest prices you've seen … " Back comes the answer from a little old lady: "Those are the devil's prices!"

Well, perhaps they are, but Wal-Mart still seems to be doing OK, and despite the violent passions they often generate, consumer boycotts have been few and far between. More importantly, the actual impact of boycotts on companies' sales has tended to be out of all proportion to the amount of media coverage they attract: in most cases, not so much a consumer "revolt" as a consumer yawn – nothing much for your average business leader to lose sleep over. But it may just be time to wake up. In the years ahead, there will be an explosion of media and consumer scrutiny – companies will face not just the odd boycott like the original sugar campaign organized by Elizabeth Hayrick, but a permanent and ongoing evaluation of their social and environmental performance. There could be a Hayrick in every household, ready to switch brands at the drop of an ethical clanger.

So no matter how good you may think business is; even if you agree wholeheartedly that the capitalist system is fundamentally a positive force in the world, the reality is that there are always going to be people who disagree. Thanks to greater ease of global communications, such critics will be more numerous, more vocal, and more able to get their message across to mainstream consumers. Those involved in business have to take account of this, just as they have to take account of more conventionally businesslike factors that may affect their ability to increase their sales and profits. For this reason, and for a number of others that we'll look at in this chapter, corporate social responsibility is now on every sensible Chief Executive's agenda – not always at the top, but it's there.

It's also on your agenda if you take a hostile view of business. If you have concerns about the way business operates, or if you don't agree that business is at heart a good thing – or even if like Doonesbury's little old lady you think that capitalism is, basically, the work of the devil – then you're presumably interested in ways to make it less diabolical. In other words, the general proposition that lies behind the concept of corporate social responsibility, that corporations should work to improve their social and environmental impact, sounds pretty unexceptional and unobjectionable whichever side of the fence you're on. But it's all very well in theory. What exactly is corporate social responsibility in practice?

One of the quickest ways of understanding the idea is to look at a company that's doing it, and doing it well. And there are probably few more impressive examples of social responsibility in action anywhere in the world than in the British home improvement company, B&Q. For British readers, this company would seem an unlikely choice. It's famous for its cheap prices, cheery ad campaigns and big shed-like warehouses all over the country. But corporate social responsibility? Do me a favor ...

That alone is a reason why B&Q is interesting. It has spent the past ten years or so developing one of the most thoughtful, rigorous and systematic approaches to corporate social responsibility that you'll find anywhere – and yet few of its customers would know about it. B&Q has been a pioneer of corporate social responsibility simply because it thinks it's the right way to run a business. Another reason that B&Q makes an interesting story is that it is a major mass market operator, not a niche, "ethical" brand on the fringes of the marketplace. Moreover, it is a hugely successful company – the clear market leader in the UK and Europe, and a strong financial performer. The company has stores in China, Taiwan and Poland, and recently merged with the French chain, Castorama. B&Q buys over 40,000 products from 60 countries. It is a big, globalized business. And it demonstrates in a powerful way that corporate social responsibility can fit happily with popular appeal and commercial success.[2]

The story began over ten years ago, when B&Q's then Marketing Director, Bill Whiting (later to become the company's Chief Executive) was asked by a journalist at a press conference how much tropical hardwood B&Q stocked. When he confessed that he didn't know, the journalist replied, "Well, if you don't know, you don't care." Stung by the comment, Whiting decided that he ought to know. So he hired a scientist, Dr Alan Knight, to become B&Q's environmental specialist. In the days before such people became two-a-penny in big corporations, it was an unusual appointment.

Knight's first task was to tackle the timber issue. The main social and environmental problems associated with timber are the uncontrolled removal of tropical rainforest; cutting techniques which clear areas of timber in a way that damages the local environment, and the consequent negative impact on the communities of the people who live there. The phrase which is used to describe timber sourcing which avoids these harmful effects is "well-managed forests," and in 1991, B&Q announced that within five years, it would only buy timber from such forests (an indication of the time it can take for a big corporation to change the complexities of its supply chain). But in 1991, there was little expertise about "well-managed forests," and how such forests could be used to meet the business needs of companies like B&Q. So Alan Knight decided to set up a new forestry project in order to create a practical laboratory for the whole range of social and environmental responsibility issues linked to timber. The project was located in Papua New Guinea, an area with huge potential for timber logging, and a consequently high incidence of destructive techniques practiced by overseas companies that had bought up the logging rights from local communities.

Early on, Knight took B&Q's Managing Director to Papua New Guinea to see the project in action on the island of East New Britain. The idea was to test mechanisms through which local communities could be trained to manage their own forests in an environmentally responsible way – for example using portable sawmills which allow them to harvest only the high-value timber, minimizing environmental damage and safeguarding future yields. Another element was to develop a system for the independent verification of well-managed forests, so that not only B&Q, but other purchasers of timber worldwide, could be sure about where it came from and how it was produced.

This hands-on approach led to a number of successful outcomes. B&Q gained valuable expertise which enabled it amongst other things to help create the Forest Stewardship Council in 1992, an independent NGO that would develop a credible system of independent certification and timber labelling and which is now the leading global player in this area. B&Q itself purchased some of the timber produced from its pilot project, and local villagers saw not only their incomes rise and their skills increase, but their communities revitalized through transport links that enabled them to trade with other villages. And by taking action itself, B&Q was able to meet the target it had set itself for sourcing timber from well-managed forests: a significant competitive advantage given subsequent growth in regulation.

But timber was just the beginning. Over the years, B&Q continued to innovate, setting up systems to audit its suppliers on the social and environmental impact of their products, developing new product ranges with less harmful environmental effects (like peat-free soil, paints labelled with their solvent content, and locally sourced charcoal that supports woodland wildlife in the UK), and creating partnerships between its stores and local disability groups to develop training in disability awareness and to improve the service disabled people would get in B&Q stores.

One of the key features of B&Q's approach to corporate social responsibility has been its hands-on, project-based attitude. For example, rather than accepting internationally agreed codes of practice on employment conditions in developing countries at face value, B&Q wanted to make sure they really worked. In China, for example, where B&Q buys products from over 350 different factories, the company set up pilot projects to find the best ways of improving factory health and safety, and living conditions for workers. Based on these projects in Kantong Province, one at a toilet-seat factory, the other at a cast-iron bench factory, B&Q realized that simply asking factory owners to comply with a code of practice wouldn't work. Improvements would not be sustained, there would be no training in the management issues involved, and no way that B&Q could guarantee high standards without permanent inspection teams.

So based on these findings, and those from a whole host of similar in-depth initiatives in the Philippines, India and elsewhere, B&Q has developed its own, far more progressive approach. This involves training and inspiring factory owners and managers to see improved working and living conditions as a way of becoming better businesses, rather than as a cost imposed by arrogant westerners. In this way, B&Q would not only be better able to guarantee the quality of its products, but the local factories would be able to win new contracts to supply others demanding similar standards. Wherever possible, B&Q tries to avoid boycotting suppliers as this offers no scope for improving conditions by working with them and passing on knowledge and expertise – and of course the money to fund improvements. Instead, the company has a sophisticated system for grading its suppliers on social and environmental criteria, and a range of management tools to help meet local needs while satisfying B&Q's business requirements.

The great thing about B&Q's attitude to corporate social responsibility is that it runs right through the business, and is manifested in all sorts of ways – from cash grants and free materials donated to local schools and community groups that want to carry out neighborhood renewal schemes, to its decision a few years ago to open a store staffed entirely by workers over 50 to demonstrate its commitment to employment diversity. The reason corporate social responsibility has become so embedded in B&Q's corporate culture is that the company's senior management are committed to it, and want to get involved in the details – for example, a photograph of a worker at a B&Q supplier in India pouring molten brass in bare feet was shown at a board meeting and prompted immediate action. This board-level enthusiasm has translated into a company-wide understanding of the issues, and of their importance to the business.

B&Q has benefited in a whole range of ways from its corporate social responsibility culture: reduced costs, better supplier relationships, greater staff pride and customer loyalty to name just a few. But those are seen as welcome by-products. The motivation is more subtle. In part, it's based on a belief that trade helps social development and the reduction of poverty, and more importantly, on a recognition that big business doesn't have to be a source of exploitation in developing countries. B&Q's story demonstrates that corporations can be a major force for change by working with NGOs and others to tackle in a practical way the complex issues involved in managing a global supply chain. The other reason B&Q takes social responsibility seriously is that it's nothing more (or less)

BISHOP BURTON COLLEGE
LIBRARY

than the manifestation of its corporate mission. The company's stated purpose is to "be the best at giving people the inspiration, confidence and solutions to create homes to be proud of" and B&Q's values are articulated as follows: "Can-Do, Down to Earth, Customer driven, Striving to be better, and Respect for people." As Martin Toogood, B&Q's former Managing Director put it, "How can our customers be proud of their home if they learn that our products such as brass handles, rugs or lampshades were made in sweatshops or by exploited children? How can B&Q claim to respect people without attempting to improve the quality of life of people who make our products?"

––––––––––––––––––––

The B&Q story is a great practical example of corporate social responsibility, but it's by no means typical, either in the detail of what the company is doing or in the reasons for doing it. It's easy to agree in theory that businesses should assess their social and environmental impact, and then try on an ongoing basis to improve it. Who could argue with that? But unfortunately, life is not so simple, and there's a lot more to corporate social responsibility than a generalized commitment to doing good. For a start, it's a moving target, with definitions changing all the time. Second, it's not quite as bland a concept as "doing good." Corporate social responsibility is usually taken to mean companies doing things over and above their legal obligations in order to serve the "public interest." The checklist of what this might involve will vary depending on who you talk to, but the items tend to include the treatment of employees, human rights, environmental protection, support for local communities, and ethical behavior towards customers, competitors and suppliers.

So the aim of this chapter is twofold. For those who've never encountered the concept of corporate social responsibility before, it's intended as an eye-opener, to show that far from arrogantly ignoring the various criticisms that have been made of it in recent years, much of the business world is frantically trying to figure out how to respond to those criticisms. Most companies are years behind leaders in the field like B&Q, but many are – or claim to be – on the same road. Our aim is to disentangle corporate spin from corporate progress, and to place social responsibility in its proper business context. For those who are familiar with the movement, this chapter is intended more as a prelude to Chapter 4, in which we show what corporate social responsibility could become, and offer a new interpretation of it that would unlock dramatically improved commercial and social gains.

Despite the superficially uncontroversial nature of the idea that companies should try to improve their social and environmental impact, the responsibilities of business are a matter of considerable debate. But it's an odd debate. It's odd because on one level, the rhetorical level, there's almost universal consensus. Corporations, governments and NGOs all sing from the same hymn sheet these days: there are many social problems in the world, business is powerful and can help, the way to do it is for companies to be more socially responsible, bob's your uncle. But if there is such a love-in of mutual agreement and collective enthusiasm for corporate do-gooding, you can't help but wonder why there are any social or environmental problems left in the world at all. As Oded Grajew of the Instituto Ethos in Brazil puts it in Simon Zadek's book *The Civil Corporation*: "If business is so powerful and now doing so much good, how come so much is still wrong in the world?"[3]

He has a point. Behind the rhetoric of optimistic consensus, there are clearly substantial and problematic issues to be resolved. If big corporations are so wholeheartedly behind corporate social responsibility, why are they being attacked like never before for being anti-social? Are they only claiming to be socially responsible in order to avoid being attacked, or are they genuinely changing but at the same time failing to persuade us of their sincerity? Are they biting off more than they can or should chew by initiating social and environmental strategies; or are they barely scratching the surface of what society expects them to do and indeed, what they are capable of achieving? Are they collaborating in a dangerously radical experiment which will damage the capitalist system; or are they merely reinterpreting a traditional aspect of good business practice for the modern era? Is all this talk of corporate social responsibility just a temporary fad arising from years of uninterrupted economic growth, about to be washed away by the storms of recession, or is it a lasting evolution in the way business is done? What about the politicians – are they abdicating their own social responsibilities by encouraging business to get involved in issues that were previously felt to be the job of government, or are they cannily enlisting the support of a powerful additional force in pursuit of their objectives? Your answers to these questions will probably depend on your own experience and your own views about business and society, and this is what makes corporate social responsibility (despite the superficial consensus supporting it), such a problematic phrase and such a divisive doctrine. But there's actually no need for confusion or dis-agreement: there's a way of looking at the role of business in society which brings together skeptics, evangelists and agnostics behind a single and consensual rallying point. That's the aim of this chapter: but first, it's worth looking at the widely diverging views that currently characterize discussion of this issue.

The first point to make is that most people have barely even heard of corporate social responsibility, and would be amazed if they lifted the stone of contemporary business activity and saw the armies of consultants, experts, charlatans and do-gooders scurry-ing around inside and outside companies trying to help them become more socially responsible. B&Q's customers would certainly be amazed to learn how seriously the company takes these issues. And two groups of people in particular, investment analysts and journalists, tend to be astonished when they find out how far the shock troops of responsible business have advanced down the boardroom table.

Within business itself, opinion is divided on corporate social responsibility. Some corporate leaders see the whole thing as a bit of a joke, swaggering about in a rather dated and quite tiring "greed is good" routine, lampooning "all this social rubbish" as the exclusive preserve of weirdoes, pinkoes and tree-hugging loons. Incidentally, these same bosses will quite happily put their name to corporate statements of social responsibility, share backslapping platforms with fawning politicians, and sanction expenditure on community projects or charitable donations: but just as long as no-one inside the company develops the subversive notion that this type of thing is in any way important to the success of the business. It is only, as these skeptics might say, the icing on the shit.

At the other end of the scale are those chief executives who have embraced corporate social responsibility with all the zeal of the convert, spending vast sums on "social audits," "environmental assessments," and "stakeholder dialogues". Curiously, the companies whose hearts are most visibly fixed to their pinstriped sleeves tend to be the ones that attract the most frequent and venomous attacks from anti-business critics. In part, this reflects a natural time lag between a company changing the way it operates and the rest of the world noticing; in part the depressingly unfair tendency of some anti-capitalists to attack the very companies who have the courage to put their head above the parapet and make a public commitment to social responsibility (alleged hypocrisy is so much more enticing a story that mere transgression), and in part, the mixed response to the business evangelists in this area reflects the fact that even those companies in the vanguard of the corporate social responsibility movement, substantial though their progress has been, have only grasped half the story. They've accepted the need for social responsibility *within* their companies, but they haven't realized that this will fail to translate into substantial business – or social – benefit unless they exert social leadership *outside* their companies. This point is the first of the two key changes that are essential if corporate social responsibility is to fulfil its potential, and it will be explored in the next chapter.

In between the two caricatured extremes of the skeptics and the evangelists lie the agnostics: the companies who feel that they probably ought to be doing something about corporate social responsibility but don't know quite what. Should they have a lot of it, or just a little bit? Should they do it themselves, or bring in some consultants? Should they wait and see what their competitors do, or should they move first? Should they – oh hell, there are more urgent things to worry about. And then finally there is the group that constitutes the overwhelming majority of the companies on earth – small businesses. Assuming they've heard of it, their view on all this is usually quite straightforward: it's got nothing to do with them, being of relevance only to the big bad multinationals that get it in the neck from the protestors and activists. This is an understandable attitude, but none the less wrong for that, and if you want to get a sense of how small companies could play their part in the corporate social responsibility movement, a good first port of call is the British think tank the Institute for Public Policy Research (ippr.org), which has carried out a number of studies in this area.

Quite apart from the range of views within the business community, there's a good old-fashioned academic and media brouhaha as well. The leading writers on anti-globalization treat corporate social responsibility with a degree of wary skepticism, occasionally tipping over into outright hostility. Noreena Hertz, for example, in *The Silent Takeover*, warns against over-reliance on corporations for our social and environmental protection, worrying that commitments to corporate social responsibility might be easy for corporations to make when economies are strong, but could be ditched quickly as times get tougher. Hertz goes on to raise concerns about the quid pro quo when business gets involved in social issues: "Is there a price that will be exacted for acts of corporate benevolence? Today Microsoft puts computers in our schools; will it tomorrow determine what our children learn ... do we want to live in a world in which commercialism takes advantage of shortages in funding and rides off the back of children's learning?"[4]

Both of the issues Hertz raises: the viability of corporate social responsibility in straitened economic circumstances, and the appropriate balance between commercial and social priorities, are crucial. Perhaps perversely for anti-business critics, the answer to the first point lies in being more businesslike. In general, it benefits no-one if activists, consumers, opinion-formers, investors – or indeed business people and their employees – come over all pie-in-the-sky, la-la land "oh who cares about the business case, companies should do it because it's the right thing to do" about corporate responsibility. Whether someone thinks it's the right thing to do or not may be a diverting question, but the important thing is that it gets done – and for most companies, it will only get done if it makes sound business sense. There *is* a strong business case for companies to change, even to change radically, in order to adopt new social values and environmental standards, but too often this case is made lazily, inaccurately, and unconvincingly. In particular, there is a tendency to over-hype the short-term benefits of corporate responsibility, whereas the real gains are likely to be seen in long-term survival and profitability. Hertz is spot on to warn that recession, or the fear of it, could threaten recent advances in this field, but the only answer is more rigor and less rhetoric. As for the second area of concern that she identifies (that of companies straying too far into social territory), you may at first cry "I should have such problems": if only there was sufficient social activism in the corporate sector today to warrant alarm. But that's no reason not to be mindful of the potential conflicts of interest that may arise in the future.

Where Noreena Hertz raises legitimate concerns about corporate social responsibility, Naomi Klein tends simply to raise her hackles. But she's on shaky ground as she argues in *No Logo* that the corporate social responsibility phenomenon is no evidence of a systematic or sincere change of heart in big business: "It's tempting to take the dramatic shift in direction on the part of so many multinationals as a massive victory for the campaigners who have battled the Nikes and the Shells all these years. Maybe corporations really have seen the light, and we're all on the same page now ... There is no doubt that companies like Nike have learned that labor-rights abuses can cost them. But the spotlight being shined on these companies is both roving and random: it is able to shine down on a few corners of the global production line, but darkness still shrouds the rest. Human rights, far from being protected by this process, are selectively respected: reforms seem to be implemented solely on the basis of where the spotlight's beam was last directed. There is absolutely no evidence that any of this reform activity is coalescing into a universal standard of ethical corporate behavior ... instead, what we have with the proliferation of voluntary codes of conduct and ethical business initiatives is a haphazard and piecemeal mess of crisis management."[5]

Klein is right in one respect: there *is* piecemeal application of social responsibility practices. But she's wrong to locate the problem within individual companies. Those companies who have made a commitment to social responsibility – most famously, Shell, bp, and Nike (although there are plenty of others) – have instituted thorough overhauls of their entire range of business processes in line with globally agreed standards of social and environmental concern. It would be imbecilic for such companies to make a great play of their new-found responsible credentials only to implement them in a half-hearted way – and whatever else they are, these companies are not run by imbeciles. Of course it will always be possible to identify individual lapses even amongst the pioneers of corporate social responsibility: as the activists never tire of pointing out, these are sizeable organizations with footprints that cover much of the globe.

But such lapses, if and when they occur, shouldn't drown out a fair hearing for the overall message of positive change, any more than an organization like Greenpeace should expect its basic message to be called into question because, to take a real example, it got some of its oil tests wrong when criticizing Shell over its planned disposal of the Brent Spar platform in the North Sea. Greenpeace immediately acknowledged its error (an error which did nothing to invalidate its overall position on the planned disposal), and successfully persuaded Shell to recycle the platform so that parts of it are now being used in a port in Norway. Along the way, Greenpeace contributed to a ban on the dumping of decommissioned oil and gas rigs in the North Sea and north-east Atlantic, and played a major part in Shell's wholehearted and sincere transformation into a company taking social and environmental issues seriously.[6] But the simplistic and incorrect taunt that "Greenpeace got it wrong on Brent Spar" has dogged the organization ever since – just as many corporations are unjustly dogged by one lapse which they have in any case put right. It's childishly fat-headed to let high-profile incidents determine judgments about corporations which can only properly be made in a thoughtful, forensic, balanced and long-term manner. Corporations, like the rest of us, make mistakes: the important questions are whether they openly acknowledge mistakes and try to correct them, and whether their basic motivations are well-intentioned and benign. The real issue here is the number of companies that have not yet even accepted the need for responsible business practice, and Klein tends to undermine her own argument with her carping and rather grudging reaction to those that have. It suggests that her most firmly held conviction is not that corporations should change how they behave, but that they must be attacked and criticized come what may.

––––––––––––––––

Another strand of opposition to corporate social responsibility is the fear that it will offer succour to governments seeking to reduce their own support for public services, confident that business will fill the ensuing gap. George Monbiot has argued this point forcefully: "If the state is failing to supply enough school books, or, in sub-Saharan Africa, AIDS education programs, it's because decades of corporate lobbying have ensured that its scope and its spending have been curtailed. As companies appear to fill the gaps they have helped to create, they can present themselves as indispensable vehicles for social provision, enabling them to argue for a further reduction in state services. Gradually, universal public provision gives way not … to a new inclusive modernity, but to an old-fashioned philanthropy, in which the survival of the poor depends on the whims of the rich."[7]

The fundamental point here is a serious one: if business social responsibility becomes a Trojan horse that substitutes corporate provision for state provision, this would indeed be a worrying development – not least for reasons of accountability. But that's not how it is. Monbiot is misleading in characterizing this as an inevitable zero-sum game: in the UK, for example, while corporate expenditure on social activity is rising, so too is public spending. Corporate social responsibility, at least in the form which is advocated in this book, is a way for the business sector to add its weight to existing mechanisms for delivering social progress. It is not an "either or" scenario.

The Monbiot critique is flawed in another sense, which is its fond assumption that businesses are so determined to exert their control over society that they choose to spend their time and money in order to "argue for a further reduction in state services." Even if one accepts the point that state services are being reduced, rather than simply being provided in new ways by new suppliers, the argument doesn't stack up. Corporate lobbying focuses on narrow areas of self-interest to the companies concerned. Most of the time, it's all about the thing that matters most to businesses: interest rates. For the small number of companies who are actually seeking to provide public services (like construction companies competing for contracts to build and manage schools and hospitals) it is undoubtedly the case that their commercial interest is best served by the state stepping aside, and they will certainly be arguing forcefully for that to happen. But corporate social responsibility encompasses the entire business world, and the idea that firms like

Shell, Microsoft, Nike or Coca-Cola even have an opinion about, say, the level of state spending on health or education, is simply a nonsense. Where there is pressure for less government and lower taxes, it is created not mainly by corporate lobbying, but by a combination of more cosmic factors: the perceived economic and social failure of other approaches, the intellectual victories of the right and the centre-left, and the fact that people all over the world have consistently voted for it.

Monbiot may be right in arguing that companies always want lower taxes – but then, they're not alone in that. Who wants to pay more taxes? Certainly not the electorates of most western democracies, who over the past few decades have conspired with their political leaders to bid down tax rates. For all the talk of a new mood in which voters are happy to pay more in tax in exchange for better public provision, there's not much sign of it happening, and not much evidence that voters believe higher taxes will guarantee better public services anyway. Mrs Thatcher always had a ready answer when people told her they'd be willing to pay more tax. She'd give them the address of the British Treasury, saying "Go on then, there's nothing stopping you. Send them a cheque." Flippant this may be, but it does make a wider point: that it's a bit rich to condemn companies for pressing for lower taxes when that's exactly what citizens regularly do.

Interestingly, it's possible to detect an emerging critique of corporate social responsibility which also lasers in anxiously on what constitutes a desirable mix of state and business roles, but from the free market right rather than the radical left. A significant body of opinion is explicitly hostile to the idea that companies should do anything other than maximize profits while obeying the law. Those that support this line of thinking take their cue from the Nobel Prize-winning economist Milton Friedman who wrote: "Few trends could so thoroughly undermine the very foundations of our free society as the acceptance by corporate officials of a social responsibility other than to make as much money for their stockholders as possible. This is a fundamentally subversive doctrine. If businessmen do have a social responsibility other than making maximum profits for stockholders, how are they to know what it is? Can self-selected private individuals decide what the social interest is?"[8] Friedman puts it more pithily still, in a phrase frequently recycled by critics of corporate social responsibility: "the social responsibility of business is to increase its profits." The most prominent champion of this hostile approach is David Henderson, the former OECD economist, and his arguments have been given some prominence by Martin Wolf of the *Financial Times*. In summary, the view from this camp is that while there's nothing wrong with companies meeting basic requirements on environmental protection, health and safety and so on, the current corporate social responsibility doctrine has gone way overboard, and will end up making everyone worse off by undermining the commercial performance of corporations by saddling them with unnecessary costs. These critics argue that corporations have run up the white flag and simply caved in to a tiny coterie of unaccountable pressure groups whose alarmist scare tactics on environmental and social issues are based on an ignorance of how the world actually works.

There's some truth in such critics' analysis – particularly in their robust defence of the social benefits of capitalism and globalization even without corporate social responsibility. But their conclusions can seem too purist for a commercially-focused CEO to endorse comfortably. For many companies, brands have replaced physical assets like factories as the most valuable aspect of their business. Indeed, for some companies, their brand is pretty much all they've got over the long term. Corporate social responsibility is deeply connected with brand reputation and the emotional component of a brand's strength, and therefore cannot be ignored, as we will see. In any case, the point has often been made that in comparison to some of the things on which corporations have tended to throw their money around, for example, as the *FT* put it, "the merger mania of the 1990s, long after it had been shown that most acquisitions destroyed shareholder value ... or squandering billions of dollars on fatuous dotcom ventures during the technology boom that went bust,"[9] corporate social responsibility is pretty sensible, and is potentially a cost effective way of communicating brand values while actually doing some good.

The general enthusiasm for corporate social responsibility is shared by the public and voluntary sectors of society too: politicians and non-governmental organizations are falling over themselves to show their backing for the idea and to champion the case studies of companies who are doing it. One of the first was Tony Blair, who said in early 1998: "The 21st century company will be different. Many of Britain's best known companies are already redefining traditional perceptions of the role of the corporation. They are recognising that every customer is part of a community, and that social responsibility is not an optional extra."[10] Blair's Government was the first in the world to appoint a minister for corporate social responsibility, though Kim Howells, the original occupant of the post, spent so much time preaching to the converted that he was quickly and rather cruelly dubbed "the Minister for Corporate Social Responsibility Conferences."

It's not just national governments that have embraced the concept: in January 1999, Kofi Annan spoke to the Davos meeting of the World Economic Forum about the importance of business taking social and environmental issues seriously, and this led to the establishment of the United Nations Global Compact, described in its own promotional material as a "challenge to world business leaders to help build the social and environmental pillars required to sustain the new global economy and make globalization work for all the world's people."[11] Blimey. The UN Global Compact is apparently a "value-based platform" – whatever that is – "designed to promote institutional learning," and is based on nine principles which are worth quoting in full as they provide a pretty accurate flavor of the burgeoning mass of statements and codes of practice which have popped up over the last few years under the social responsibility banner. The nine principles are organized into three categories, human rights, labor, and environment. They take the form of challenges issued by the UN Secretary-General to the business leaders of the world:

1. Support and respect the protection of international human rights within their sphere of influence.
2. Make sure their own corporations are not compliant in human rights abuses.
3. Freedom of association and the effective recognition of the right to collective bargaining.
4. The elimination of all forms of forced and compulsory labor.
5. The effective abolition of child labor.
6. The elimination of discrimination in respect of employment and occupation.
7. Support a precautionary approach to environmental challenges.
8. Undertake initiatives to promote greater environmental responsibility.
9. Encourage the development and diffusion of environmentally friendly technologies.

The Global Compact website (unglobalcompact.org) will give you chapter and verse on how the whole thing works, as well as many interesting case studies: but if you can't be bothered with that, the idea is that in order to qualify as members of the scheme, companies have to send a letter to Kofi Annan signing up to the nine principles, and then commit to various activities such as becoming advocates of corporate social responsibility, "posting concrete steps" on the website, and engaging in "thematic dialogues" every now and again. The whole thing is branded with Kofi Annan's worthy, if somewhat baffling, quote: "let's choose to unite the powers of markets with the authority of global ideals." Founder corporate members of the Global Compact included bp, DaimlerChrysler, Unilever, Ericsson, and Nike.

A recent spat over the UN Global Compact shows how treacherous these social responsibility waters can be. A large number of NGOs have criticized it in quite violent terms: this comment from Greenpeace International and the Third World

Institute is typical, alleging that the Global Compact would enable corporations "to wrap themselves in the flag of the UN in order to bluewash their public image, while avoiding significant changes in behavior."[12] Not true, says the UN, expressing "the hope and expectation that through the power of dialogue, transparency, advocacy and competition, good practices will drive out bad ones."[13] Probably best to stay out of this one …

And it's no surprise that the World Economic Forum (motto: "Committed to Improving the State of the World") has added its voice to the good citizen chorus. Delegates attending its 2002 meeting (symbolically relocated from Davos to New York) found a statement on global corporate citizenship, signed by nearly 40 top CEOs, waiting for them in their hotel bedrooms. You can get your very own copy by visiting weforum.org.

Quite apart from the backing for corporate social responsibility that's come from existing organizations, you could fill an entire conference hall with representatives of the new organizations that have sprung up specifically to promote this agenda. The first and biggest of these is Britain's Business in the Community, whose origins lie in a conference held at Sunningdale in the early years of Mrs Thatcher's government. Tom King, then a minister in that government, invited a group of American business leaders to talk to some of their British peers about the work that had been done by US companies in the 1970s to regenerate urban areas in the United States. Impressed and inspired by these examples of business playing an active social role, the British contingent decided to form a club to promote similar work in the UK. The inner city riots which hit Britain in 1981 gave added urgency and relevance to their efforts, which led to the creation in 1982 of Business in the Community. With Prince Charles as its President, the organization has become a respected fixture in the British corporate scene, and has contributed more than any other player to the emergence of the UK as such a developed and sophisticated market for corporate social responsibility. It's worth going along to any major Business in the Community function simply to see the splendid Julia Cleverdon, the organization's Chief Executive, in action. Cleverdon most resembles the charming but fearsome headmistress of a British public school on annual prize-giving day. Woe betide any Chief Executive that doesn't get stuck in to one of her seemingly endless supply of neatly branded community involvement initiatives.

Business in the Community has been joined by countless other organizations around the world with a similar remit – most notably Business for Social Responsibility in the US, which the jeans maker Levi Strauss played a key part in establishing, and CSR Europe, which is an umbrella organization for, amazingly enough, corporate social responsibility in Europe. Some, like the Global Reporting Initiative and the Institute for Social and Ethical Accountability, focus on helping companies audit and report on their social and environmental performance; some like Sustainability and the New Economics Foundation combine the functions of think tank and management consultancy. Others are more informal groupings of business people who are interested in the area, like the London Benchmarking Group, through which leading British companies have developed a mechanism for measuring their community contribution, or Net Impact in the US, which humbly describes itself as follows: "Net Impact is a network of emerging business leaders committed to using the power of business to create a better world. It is also the most progressive and influential network of MBAs in existence today. Originally founded as Students for Responsible Business in 1993, Net Impact has developed from a great idea shared by a few business students into a mission-driven network of 5,000 leaders for better business."[14]

Interestingly, the thinking and vocabulary of corporate social responsibility may be older than many of its new adherents might think. A researcher at Warwick Business School discovered documents showing that business people in India were using the precise terminology of the contemporary social responsibility scene, but nearly 40 years ago. A 1965 seminar in New Delhi on "social responsibilities of business," described a company as "a corporate citizen," included a declaration that called for "open, regular stakeholder dialogue, social accountability and openness and transparency," and "a social audit by trained and professional observers for factual assessment of a company's social performance."[15] There goes British author and campaigner Will Hutton's crown as the man who invented the stakeholder concept.

There are a host of standards and accreditations that companies can adopt in order to demonstrate their social and environmental credentials, and to provide a framework for improving their performance. Get ready for a hefty serving of alphabet soup: these kitemarks include the Geneva-based International Organization for Standardization's ISO14 000, which is a standard for environmental management, SA8000 which is a global trading standard, and the UK's Ethical Trading Initiative (ETI) which is "an alliance of companies, non-governmental organizations and trade union organizations that is working to improve conditions of employment in the supply chains delivering goods to consumers in Britain ... the employment standards adopted by ETI members are international standards that come from the Core Conventions of the International Labour Organization ..." The ETI website (ethicaltrade.org) provides full information on what the code of practice means in practice, as well as links to many of the other standards that companies are adopting: the most significant point, however, is that most of Britain's best-known retail chains are members, including Sainsbury's, Marks & Spencer and Tesco – another indication of mainstream support for corporate social responsibility. On the back of this increasing interest, many new publications have sprung up, including *Corporate Citizen* magazine, the *Journal of Corporate Citizenship*, and probably the most comprehensive and accessible, *Ethical Performance* magazine, which offers up to date information on latest developments in the field around the world. To gain a quick overview of just how much is going on in this area, it's really worth visiting their website at ethicalperformance.com. And for interviews with key players and in-depth analysis of the issues, see *Ethical Corporation* magazine, or visit ethicalcorp.com.

There are now literally hundreds of organizations around the world whose sole aim in life is to promote and contribute to corporate social responsibility. That's before we even mention the new breed of consultancies and marketing agencies that have been established, as well as the investment that existing business services firms have made in developing a competence in what only a few years ago they would have ridiculed as hippy nonsense. All the major accounting firms offer their clients some form of social auditing service (although in the light of Enron, you might well suggest that they start by looking at their own standards), and every PR company and ad agency worth its salt is getting in on the act too. The reason for going on about all this is not to attempt any kind of comprehensive survey of the expertise that's out there, but simply to make the point that someone's paying for it: and that someone is, frankly, business itself – either in the form of membership fees and sponsorship of corporate social responsibility organizations, or fees paid directly to consultants and suppliers of services. In other words, big business is interested: corporate social responsibility is not just the kooky obsession of a few maverick companies like Ben & Jerry's or The Body Shop. If you want to find out more, the best places to start are five excellent websites: business-impact.org, iosreporting.org, global-reporting.org, csrforum.org, and zadek.net.

In case you're worried that this is straying too far away from the nitty gritty of real business people and what they think about corporate social responsibility, let's bring on those red-blooded bastions of capitalism, the Dow Jones and FTSE stock markets, and the ever-strengthening armies of socially responsible investment funds, or ethical investing as it's also been dubbed. Here you'll find an exhilarating market-based approach, providing investors with the chance to put their money into companies with a good track record on social responsibility. The idea is simple: more and more people are interested in knowing that the companies they invest in are socially and environmentally responsible, so let's set up funds that single out those companies and exclude the ones that don't come up to scratch. The key commodity here is information:

information about the actual social and environmental performance of the world's biggest companies. Unless you can demonstrate with hard facts that what you're doing in your business qualifies you for inclusion in ethical funds, then you won't be included – and your shares won't be bought by those customers who invest on this basis. If you're looking for an accurate picture of the extent to which corporate social responsibility has genuinely caught on in the business world, there's no better place to look than here, in the stock markets of the world which are the throbbing heart of the capitalist system.

Anyone can put out glossy brochures banging on about social and environmental care; it's easy to make speeches and go along to government campaign launches; it won't break the bank to become a member of a few business social responsibility organizations – but stock markets pose a stiffer test. First of all, they deal in actual performance, not aspirations or commitments; and second, they reveal consumer preferences in the most direct and honest way, through buying and selling. The need for information to give these markets is prompting business to take a closer look at the issues that come under the heading of corporate social responsibility.

The first mainstream toe to be dipped in these waters came at the end of 1998, when the Dow Jones Index, in association with Sustainable Asset Management, launched five "sustainable" indices which make up what is known as the Dow Jones Sustainability Group Index. Sustainability is a term which, like corporate social responsibility, basks in a warm glow of generalized acceptance and support while prompting violent disagreement over what it means precisely and how it should be implemented. The most commonly accepted definition of sustainability was provided in the 1987 Brundtland Commission report to the UN, and it reads as follows: development which "meets the needs of the present generation without compromising the ability of future generations to meet their own needs."[17] OK, it's vague, but you kind of know what they mean. Don't you? Anyway, to qualify for inclusion in the Dow Jones Sustainability Group Index, companies have first of all to be part of the mainstream Dow Jones Index. They're then assessed annually to see if they satisfy five specific sustainability performance criteria. Now take a deep breath: here come the criteria.

The first is *innovation* – investing in product and services innovation that focuses on technologies and systems, which use financial, natural and social resources in an efficient, effective and economic manner over the long term. Second, *governance* – setting the highest standards of corporate governance, including management quality and responsibility, organizational capability and corporate structure. Third, *shareholders* – meeting shareholders' demands for sound financial returns, long-term economic growth, long-term productivity increases, sharpened global competitiveness, and enhancing intellectual capital. Fourth, *leadership* – leading the industry towards sustainability by setting standards for best practice and maintaining superior performance; and finally, *society* – encouraging long-lasting wellbeing in communities where companies operate, interacting with different stakeholders, and responding to their specific and evolving needs – thereby securing superior customer and employee loyalty.

Got all that? Great.

At the time of writing the index included 312 companies from 62 industries in 26 countries. Recent new entrants included Michelin, Ericsson and the Swiss pharmaceutical company Roche (an odd choice given its implication in what the European Commission described as the biggest ever price-fixing cartel it had ever investigated), while companies that were removed for failing to satisfy the criteria included Disney, Benetton and the British media company Pearson. The Dow Jones Sustainability Index has been widely adopted elsewhere – it's now used by 30 financial institutions in 12 countries (including Germany, Australia, and Japan) as the basis for ethical investment funds.

In the UK in July 2001, the Financial Times/Stock Exchange index – the famous footsie – decided to launch its own version which goes by the more catchy (if rather cheesy) name of FTSE4Good. FTSE4Good assesses companies according to three criteria: working towards environmental sustainability, developing positive relationships with stakeholders, and upholding and supporting universal human rights. At the latest count, FTSE4Good represented over a third of all the companies in the main FTSE index. (Incidentally, an intriguing Autumn 2001 addition was the stricken telecoms company Marconi, which just goes to show that catastrophically inept management and disastrous commercial performance are no barrier to being judged socially responsible. But let's not be snippy ...)

Before getting too carried away with the value and impact of ethical investing, it's important to remember that it's still a minority of all stock market activity, but more importantly, that there's a great deal of difficulty with the assessments made in pursuit of it. Social responsibility is a subjective judgment and there's disagreement over what it means. Different people, depending on their personal values and beliefs, will have profoundly different views as to what makes a company responsible or not. Some, for example, question whether oil companies like bp and Shell should be included in the FTSE4Good index since they believe that the nature of these companies' business is inherently bad. Others, perhaps to the surprise of anti-globalization activists, would argue that Shell and bp in particular have led the world in figuring out how to satisfy consumer needs while respecting the environment, human rights and so on, and should therefore be ranked top of the list in any ethical investment league table. Agonizing over this type of dilemma is going to become increasingly commonplace given how rapidly the socially responsible investment sector is growing.

It now accounts for nearly 15 per cent of all investment in the United States,[18] and is growing rapidly in many markets around the world. It's still relatively small outside the US – even in the UK, Europe's most advanced market, this type of investing accounts for only around 1 percent of total assets – but there's no reason to suppose that the rest of the world won't follow the United States' lead. As UBS Warburg put in its August 2001 report on "Sustainability Investment": "The situation is reminiscent of the story of the two shoe salespeople dispatched to sell shoes in a new market: one salesperson, having thoroughly assessed the situation, reported back to head office that there is absolutely no demand for shoes in the new market because no-one wears shoes. The other salesperson calls the office and asks for a huge quantity of shoes to be sent immediately for the same reason – that no-one wears shoes and everyone needs them. We are firmly in the latter camp."[19]

The idea behind ethical investing is not particularly new: in the 1920s, for example, when the Methodist Church started investing in the stock market, it refused to buy shares in companies that were associated with alcohol, tobacco or gambling. The first explicitly ethical investment mutual fund was set up in America in 1971: the Pax World Fund was established to provide a way for people to invest in companies that had nothing to do with the Vietnam War, and similar funds followed in the 1980s to enable investors to avoid companies that were involved with South Africa's apartheid regime. But these historical antecedents of the current boom in ethical investing were niche players, with extremely clear criteria for those investors who took an interest in the issues. Refusing to invest in companies involved with alcohol, for example, requires no great exercise of Olympian judgment or forensic skill. But today, socially responsible investing is moving into the mainstream, and indeed will eventually become the norm if current growth trends continue. This means that the criteria for judging companies' social and environmental responsibility need to be far more sophisticated, as they'll have to be applied to all businesses, including many which are controversial in one way or another.

So in today's stock market scenario, what makes a company ethical, or socially responsible? There's a philosophical answer, and a practical answer. The philosophical answer is to decide whether you favor what's known in the jargon as negative screening or positive screening. Negative screening weeds out companies who operate in certain industries that are considered to be unacceptable, for example the oil industry, the arms trade, alcohol, tobacco, and gambling; who operate in unacceptable territories, for example countries with oppressive regimes like Myanmar; or who engage in "unacceptable activities," like animal experimentation, anti-trade union activity, or Third World exploitation. Positive screening, on the other hand, singles out and selects companies who go out of their way to provide long-term benefits to communities and the environment. Characteristics of such companies could include a commitment to energy conservation, a strong community investment policy, a good safety record, and a full and open disclosure policy which informs the public about every aspect of its activities.

Clearly, there's a problem with negative screening, in that it relies on a wholly subjective assessment of what's good or bad. Is nuclear power in or out? What about tobacco? Both these activities are legal and play a major part in our society. Yet companies engaged in these activities are excluded from many ethical funds without any regard to whether or not they carry out their controversial activities in a responsible manner. As Gareth Davis, Chief Executive of Imperial Tobacco has put it: "as a big UK manufacturer of a legal but controversial product, Imperial Tobacco aspires to apply recognized criteria for good corporate governance, employee relations, health, safety and the environment and wider community relations. We believe investors would be better served by a set of indices that represent a fair and objective assessment of identifiable business practices, rather than measures based on inclusion criteria that are completely inflexible and a subjective opinion of a company's products."[20] There's no right or wrong answer to this: on the one hand, it's clearly desirable for all companies to behave in a responsible way, and as long as Imperial Tobacco is permitted by law to make cigarettes, surely it's right to recognize and encourage any steps it may take to do what it does more responsibly? On the other hand, if investors interested in social responsibility believe that tobacco companies are beyond the pale, then they have every right to insist that ethical funds exclude them. As ever, the only sensible way out of a dilemma of this type is to let the market decide. This is exactly what is happening, as investors make their own choices about which funds to select, enabling subjective opinions to find a commercial expression.

The practical answer to the question of what makes a company socially responsible or not is provided by the various organizations that have been set up specifically to carry out research on corporate behavior and then to assess how companies perform. In short, they rate companies on how socially and environmentally responsible they are. Their assessments are provided to the managers of ethical investment funds so that they have concrete information on which to base their decisions about which companies meet whatever social and environmental criteria their particular fund uses. The FTSE4Good, for example, uses data from EIRIS (the Ethical Investment Research Service, set up as a charity in 1983 to provide information on company activities). Another leader in the field is the Pensions Investment Research Company (PIRC), and a glance at their website (pirc.co.uk) will offer you a glimpse of the general approach and specific details that such rating organizations use when deciding how socially responsible companies actually are.

It's easy to get strung up, bogged down and monumentally confused by this whole area. Who are these anonymous people that decide what's socially responsible or not? How can we be sure they get it right? How can they possibly know what's going on in every nook and cranny of a huge company? What right have they got to make ethical decisions? Is there any company out there that's genuinely responsible – what about companies that produce food that gives people heart disease? What about companies whose advertisements for toys lead children to drive their parents to distraction and the brink of poverty with their unceasing demands for the latest gizmo? What about companies that make hair care products for frequent use causing irresponsibly high consumption of water? What about Microsoft? Surely we all hate Bill Gates ... and so on. Even in the so-called responsible business sector, people could raise perfectly valid concerns: what's so ethical about The Body Shop, marketing flim-flam, superfluous cosmetic products and forcing its logo into every available shopping mall and high street? What's so good about Ben & Jerry's with its tacky tubs of obesity-inducing junk food? What about all those organic producers? They may not pump chemicals into the soil but how do they treat their farm workers? Are they granted collective bargaining rights, as prescribed by the International Labour Organization?

Anita Roddick would say that people will always want to look after their bodies, and so she's proud to have created a brand that helps them do that in a more responsible way; she'd argue that The Body Shop has led to a cultural revolution on the issue of animal testing, and she's right on both counts. Ben, Jerry, and their new owners at global food giant Unilever would say that people will always want ice cream, and that it's better to supply it in a way that supports local communities; and they're right. Organic farmers would say that people will always need food so why not find ways of providing it that don't pollute the earth and put dodgy toxins into people's bodies? They're right too, but the fact that all these people are right doesn't give them a monopoly on virtue.

You could quite easily argue that the corporations which make the greatest single contribution to human happiness and global development, and have done for years, are in fact those wicked oil companies. They enable us to move around, keep warm, use plastic, have cosmetics, on and on it goes: if it happened in the twentieth century, oil had something to do with it. But we're back to the half full/half empty debate. If you view the twentieth century not as mankind's greatest, but as his most destructive and irresponsible, it's no wonder that you hate the oil companies and would want them flung out of every ethical fund.

There are endless potential concerns about the products and services we consume, and the fact that anyone may have such concerns automatically makes them valid. But that doesn't mean that the fledgling infrastructure for socially responsible investing can instantly accommodate them: the world is not black and white, and as we saw in Chapters 1 and 2, it's important to remind ourselves of the positive aspects of capitalism and business even while making legitimate criticisms. It's also important to remember that companies only exist if they can sell their products or services to someone, and that this in a broad sense constitutes society's approval of their activities. The remarkable recent growth of socially responsible investing is just one further indication of the way in which corporate social responsibility is becoming a serious and mainstream concern for business, but it's not exact, and there will always be anomalies. It's a new development that's still finding its feet, but on the whole, it can only be a good thing if it encourages companies to think about social and environmental issues that previously didn't concern them. But it's not just a challenge; it's also an opportunity for corporations, a chance to redefine their brand and their strategic direction.

To the extent that it provides fuller and more accurate information about companies and their products, it's a tremendous step forward in the development of the free market economy, since the more information that's available to buyers and sellers, the more efficiently markets work. And therefore the ultimate, and the only truly democratic, test of whether a company is sufficiently socially responsible will come from its customers. If customers are happy to do business with a company, who is anyone else to tell them they're wrong? So the pressure for companies to disclose information on their social and environmental performance in order to respond to the demands of stock markets is clearly in the consumer interest too, as it enables customers, as well as investors, to make better informed choices. If they ignore social and environmental factors, so be it: but thanks to developments in socially responsible investing and in corporate social responsibility generally, at least people will increasingly have the information to make their own decisions rather than having those decisions made for them by lawmakers and bureaucrats, or influenced by the often unbalanced opinions of activists with an axe to grind. But these considerable benefits are not even vaguely being realized at the moment. It is in this area of information provision where the second of the two key changes in corporate social responsibility will be required – the first, remember, being the need for corporations to take on the mantle of social leadership as well as social responsibility. These two changes are desribed more fully in Chapter 4.

But we won't be able to form a confident opinion about where corporate social responsibility needs to go next unless we understand how it's got to where it is. Is it just part of the evolution of capitalism, the tendency for corporations to make things better, to adhere to higher environmental and social standards (either through competition or regulation)? How has the doctrine accomplished such a comprehensive clean sweep of approval? On the other hand, what about the concerns? Is it possible to construct a working and realizable synthesis which takes account of criticisms such as those of David Henderson – that corporate social responsibility has gone too far; as well as satisfying opponents like George Monbiot who argue that this is all just a cover-up, and that we're in danger of reversing social progress by reviving a pernicious Victorian approach where social issues depend for their resolution on the philanthropic whim of unelected fat cat executives? And is it really all that it's cracked up to be anyway – what about all the companies that still act as if they're lukewarm about the idea, despite public statements to the contrary?

It's often claimed that consumer pressure is one of the main forces prodding companies in a more socially responsible direction. Practically every week sees the publication of a new opinion poll somewhere in the world "proving" that social responsibility is good for business.[21] Some of them focus on employees, indicating that people would prefer to work for companies that demonstrate high social, ethical, and environmental standards, and that a company's reputation is more important than salary and benefits in determining whether or not people want to work for that company. If true, this would indeed be significant news since recruiting skilled workers, keeping hold of them, and keeping them

motivated is a hugely important objective for most businesses –
and the costs of failing to do it right are considerable. Other
opinion polls suggest that consumers increasingly expect companies to be socially responsible, and that they're more likely than
before to take such considerations into account when making their
purchasing decisions; for example, they would switch from Ford to
Toyota if Toyota had greener credentials than Ford, or if by buying
a Toyota they helped support conservation initiatives (as long as
price and quality issues were about the same).[22] Again, this would
amount to something of a Holy Grail for businesses as it becomes
more and more difficult for them to create product and service
advantages that aren't quickly matched by competitors. Any
method of guaranteeing a customer's preference is bound to be
attractive, and if it helps society in some way, so much the better.
Still more polls show that consumers are more prepared than ever
before to boycott companies and their products if they hear that
they've made some kind of ethical *faux pas*.[23] This finding is
potentially the most terrifying for business leaders: no-one wants to
risk a concerted campaign against their product, not just because
of the drop in sales, but because of all the knock-on effects and
costs, including those associated with rebuilding a damaged
reputation. As Warren Buffett, probably the world's most respected
investor, once said, "it takes twenty years to build up a reputation
and five minutes to ruin it."[24] The final category of opinion polling
in this area is the type which invites people to rank companies
according to whether or not they think they're socially responsible,
asking whether companies and brands should be doing more to
prove how nice they are.[25]

The trouble with such surveys, and the reason that they're not
taken terribly seriously by the business community, is that they're
all attitudinal, rather than behavioral. If someone comes up to you
in the street and asks you a bunch of questions about social
responsibility, it's highly likely that you'll be positive about the
subject: after all, who wants to be seen as a nasty, flinty-hearted
skinflint who's only interested in results, results, results? Actually,

there *are* some people like this: the answers to questions about social responsibility usually feature percentage scores in the high 70s and 80s agreeing with the positive point of view – which always leaves at least 15 percent of the public who rather heroically stand out against the incoming tide of compassion and caring, insisting that they couldn't care less whether companies are socially responsible and wouldn't boycott an unethical product if their lives depended on it. But most of the time, people give what they think is the "right" answer to questions of this kind, and it doesn't necessarily follow from this that they actually behave in the way they say they would. This mirrors the political arena where voters tell pollsters they'd happily pay more in taxes in order to get better public services and then promptly vote for parties that promise not to increase their tax bills. It's all very well for consumers to call upon the businesses of the world to become more socially responsible, but they usually haven't the faintest idea what this would mean – for example in terms of cost increases that might raise the price of the products they buy.

While the drawbacks of such attitudinal research are plain to see, actual behavior provides no more convincing an argument in the promotion of social responsibility. As we've already noted, the real sales impact of even the most high profile ethical boycotts has been slight, and there's no evidence that companies with a dubious reputation have difficulty attracting top quality staff. Furthermore, there are plenty of examples of companies which have made a great play of their social and environmental credentials only to come a cropper for good old-fashioned business reasons – The Body Shop and Levi Strauss are two of the most prominent. Of course, this is not to say that these companies experienced trading difficulties *because* of their commitment to social responsibility, merely to make the general point that social factors have not in the past proved to correlate with commercial performance one way or the other, and can't solve basic business problems.

Another set of arguments that is used to try and gain general acceptance for social responsibility is based on analysis of long-term company performance. In the 1980s, Arie de Geus carried out research into the lifespan of various companies in the US, Europe, and Japan, and examined their characteristics. He reported that on average companies stayed in existence for twelve years; that the really major companies that could be described as pillars of their economies lived for around forty years, and that those which survived longer were the ones that saw their role not merely as profit generators but as members of the community.[26] Similarly, James Collins and Jerry Porras, in their book *Built to Last*, present evidence that the world's most successful companies are those that have some kind of social vision beyond making money, and are prepared to stick to their core values even if that sometimes means sacrificing profits in the short term.[27] Entertaining and inspiring these tales may be: but they still don't add up to a convincing case for corporate social responsibility since there's no evidence of a causal link between a company's long-term success and its social values. While it may be true that great companies are great because they have an element of social and environmental concern, it could equally be true (and is frankly more likely) that they're successful for a whole host of other reasons like good management, skilful marketing and a culture of innovation, and that their community credentials are a happy coincidence.

Alright then, let's pull another arrow from the social quiver. What about the performance of socially responsible stocks? Do they indicate that companies rated as good citizens do better financially, at least in terms of their share price? Er, not really. While it's true that the five-year return on equity of the Dow Jones Sustainability Group Index was higher than that for the Dow Jones overall,[28] and there are some studies showing ethical funds outperforming other funds,[29] there's no evidence that this superior return is a *result* of their social or environmental qualities. It could just as easily be due to the composition of the funds, in other words the type of companies and industrial sectors represented. Compared to the mainstream stock market funds, the ethical funds include fewer "old-fashioned" industrial companies, and more stocks in "new economy" sectors such as telecommunications. Guess what – over the past few years there's been something of a boom in that type of share. So the fact that some ethical funds did better than some funds based on other criteria reflects nothing more than economic and investing trends generally. However, it *is* true to say that investing according to social and ethical criteria certainly seems as likely to make you money as any other rationale for stock picking.[30] In other words, there's no financial sacrifice involved in being responsible in your investments – and that in itself is a hugely important message given the somewhat patronizing approach that certain financial services executives take when it comes to this sector ("well it's all very nice but it's never going to make you money"). There's no need for the advocates of socially responsible investing to overstate their case, claiming that social responsibility is guaranteed to improve financial performance – but it's equally misleading for skeptics to claim that it's bound to impair profitability, growth, or any of the other conventional measures of business success.

So if it's not really proven that social responsibility improves a company's financial performance, if it's not guaranteed to win new customers, if it can't on its own make sure that companies recruit the best workers, if there's no real evidence that it's been the magical "x factor" that explains the success of enduring businesses, why is corporate social responsibility increasingly catching the eye of Chief Executives, albeit in a haphazard way?

Is it something much more human, much simpler, at work? Could it just be that business people would actually like to help make the world a better place – or at least, to avoid making it a worse place? After all, with certain famous exceptions, business people are not monsters. They're human beings, and when they leave their offices and factories at the end of the working day, there's no reason to suppose that their personal and social values are any different from, say, those of a nurse or a charity worker. Fundamentally, all people, including business people, want pretty much the same things: a secure future for themselves and their

BISHOP BURTON COLLEGE
LIBRARY

family, a safe and clean neighborhood, a world in which opportunities are growing and in which poverty and injustice are falling.
In the past, people in business have rarely felt able to introduce
such values to the daily grind of their jobs – but maybe that's
changing. Maybe the real explanation for the growing commercial
appeal of corporate social responsibility is cultural rather than
economic. Talk to the most recent graduates from Harvard Business
School or INSEAD, and it's likely many will be openly grappling
with a once-hidden dilemma: how to forge a career in business
without feeling ashamed of the social and environmental
consequences of their work? It doesn't matter whether this feeling
is justified or not, the fact is that it's there on the part of many
budding business people. Net Impact in the US is just one visible
example of this trend, as are the growing number of business
schools that offer courses in social responsibility alongside the
conventional business training received, and the willingness, even
eagerness, of many major corporations to send their executives on
career development programs that include an explicit social
responsibility dimension.

Of course, the idea that business people might care about social
issues is nothing new. As Anita Roddick points out, "the truth is that
business as it is generally understood now, with its narrow
concentration on profit, is not actually a very old idea. For most of
history, excessive money-making has been consistently condemned
as sinful and even after the Protestant Reformation changed society's
attitude to business enterprise, corporations were chartered
according to the duties they owed to the community as a whole.
Queen Elizabeth I chartered the early trading corporations with this
duty to the wider community central to their purpose. In many ways,
social responsibility in business means reaching back to the original
tradition that has been mislaid somewhere along the way."[31]

The advent of capitalist enterprise ushered in a whole new
interpretation, with industrialists raising two well-manicured fingers
to accusations of rip-off and reckless plundering in the form of good
works and philanthropy. Ever since the process of industrialization

began, big business has spent big bucks on social projects: think of names like Rockefeller, Ford, Carnegie, Guggenheim, Rowntree, Cadbury. All of them invested fortunes in charitable foundations, arts and education projects, social infrastructure – you name it. Or rather, they named it, since most of these projects bore the branding of their generous benefactors. Their motivation was mixed. Certainly, there was amongst many of these giants of capitalism a genuine and sincerely held belief that it was the duty of the successful entrepreneur to "give something back": here's Andrew Carnegie, who made his fortune in steel and then went on to be one of the all-time great philanthropists, amongst other things pretty much launching the concept of the free public library, of which he built thousands: "This, then, is held to be the duty of the man of wealth: first, to set an example of modest unostentatious living, shunning display: to provide moderately for the legitimate wants of those dependent on him; and after doing so to consider all surplus revenues which come to him simply as trust funds which he has strictly bound as a matter of duty to administer in the manner which, in his judgment, is best calculated to produce the most beneficial results for the community."[32]

It wasn't all strictly altruistic, though. Some of the very first industrialists, particularly those with fervently-held religious views like the great industrial scions of the Quaker movement, provided social protection for their workers because no-one else would – this was in the days before the advent of the welfare state – and because it was in their commercial interests to do so. Educated workers housed in decent conditions and fed properly simply worked harder. The doctrine has since been described as "enlightened self-interest." The Bournville Village, a model "garden town" built for their workers by the Cadbury chocolate brothers outside Birmingham, England, is just one of the many physical manifestations of this philosophy. But it's simplistic and in many cases plain wrong to trace, as some writers have done, a continuous link between yesterday's philanthropy and today's corporate social responsibility. Corporate social responsibility is about how a company behaves, about the way it does business, all the time. Old-fashioned philanthropy was often completely divorced from actual business activity: it was carried out, if you like, after-hours. Nothing illustrates this better than two contrasting quotes from one of the most famous businessmen of all time, John D Rockefeller. First of all, take a look at these words of his, enshrined on a bronze plaque in Rockefeller Plaza, New York City. It's barely conceivable to imagine one of today's CEOs speaking in these terms:

"I believe in the supreme worth of the individual and his right to life, liberty and the pursuit of happiness.

I believe that every right implies a responsibility; every opportunity, an obligation; every possession, a duty.

I believe that the law was made for man and not man for the law; that government is the servant of the people and not their master.

I believe in the dignity of labor, whether with head or hand; that the world owes no man a living, but that it owes every man an opportunity to make a living.

I believe that thrift is essential to well-ordered living, and that economy is a prime requisite of a sound financial structure, whether in government, business or personal affairs.

I believe that truth and justice are fundamental to an enduring social order.

I believe in the sacredness of a promise, that a man's word should be as good as his bond; that character – not wealth, or power, or position – is of supreme worth.

I believe that the rendering of useful service is the common duty of mankind and that only in the purifying fire of sacrifice is the dross of selfishness consumed and the greatness of the human soul set free.

I believe in an all-wise and all-loving god, named by whatever name, and that the individual's highest fulfilment, greatest happiness and widest usefulness are to be found in living in harmony with His will.

I believe that love is the greatest thing in the world; that it alone can overcome hate; that right can and will triumph over might."[33]

Reeling from this overblown but doubtless well-intentioned rhapsody of rhetoric, oozing wisdom and compassion like Gruyère in a fondue, you might be tempted instantly to crown Rockefeller the king of corporate responsibility. That is, until you read some other words of his: "I am prepared to pay someone a salary of one million dollars, but he must display certain characteristics: he must be able to glide over every moral restraint with almost childlike disregard … and has, besides other positive qualities, no scruples whatsoever and be ready to kill off thousands of victims – without a murmur."[34] Nice. Would the real John D Rockefeller please stand up?

The truth is, they're both real. Oddly enough, traditional business people were – and many still are – almost miraculously agile in compartmentalizing different aspects of their lives. A more modern version of the potential conflict in values was graphically illustrated a few years ago during "Take Your Daughters To Work Day," a US scheme now replicated in Britain, where parents are encouraged, as you've probably guessed by now, to take their daughters to work for a day, the idea being that young women would grow up to be familiar with workplace environments and therefore less likely to be culturally cowed into accepting that their only role in life is to look after the kids and make cookies. A few years ago, a participating British father was interviewed about his experience. His reply was supremely poignant. He reported that while he found it straightforward enough to take his daughter to work, taking himself to work proved far more problematic. What he meant was that having his daughter sit with him in his office all day brought home to him that he was in actual fact two different people. At home, a loving and compassionate father; at work, a ruthless bully. He found himself embarrassed to behave in front of his daughter as he would normally have behaved in the workplace. She simply wouldn't recognize this snarling corporate gauleiter as the father she knew and loved. In a tiny way, this brings home an enormously important point about corporate social responsibility, one that is nearly always overlooked. It could just be that a new generation of senior executives, many of them with socially liberal values established during their formative years in the 1960s, and crucially, many of them women, is starting to change the conventions of doing business. Like the new generation of business school graduates, they're starting to take themselves – and their values – to work every day.

So, are the first green shoots of business liberalism starting to peek through into our barren capitalist world? Perhaps we should all raise a glass or two to phenomena like the decline of formality in the workplace, increased time flexibility, the fashion for open-plan office layouts, and the trend towards more consensual and open relationships between people at different levels in the corporate hierarchy. Corporate social responsibility not only encompasses many of these developments, but goes far broader and is therefore of far greater significance. But let's not get too excited: one dress-down Friday does not nirvana make.

In reality, many companies still ape the compartmentalism practiced by the very first industrialists. It's probably the aspect of business behavior that's changed least over the past hundred years. The belief that being a good corporate citizen involves little more than developing a generous and thoughtful program of philanthropy and good works is still a powerful one for many CEOs, whatever their claims about "aligning their social investment strategies with the core business," or similar guff. There's absolutely nothing wrong with a generous and thoughtful program of philanthropy and good works: but let's not pretend that it's got much to do with running a business responsibly. It's the worst form of hypocrisy to invest time and money in charity and community projects while treating your own workers in a high-handed, arrogant, or exploitative manner. Only when social values permeate every aspect of a company's operations, when social objectives are included in every worker's job description could that company be described as truly embracing corporate social responsibility. And it will be particularly interesting to see how corporations that have signed up to social responsibility respond to the testing times of recession: will lay-offs be less brutal now that there's a corporate citizenship department? When number-crunching business skeptics question the value of corporate social responsibility, it's usually because they're seeing it in this old-fashioned, compartmentalized way. From that viewpoint, they're absolutely right to question its real commercial worth: frankly, there isn't much, although it may bring the undeniable (but fleeting) pleasure of public recognition and acclaim from the great and the good. What price now the lavish philanthropy and model do-gooding of those "corporate citizens" at Enron? Proponents of corporate social responsibility now have a one-word answer when confronted by business skeptics. Enron shows us, in the most dramatic possible way, the importance of openness, transparency, and the need to embed the principles of social responsibility at every level of the corporate hierarchy.

Woody Allen famously remarked that he didn't want to achieve immortality through his work – he wanted to achieve it through not dying. In the same vein, those business leaders currently chucking money at charitable projects and unarguably admirable foundations to ensure their immortality in the pantheon of business heroes (step forward Bill Gates, Ted Turner *et al.*) would be wise to adopt Allen's aim: social responsibility is not about individual bosses being or looking good; it's about companies not dying. Because firms that fail to get their social and environmental performance up to scratch will not survive. This may sound like the sort of sweeping, overblown hyperbole that characterizes the promotion of every half-baked business idea from the need to embrace WAP technology to the vital importance of applying the principles of feng shui to the layout of office space, but for once the rhetoric is on target. And here's the real, hard-nosed, cold light of day, show-me-the-money reason why.

The fact that corporate social responsibility is here to stay is less to do with past evidence that it's good for business, and far more to do with unspecified future risks and threats. This is not an iron rule: many of the most exciting and inspiring examples of responsible business practice are being generated by passionate corporate leaders and entrepreneurs who have a wholly positive vision of doing business in a different way, doing well by doing good as the saying goes. B&Q is just one example. Such companies are growing in number – and size – all the time, but they still represent a tiny proportion of overall business activity. There will be a far more substantial impact as the big corporations slowly but surely turn their tankers around, pointing them in a more socially and environmentally responsible direction. In many cases, the hands on the tiller will belong to individual business leaders who, despite spending their careers within what the outside world might characterize as soulless corporations, have managed to retain values not entirely dissimilar to the entrepreneurs that set up ethical cosmetics companies. But the main reason the tankers are permitted to turn at all is fear rather than vision.

Business leaders, however strong or passionately held their personal belief in social responsibility, cannot act alone, and they cannot act without credible commercial arguments. They need to persuade colleagues, board members, investors that their strategy is the right one. And quite frankly, fear is an easier sell than vision. Think about it: "we have to do this or we'll go out of business" will tend to be more instantly compelling than: "if we do this, we could really do well." Of course, the choice is rarely quite so dramatic – it's not immediately a question of going out of business, but the issue at stake is whether or not companies could be negatively affected by a failure to put social responsibility strategies in place. And the answer seems to be an emphatic yes, with social responsibility emerging as a key component of what is known as risk management. Stay awake, this is important; in layman's terms, risk management is like an insurance policy in case things go wrong. Companies have learned to take the issue of risk management seriously, not least because they're required to report on commercial risks, but just as importantly because it's a vital aspect of assuring investors about the long-term prospects of the business.

It's dawning on more and more companies that social and environmental issues could pose a considerable risk to their continued commercial success. For a brilliant insight into this area, it's worth looking at *Everybody's Business* by David Grayson and Adrian Hodges.[35] It's by far the best guide to corporate social responsibility that has been produced, managing to be both comprehensive and instantly accessible, and to move easily from global issue to local application; from potential problem to practical solution. One of its key strengths is the systematic way in which it explains the huge variety of risks companies face if they ignore corporate social responsibility. It's impossible to do justice here to the wide range of examples the authors provide, but a handful will offer a flavor and show just how influential these issues are becoming in determining corporate success or failure.

Perhaps the most immediately painful threat is that of litigation, either through a class action lawsuit or through individual claims made by disgruntled employees or suppliers. There have been several high-profile examples in recent years: in the US, both Texaco and Coca-Cola have faced lawsuits alleging racism; in January 1999, the international NGO Global Exchange, along with the garment workers union (UNITE), Sweatshop Watch, and the Asian Law Caucus, filed a $1 billion class action lawsuit on behalf of 20,000 sweatshop workers on the Pacific island of Saipan, charging 17 US retailers of using indentured labor and violating human rights laws; US insurance giant American General settled claims that it charged African-Americans more for insurance than whites with a payment of $206 million; and the cost to restaurant chain Shoney Inc. to settle a class-action lawsuit brought by 20,000 employees for alleged discrimination was $132 million. For any company, such sums are not peanuts: they knock most corporate advertising and communications budgets into a cocked hat, for a start. And there's an entirely new type of legal threat emerging, in the form of foreign direct liability claims, where a parent company can be held directly responsible for the actions of an overseas subsidiary. Thor, RTZ, and Cape plc have all recently been sued in the British courts for personal injuries sustained by their workers in South Africa or Namibia.

Another area of risk is the threat to a company's reputation when it's accused of an ethical gaffe, either through lawsuits, boycotts or just good old-fashioned PR campaigns mounted by critics. While reputational damage is a less tangible cost than dollars shelled out to settle a lawsuit, it's not an insignificant factor given how important intangible corporate assets, like brand strength and general goodwill, are now considered to be. Many companies value their brand reputation on their financial balance sheets, and these figures are used to work out their market capitalization. For example 97 percent of the value of Kelloggs is accounted for by intangible brand assets; for Coca-Cola the figure is 96 percent, according to brand consultancy Interbrand.[36] Coca-Cola is, effectively, a brand manager and nothing else: all its bottling and distribution functions are carried out by wholly separate companies. Damage the asset that is the brand, and you damage the share price. As Tim Mason, Marketing Director of British retail chain Tesco has put it, corporate social responsibility is an effective way of topping up the "fund of benevolence" that every company needs if it is to prosper.

Another risk from failing to deal properly with corporate social responsibility is the risk of losing out on business. This can manifest itself in a number of ways. For instance, increasingly, public sector procurement requires compliance with social and environmental codes of practice. (Although as Ed Mayo of Britain's New Economics Foundation has pointed out, national governments could give a significant boost to corporate social responsibility by requiring far more of companies that compete for government contracts.)[37] It's particularly important for the major multinationals seeking government authority to set up in new territories: the first question often asked of the would-be investor is: "OK, but what are you going to do for us?" And it applies to small firms too, since many large companies that have adopted social responsibility themselves are introducing requirements for their own suppliers to follow suit. A creative and practical way of helping businesses of all sizes to meet these demands was launched in the UK in 2001 by GoodCorporation. The website, goodcorporation.com provides a good run-down on how it all works, and their "Charter" is a useful and short summary of the specific subjects that companies need to look at when developing their own social responsibility plans.

The growing popularity of ethical investment funds, which we looked at earlier, and the development of indices like the Dow Jones Sustainability Group Index and the FTSE4Good, leads to another fear: that a company's share price could suffer by exclusion from investment vehicles that use social and environmental criteria. And it's not just the ethical funds: since July 2000, all UK pension funds, for example, have to include their policy on social, environmental and ethical investing in their Statement of Investment Principles. They don't have to have a policy; they just have to state whether or not they've got one. Since it looks pretty antediluvian to state categorically that you take no interest in ethical issues, the tendency has been to develop investment policies along these lines. Insurance companies are following suit, which means that British corporations are now receiving questionnaires on their social and environmental performance not from (as they might see it) way-out pressure groups that they can safely ignore, but from the people they really care about: the big institutional investors.

The fear of regulatory control provides a further impetus in the direction of social responsibility. More and more national governments and international bodies like the World Bank and the OECD are introducing, or planning to introduce, requirements specifying principles, standards, and reporting guidelines in this area. The reporting requirement is particularly uppermost in corporations' minds. We're moving towards a situation where in a decade's time, companies might have to report on their social and environmental performance as rigorously as they now have to on their financial performance. The social audit business is enjoying considerable growth (though not nearly enough for some campaigners) and presents a whole new set of challenges to managers of companies. The idea behind social auditing is to conduct a thorough assessment of a company's relationships with all its stakeholders – that is, the various different groups of people that affect, and are affected by, what the company does. The usual list is: customers, employees, local communities, suppliers, govern-ments, and regulators. Some companies include the media, some go further and include what they describe as "wider society," and some even talk about "future generations" (chiefly used to take account of long-term environmental factors). Having agreed who its stakeholders are, the next step is for a company to figure out its impact on those stakeholders, and what impact those stakeholders have on the company. This is usually done by a combination of interviews and questionnaires, and the monitoring of various objective benchmarks such as speed of response to customer complaints, provision of facilities for disabled people, percentage of buildings compliant with adopted environmental standards, and so on. The final step is for the social audit to be verified independently by an expert, much in the same way as a company's annual report and accounts are signed off by recognized accountancy firms.

Frankly, very few companies currently undertake social audits with any degree of rigor, although there are more and more examples of glossy social reports and websites which act as a compendium of all the good things that a company thinks it's doing. The New Economics Foundation, one of the pioneers of social auditing in the UK, published a critical survey in 2000 which pointed out that fewer than one percent of the companies listed on the New York or London Stock Exchanges report on their social performance, that "social reporting has been captured by the marketing departments" and that it "ignores the most important facts."[38] On the other hand, it *is* interesting to look at the best of them, simply to understand just how complex many of these social and environmental issues are for companies, and the level of detail they need to go into in order to make sure they're not leaving themselves exposed to dangerous risks. The social reports that seem to win all the prizes at the newly instituted Social Reporting

Awards (now there's a ticket you'll want to get your hands on) are those produced by UK companies the Co-Operative Bank, Shell and lottery operator Camelot; and by Canadian bank Van City. Alternatively, you could look at one of the following company's reports, which were rated as in the top 20 in the world by the consultancy Sustainability: BAA, Novo Nordisk, British Airways, Bristol-Myers Squibb, Volkswagen, ING, Eskom, and United Utilities. Anti-globalization activists tend to brush off the entire social reporting phenomenon as yet another example of companies trying to pull the wool over the eyes of concerned citizens, but Grayson and Hodges sum up the position well in *Everybody's Business*: "While it may seem as if business is damned if it does report and still damned if it does not, the pressures on companies are pushing towards higher standards of accountability and demanding hard evidence of performance. This will need to be made available to internal and external stakeholders, in forms and formats that permit more accurate benchmarking."[39]

There's one last point to bear in mind. Corporations, like human beings, prefer to shape their own destinies than to have their destinies shaped for them. As CEOs and their attendant throngs of subordinates, advisers, consultants, and lickspittles survey the world from their corporate eyries, they detect change in the air. They see the media taking a far keener interest in the intricacies of the capitalist system. They see anti-globalization activists managing to undo in five minutes on a radio phone-in the work of hundreds of thousands of dollars worth of corporate communications "strategy." They see, like Gulliver, swarms of Lilliputians: the bureaucrats eager to tie them down with ever more onerous regulations and controls. They see politicians as fair-weather friends, worryingly prone to tossing the electoral dogs some juicy business bones. What are they to make of it all? Stand by and let it happen? No: better to act now, and head off the dangers that lurk in the long shadows cast by the anti-capitalist movement. By participating in the debate on corporate social responsibility, companies believe, rightly, that they can shape it to their advantage. By acting on corporate social responsibility, they know they can ensure that it works for them.

This is not surrender, as the free-market critics have claimed. This is sound strategy; this is survival.

When you consider the range of pressures that are leading companies in the direction of social responsibility – for instance, the fear of litigation, the fear of a damaged reputation, the fear of being excluded from social investment funds, the need to comply with legislation and regulation – it's pretty clear that the classic and rather pious mantra endlessly trotted out in connection with corporate social responsibility, that being a good citizen is good for business, gives a misleading picture. The formulation that really cuts the mustard in the boardroom is that being a bad citizen is bad for business. To put it another way, eliminating the negative currently takes precedence over accentuating the positive. This is not to ignore or undermine the many excellent examples of projects and strategies that fall into the latter category, nor should it be taken as a dismissal of the many people in business today who are passionate about helping their companies to be more socially responsible simply because they think it's the right thing to do. Furthermore, you might well point out that eliminating the negative is not a bad start. But let's be honest about it. To really understand what's going on in this area, and to be in a position to constructively shape its future, we have to acknowledge that fear of exposure and the need for compliance are the most powerful forces galvanizing the majority of active corporate citizens.

Although (as we shall see in the next chapter) there's a lot wrong with this state of affairs, it could be argued that putting the case in these terms is actually more credible than claiming that corporations have suddenly "seen the light." If your starting point is a mistrust of capitalism and business in general, you're not likely to be persuaded that companies can be good eggs if they suddenly come over all soft and gooey without explaining why. Frankly, you're more likely to believe it if they admit that they're only doing it to make more money, or at least, to avoid losing money. That line of argument has two distinct merits: first, it happens to be true, and second, it chimes with nearly everyone's instinctive beliefs and prejudices about business. Whether we think business is only interested in making money (and that's a bad thing), or whether we think business is only interested in making money (and that's a good thing); at least we can agree on the money point. (If we're somewhere in the middle, fondly believing that capitalism should always have been about making money and pursuing social objectives at the same time, then hey – there's nothing to worry about since our time has clearly come.)

And so here's our first stab at consensus-building; our first little synthesis. We've shown that it's in corporations' commercial interests to be more socially responsible, if simply to avoid future risks and threats. If you're cynical about all this social responsibility talk, judging it to be nothing more than a monumental cover-up, don't worry: they really mean it because after all, they're only doing it for the money. On the other hand, if you're concerned that it's all just a fashionable distraction or even worse, something that could undermine competitiveness, don't worry: it'll be good for business because after all, they're only doing it for the money.

By claiming anything other than commercial motives, by arguing that they're changing their ways, turning over a new leaf and joining the side of the angels in verdant pastures new because they woke up one day feeling like a corporate merger between Mother Theresa and Princess Diana, companies actually end up with the worst of all worlds. Anti-capitalists don't believe them, if anything hating them even more for being "hypocrites" or for "greenwashing," while red-blooded free marketeers just think they've lost the plot. Those who don't have strong feelings either way, but have a vague suspicion that companies are secretive manipulators who are probably up to no good; these people (the majority of people by the way) just let it wash over them, seeing it as just another form of corporate spin. This partly explains the general derision that has greeted most attempts by major corporations to communicate any advances they have made behind the flag of social responsibility. Even though their motives are mixed, and undoubtedly include a healthy dose of genuine and sincere conviction that this is the right way to do business in the twenty-first century, these companies would be far more convincing if they set out their stall with a little less gloss and a little more candor.

But most of all, businesses should realize that corporate social responsibility is simply not enough: it's the first step on the road, not the final destination. You can imagine the horror such a pronouncement might cause some weary Chief Executives, still reeling from the hard work involved in implementing social responsibility. But the reason it's not enough should be obvious to any commercially-minded CEO. The fact is, corporate social responsibility is catching on, as we've shown in this chapter. And what does that mean? It means that all your competitors are either doing it now, or will be doing it soon. Social responsibility will become what fancy consultants sometimes describe as a "hygiene factor," a *sine qua non*, a basic requirement of doing business. In other words, there won't be many opportunities to make money from it, any more than a business would consider the use of PCs a surefire way of increasing market share. To really benefit from playing a positive social role, companies will have to take social responsibility one step further, and embrace a new concept: corporate social leadership.

4

Leadership

Imagine there's a global oil company which a few years ago decided that, like one of its major rivals, it would wholeheartedly embrace the corporate social responsibility doctrine. This company proceeded to invest considerable human and financial capital in a thorough overhaul of every aspect of its business. Dialogue was undertaken, managers retrained, systems reviewed, codes of practice drawn up and implemented, new green technologies developed. Although it never had any doubts about how difficult it would be – and how long it would take – to effect the transformation it sought, it was confident that it had put in place the building blocks that would eventually turn it into the very model of a responsible twenty-first century corporation. This confidence was amply repaid as former critics (including some of the most vocal environmental pressure groups) acknowledged, sometimes grudgingly, sometimes enthusiastically, that it really was changing – unlike some other companies in its sector. It won plaudits galore from the social responsibility community for its visionary stance and its measurable progress. This forward looking company then decided to tell the world that it had changed. "We're no longer a destructive oil company," it announced. "We're a responsible energy company. Look, we even have a new logo to prove it, and our name no longer means what you thought it meant. We've moved beyond all that." Cue sniggers from the general public, who, not having benefited from five years of education in the tricky subject of corporate social responsibility, simply don't get it. Worse still, many of them don't buy it, because they see no practical demonstration of what is meant by this new corporate vision.

This company, alright then, bp, got almost everything right. It has clearly embarked on an exciting and positive journey. Its Chief Executive, John Browne, is obviously a businessman of quite exceptional calibre, demonstrating remarkable vision and leadership. Over time, it will no doubt succeed in proving that "beyond petroleum" is not just a slogan. For a snapshot of bp's progress, visit www.eco-connect.co.uk, a remarkable picture of what bp sees as the petrol station of the future. Except it's not imaginary: it actually exists in Hornchurch, England. But bp could have won more people over, and quicker. It could have explained to the masses, and not just the cognoscenti, why it had set out on a new corporate strategy. It could have presented the arguments in a full and reasoned way, eschewing simplistic assertions and instead explaining some simple truths: that the hydrocarbon century is over; that oil will get more expensive to find and will eventually run out; that if it is to survive and prosper bp needs to develop renewable energy sources. It could have made the point, with brutal directness, that although it's in the interests of environmental protection for bp to act in this way, the main reason for it doing so is commercial. It's about profits. Then people would have instantly understood, and readily believed. In the process, a powerful educational purpose would have been served, drumming home the message that commercial and social objectives can go hand in hand, not just because a big company has said so but because a big company has explained why it's so.

But that's just the beginning. In the previous chapter, we asked why it was that companies developing impeccable social responsibility credentials remain the targets of criticism and suspicion. In part, this is due to the sort of communication issues outlined above. But far more fundamental is the fact that even the leaders in corporate social responsibility have only grasped half the story. It's not enough to be socially responsible within your business. You need to demonstrate social leadership outside your business. It's not enough to change your company. You should use your company to change the world. That is the truly progressive course, and that is the way to persuade the world that you're truly responsible. Because leadership requires mass engagement; whereas responsibility can happily remain a well-kept secret, and usually does. Social leadership is the key to seeing this whole area as an opportunity rather than a challenge. And it's the way to transform that key corporate asset, the brand. Corporations find it harder and harder (and more and more costly) to cut through media clutter in a way that appeals to their target audiences, and particularly to do this in a way that engages with people emotionally. That's why companies sponsor people's passions, like sports and the arts. Social leadership gives businesses a new and more effective weapon in the battle to win people's hearts and minds – and wallets.

What does this mean if you're a company like bp? It means using all the resources at your disposal to bring about social change that matches your business strategy. If your strategy is based on environmental responsibility, then don't just be environmentally responsible yourself: encourage and help your customers to be environmentally responsible too. In a myriad micro ways, you, as a big global company, can make more of a difference to social behavior than any pressure group, or even many governments. The ideas you're about to see may not individually seem that big, but collectively they tell a powerful and convincing story about bp and would make a significant contribution to the advancement of the green agenda. Here are some ways for bp to match corporate social responsibility with corporate social leadership, throwing its full weight behind social change and environmental concern.

Imagine you're the boss at bp. You want more people to buy your petrol. But you also say you want to promote environmental responsibility. Contradictory aims? Not necessarily. Why not run campaigns that encourage more responsible car use? Integrate these into your marketing initiatives by creating sales promotions that give customers vouchers that they could exchange for bus or train tickets every time they buy your petrol. You could turn it into Green Miles, the twenty-first century version of Air Miles. Collect enough and you could win a bike, or an environmentally responsible tourism holiday for your family. It's more of an incentive to use bp than cheap wine glasses or tacky gifts that no-one really wants. The message to the public is straightforward: when you do need to buy petrol, we want you to buy ours – but think about ways to use less of it. That'll show people that bp is serious about the environment, and has the added benefit of helping governments around the world with one of their biggest headaches, the seemingly remorseless rise in car usage.

Instead of sponsoring the same upmarket arts events as every other big corporation, start sponsoring innovative projects that fit your new social purpose. What about sponsoring the creation of new cycle lanes, schemes that offer free bicycles for people to borrow in town centres, or car-free days in major world cities? Why not help reduce rush-hour traffic by supporting school bus services? How about raising awareness of carbon offset programs, which are now a part of the Kyoto Treaty on climate change? The idea is to link economic activity with the planting or protection of trees that suck out an equivalent amount of carbon dioxide. You could use this to boost petrol sales too – "every time you fill up your car, we'll plant a tree." Imagine that: you could help every bp customer to become carbon neutral. The same goes for air travel, proportionately a far bigger polluter than road travel anyway. A big chunk of your business is the supply of fuel to airlines. Why not work with your airline customers to create carbon neutral flights – it's been done in Costa Rica. Imagine if people sat down in their aeroplane seats to see a card that said: "thanks to bp, today's flight will not add to the level of carbon dioxide in the atmosphere." Wouldn't that start to convince the skeptics that bp is serious about the environment?

You could take it further: every government in the developed world is wrestling with the problem of waste, and how to create public enthusiasm for energy efficiency, recycling, and environmental awareness on an individual and family level. Show you can help by supporting kerbside recycling schemes, encouraging customers to separate their waste, to start composting their biodegradable rubbish. You already do so much innovative work in environmental protection anyway – but no-one knows about it because customers aren't involved. Look at some of the bp projects that are already underway: the water recycling systems for car washes in Spain and Portugal; the wildlife sanctuary in Malaysia that protects endangered species of turtles and runs educational camps to help local communities understand green issues; the work with the World Wide Fund for Nature in China to train teachers in environmental education.[1] There are countless such schemes throughout bp, all around the world, but they're kept separate and hidden from the general public. What can you do? You could take out ads, create websites, publish reports – as you are doing – simply telling people about these and similar projects. But would anyone really believe them? They might well think, unfairly, that you'd just plucked out a few good news stories for the sake of improving your image. The way to be credible lies not in trying harder to *communicate* what you're doing in corporate social responsibility, but to actually *demonstrate* corporate social leadership. And the beauty of it is that by involving your customers in a direct way, it's more likely to help your business in a direct way.

This is an essential lesson for corporations, but it cuts both ways. You can't have pretensions to social leadership unless you've put the work in place on social responsibility. A graphic illustration of this is provided by one of bp's competitors, Exxon Mobil/Esso. As we noted earlier, Esso chose not to follow bp and Shell down the high-profile social responsibility path and as a result has become the target of a worldwide boycott. (Whether or not this hits Esso's sales at the petrol pump, it's already having all sorts of unwelcome side-effects – for instance, business customers are coming under pressure to avoid Esso as their petrol supplier.)[2] Amidst all this criticism, Esso's sponsorship of Britain's "National Tree Week" caused widespread mirth and/or rage towards the end of 2001. "You've got to be kidding" was the incredulous reaction from Esso's critics. Instead of helping to improve its image, the attempt to associate itself with a green cause simply did Esso further damage.

The truth is, there's very little that annoys customers more than companies banging on about how marvellous they are. Self-aggrandizing corporate chest-beating ranks alongside being put on hold for minutes on end to the sound of mangled faux-classical music, or rude and unhelpful staff, as a top source of hair-tearing rage. Yet for years this has seemed to be the format *de rigueur* for companies to communicate their commitment to social responsibility. You know the stuff: "Here at LargeCo., we care passionately about all the people we serve. That's why last year we gave $1 million to an old people's home in Connecticut. Just another example of our philosophy of putting people first," or: "It's not just grasping power-hungry executives that we help bring together at EnormousTel.Co. Thanks to a donation from the EnormousTel.Co. Foundation, Mickey Tokenista can call his mom every day. With his foot." (Cheesy picture of cute Hispanic boy with physical disability overcome by ingenious telephonic device.) Such advertisements were brilliantly parodied by the American comedienne Lily Tomlin in a sketch in which she aped the caring sharing style of a corporate representative at the "Phone Company." It went something like this: "Hi, I'm from the Phone Company. Here at the Phone Company we work hard for you all hours the Good Lord sends, handling your calls and making sure you can speak to your loved ones. And we work for everyone – oh yes, from Presidents and Kings to the scum of the earth!"

Phone companies around the world have indeed been major culprits in this type of corporate ego-massage. But the trouble with the "aren't we nice" style of corporate social communication is that it's utterly implausible. Consumers are not stupid: they understand that the purpose of business is to make money, not to make donations to charities. Social leadership is the smarter way to highlight the social benefits of whatever a company is doing. This means integrating social values into everyday business, not running public relations or advertising campaigns to highlight social responsibility or philanthropy every now and again. You'll see the "aren't we nice" stuff in opinion-former magazines like the *New Yorker, Time* or *The Economist*, or else in the Sunday newspapers – if you follow these ads on a regular basis, you'd be left thinking that it's a little like the Genesis story in the Bible: on the first six days the corporation made the profits, on the seventh it took a rest and gave them away to random charities of dubious worth. Companies need to be a lot more intelligent than this.

A small, but neat example of the difference between social responsibility and social leadership can be seen in the comparison between two ads run by British telecommunications company BT a few years apart. In the late 1990s, BT started running a TV advertisement featuring a soft-soap voice-over talking about the millions the company invests every year in social and community projects, with soft-focus images of "good causes" – happy children, contented senior citizens and so on, all set to the Elvis track, "Always on my mind." Now BT have copious market research evidence showing that when they ran this commercial, their brand approval ratings went up.[3] So who is anyone to argue with that? But still, but still … it felt wrong. Whatever the market research said (and you can make market research say pretty much anything you like), you can imagine the viewer seeing that commercial and fuming silently to themselves: "don't tell me how nice you are! What's a couple of million anyway, I keep reading in the paper about your profits running into the billions." (More recently, regrettably enough for BT shareholders, it has tended to be losses.) Alternatively it could easily have prompted something along these lines: "I don't believe it! Spending all that money trying to make out you're caring when you charge me a fortune and you haven't fixed my phone yet!" It's not enormously persuasive to promote your company's social credentials by stating what a good guy you are: far more effective to prove it, in more subtle ways. And that's what BT are now doing.

The company's most recent campaign focused on the power of communications to improve people's lives by making positive connections – "more connections, more possibilities." A series of small press advertisements show how the big social message fits in to individual people's lives in a practical and beneficial way. One ad, for example, showed a mother holding a small child. "Do you sometimes feel overwhelmed?" ran the headline. The ad then went on to suggest that by connecting with others going through the same experience, mothers might be able to pick up useful tips, and feel better about the burdens of parenting. It then listed a selection of parenting websites. Go to the websites, and you'll see that they're supported by BT. It's clever, subtle, and demonstrates the social benefits of the company's business without ramming it down consumers' throats. It's also entirely convincing because it's an integral part of the company's marketing strategy and campaign rather than an add-on extra designed to curry favor. To support the parenting charities in the first place is an example of BT's social responsibility. Raising public awareness of parenting issues and directing mothers to the organization that could help them is an example of social leadership.

This integrated, practical approach is the perfect riposte to the critics of business who take great delight in pointing out the gaps between corporate rhetoric and reality. As corporations increasingly move towards the adoption of high-blown mission statements which emphasize some great social role: "we don't make cars, we make dreams come true;" "we don't produce toys, we make children happy," it will be essential to match these aspirations with concrete actions that move beyond the current understanding of what corporate social responsibility means. By using the economic and cultural power of their corporations to help promote positive social change, business leaders will be able to tackle head on the criticism that labels existing initiatives in this area as just flim-flam marketing scams. The truth is, much of what has gone on to date *can* be categorized in this way, prompting criticism such as this from George Monbiot: "the primary purpose of these new intrusions upon the public realm is not to make the world a better place, but to raise the profile of the brand ... it is a privatization of our minds, a means of reaching those parts of our consciousness untouched by conventional advertising."[4]

He's half right, of course: the primary purpose *is* to enhance brands, and the techniques of social responsibility and social leadership *can* touch consumers in a way that conventional advertising doesn't. But this doesn't make them bad. If you give money to a charity, and this action provides you with a warm glow from having done something worthwhile – in other words, your motive is self-interest – does that invalidate your donation? The more that social responsibility is seen as a commercial activity rather than a philanthropic one, the more likely it is to be serious and sustained. This point serves to rebut two other criticisms of social responsibility that we noted earlier: Noreena Hertz's concern that it could just fall away in recessionary times, and George Monbiot's worry that it's substituting the whim of corporate philanthropy for the assurance of collective public provision.

If social responsibility *is* seen by companies as a PR exercise, then it could well fall victim to budget cuts necessitated by difficult trading conditions. But many companies are no longer seeing it in that old-fashioned way. As we saw in Chapter 3, the fears that are persuading corporations to be more socially responsible are very real ones, centred on the need to protect the business from potential risks. These are serious, long-term issues for companies, and they are unrelated to cyclical swings in the economy. In any case, the growing need for compliance with legislative, regulatory and financial market standards on social responsibility will keep the issue on the corporate agenda.

The second criticism will only be fully answered if companies embrace this first key change that's required in the way they see their social role: the change from social responsibility to social leadership. Frankly, if corporations' performance in this area is limited to getting their own house in order and then doing a bit of fundraising for social causes, either in the form of cash or equipment, then it may well be taken by government as an excuse to reduce spending. Even today, many schools build into their annual budget plans the donations they expect to receive from corporate campaigns of one kind or another. But social leadership is about far more than that. It's about using companies for social change, harnessing the resources of business and the cultural power of brands as a positive influence on social behavior in the same way that they're presently used to influence consumer behavior. This is not a substitute for government action; it's entirely complementary to it, an additional engine of social progress.

Think of the notional bp examples: the campaign for responsible car use, the Green Miles scheme, the promotion of cycling, carbon neutral journeys, changing attitudes towards green issues in the home. Some of these socially and environmentally desirable things are provided by government, but most are not; nor could they be. Particularly exciting would be the ones that involve changing the way people think and behave, for this is the area where government is inherently ill-equipped to act. Leadership of this type is not privatizing people's minds, as George Monbiot puts it (a curious choice of words, suggesting that he would prefer citizens' minds to be nationalized); it is opening people's minds, changing their minds. Surely this is an objective that everyone can support if it leads to people taking more of an interest in their own impact on the environment?

After all, this is precisely one of the courses of action recommended in Anita Roddick's breezy anti-globalization handbook, *Take it Personally.* Readers are encouraged to: "Change your lifestyle. Measure you and your family's ecological footprint and work to reduce it to the sustainable level. Focus on the action that makes the big differences (like cycling more instead of driving) instead of the small improvements (like recycling) – see People and Planet and Best Foot Forward websites."[5] Presumably Monbiot, who has criticized pressure groups for becoming too chummy and collaborative with corporations, would object if, for example, bp developed a simple consumer guide, in partnership with People and Planet or Best Foot Forward or some other eco-group, that helped households follow Roddick's advice. Isn't this curmudgeonly in the extreme? If it makes a positive difference, what's wrong with it?

Another powerful benefit of the social responsibility plus social leadership approach is that it moves beyond the rather dreary, box-ticking compliance models of corporate social responsibility that many practitioners fear will be the death of progress in this area. If social responsibility is nothing more than corporations complying with prescriptive, one-size-fits-all regulations, then there will be no scope for creativity and no incentive for companies to do anything other than meet the bare minimum requirements as laid out by government. You may say that's a good thing; that all companies should at least be required by law to meet certain standards of social and environmental behavior. Indeed: but they already are – through the mass of existing regulations and laws that control business behavior, from health and safety codes, to environmental standards, to competition policy, to anti-discrimination laws. While a general requirement for companies to report on their social and environmental performance is certainly an element that's missing, it could be argued that even that is being taken care of by the evolving requirements of stock markets for more detailed "ethical" information about companies. The version of corporate social responsibility that so enrages free market critics is the version that implies a whole new battery of bureaucratic requirements telling companies exactly what to do.

Here, again, a synthesis of superficially conflicting views is possible. For those who believe corporations don't do nearly enough on social responsibility, the best outcome will be a situation in which companies are constantly pushing forward the boundaries, permanently improving their performance. This is most likely to occur if companies, for competitive business reasons, innovate and design their own response to changing expectations. For those who believe that corporations are doing far too much already, the best outcome would be a situation in which they do only what is consistent with their commercial requirements. This is most likely to occur if companies are free to create their own individual strategies on social and environmental responsibility. Regulation is the enemy of both anti- and pro-capitalists; it is the enemy of those who are enthusiastic about corporate social responsibility and of those who are skeptical of it. Government intervention in this area would destroy both sides of the "enlightened self-interest" equation: society would lose out on the "enlightened" part, and companies would lose out on the "self-interest."

Thus it was singularly unhelpful for the European Commission to step into this arena in the autumn of 2001 with the sort of blundering, bureaucratic, heavy-handed grasping for regulatory control that would have left the five-year planners in Stalin's Kremlin in need of a stiff drink for fear that they'd over-reached themselves. The Commission's "Green Paper," Promoting a European Framework for Corporate Social Responsibility, set out in minute detail its view on what companies should do. Here are some of the suggestions[6]: codes of conduct should be applied by companies "at every level of the organization and production line," with "full disclosure of information" and "training for local management, workers and communities." "Monitoring, which should involve stakeholders as well as public authorities, trade unions and NGOs, is important to ensure the credibility of codes of conduct." Values "need to be translated into action," and "this involves practices such as adding a social or environmental dimension in plans and budgets and evaluating corporate performance in these areas, creating 'community advisory committees,' carrying out social or environmental audits and setting up continuing education programmes." Companies of more than 1,000 employees are recommended to publish an annual report on employment and working conditions, and reference is made to the Commission's "Communication on Sustainable Development" to the EU Gothenburg summit of 2001, which recommends that all publicly quoted companies with at least 500 staff should "publish a 'triple bottom line' in their annual reports to shareholders." Finally, the Green Paper calls for "social and eco labels" which "would require permanent verification at the workplace."

It's going to be fun laying into all that …

But first, it's only polite to give the first free punch to Martin le Jeune, a leading corporate social responsibility consultant who has argued that the European Union's move into this area would stifle innovation and take the initiative away from businesses, turning the social responsibility area into "a one-way street with the Commission driving the car." He warns the EU to keep its distance, adding "you might think that to be a harsh reaction to a worthy attempt to summarize where we have got to on corporate social responsibility and take the process a stage further. But I would extend the same helpful advice to any government that moves its tanks into this territory. Corporate social responsibility and governments are like alternating whisky and wine: they don't mix well, and they leave you with a nasty headache in the morning."[7] Le Jeune is right.

In many ways it's laughable that the European Commission, an outfit that is consistently criticized by the European Court of Auditors for lack of transparency, failure to comply with generally accepted accounting principles or with its own regulations even though its entire income is provided by taxpayers; a body that has done as much as any other institution on earth to keep developing countries in poverty by refusing to dismantle its trade barriers; it is just laughable that this of all organizations has the nerve to lecture anyone on social responsibility, much less instruct Europe's companies, who by and large and on their own initiative are streets ahead of those elsewhere in the world and perfectly capable of continuing to innovate in this area without the assistance of the Euro-boobies.

How much of this preaching does the European Commission practice, you may ask? Don't hold your breath for *its* social audit to hit the bookshops. It's as if bureaucrats of this type simply don't understand that innovation in the area of corporate social responsibility, as in all other areas of business performance, will come about without their well-meaning intervention, and that companies if left to their own devices and subject to a competitive commercial environment are among the most creative forces on earth. Where do they think new, clean technologies come from? Where do they think new jobs come from? The would-be regulators state in their document that there's a clear business case for social responsibility: well if there is, then why on earth does it need the European Commission to make companies do it and to tell them how to do it? Do they imagine that businesses are led by incompetent fools who are less good at spotting what's in their company's interests than officials in Brussels?

This is not some knee-jerk reaction against regulation. There's a very good reason why prescriptive regulation is a bad idea: it's likely to lead to less social responsibility, not more. If social responsibility becomes a blanket compliance requirement uniformly imposed on every company, CEOs will struggle to use it to their active commercial advantage, and will therefore be reluctant to get fully behind it. How can you distinguish yourself from your competitors if you're all following the same codes of practice? *Ethical Performance* magazine got the balance right in an editorial in its January 2002 edition, arguing that instead of introducing regulations directly requiring, for example, mandatory social and environmental reporting, the European Commission should "pursue a policy based on the principle of embarrassment. The UK's experience shows that this approach works. The UK pension disclosure regulations, widely regarded as the most effective single regulation in this area ever introduced, has worked precisely because it has embarrassed pension funds into taking action, and they are now beginning to apply pressure on companies ... such a policy would have the advantage of targeting the laggards rather than forward-thinking companies." What *will* lead to more social responsibility is for companies to see it as a stepping stone to social leadership, which is the territory in which they can genuinely demonstrate, with wholehearted enthusiasm, that being a good citizen is good for business. This is the first change we need if corporate social responsibility is to move forward and fulfil its potential, not more regulation.

And what of the second key change that is required? We mentioned it briefly in Chapter 3 in the discussion of socially responsible investing. It's another dimension of leadership and it concerns the provision of information. The more information there is, the better markets work – and this is as true of the social dimension of the market as of any other. In order to meet the demands of institutional investors who are increasingly questioning companies on their social, environmental and ethical performance, companies are collecting information on these areas with a revolutionary degree of thoroughness. For those who have chosen to publish independently verified social audits, they even have information that is backed up by a respected and independent third party. Yet at present, most of this information never finds its way beyond the small circle of corporate officials, opinion formers and investors that use it. Sure, many companies publish their social audits, often producing dedicated websites. These are all good things to do. But they don't get the information in the hands of the people who really need it: consumers, shoppers. Corporations frequently and plaintively bemoan the fact that "we do all these good things, but no-one knows about it." That's because they don't tell consumers about it, and therefore don't get the word-of-mouth effect that is the ultimate aim of business communications.

At the same time, consumers say they care more and more about social and environmental issues, but as we saw earlier, their actual consumer behavior doesn't seem to reflect these new-found concerns. That's because they don't have sufficient information to make informed choices. Partly, it's a problem of compartmentalism within corporations. The people who collect social responsibility information are not the people who design the packaging, write the letters, create the advertising, determine the store layouts. Many corporations valiantly try to provide their customers with information – after all, every McDonald's restaurant has a rack of leaflets about nutritional information and McDonald's community programs. But does anyone read them? And if they read them, would they believe them? Once again, it's that problem of perceived corporate spin. But companies who might view the prospect of an independently verified social and environmental audit as an onerous burden might see things differently if such an audit could generate information that they could give to the public, in a way that helped increase their sales.

At the moment, all the traffic on the ethical information highway seems to be in one direction: pressure groups reporting on corporate transgressions and calling for boycotts. This is the favored tactic of most campaigners. Here's Eric Schlosser in *Fast Food Nation*, explaining graphically why consumer power is the only practical solution to his critique of the US fast food industry: "Congress should ban advertising that preys upon children, it should stop subsidizing dead-end jobs, it should pass tougher food safety laws, it should protect American workers from serious harm, it should fight against dangerous concentrations of economic power. Congress should do all these things, but it isn't likely to do any of them soon. The political influence of the fast food industry and its agribusiness suppliers makes a discussion of what Congress should do largely academic. The fast food industry spends millions of dollars every year on lobbying and billions on mass marketing. The wealth and power of the major chains make them seem impossible to defeat. And yet those companies must obey the demands of one group – consumers – whom they eagerly flatter and pursue ... Nobody in the United States is forced to buy fast food. The first step toward meaningful change is by far the easiest: stop buying it. The executives who run the fast food industry are not bad men. They are businessmen. They will sell free-range, organic, grass-fed hamburgers if you demand it. They will sell whatever sells at a profit. The usefulness of the market, its effectiveness as a tool, cuts both ways. The real power of the American consumer has not yet been unleashed. The heads of Burger King, KFC, and McDonald's should feel daunted; they're outnumbered. There are three of them and almost three hundred million of you. A good boycott, a refusal to buy, can speak much louder than words. Sometimes the most irresistible force is the most mundane … even in this fast food nation, you can still have it your way."[8]

The usefulness of the market cuts both ways … indeed it does, and by providing better and more credible information about their social responsibility activities, companies could harness the favorite tool of the anti-capitalists to their own commercial advantage. We began Chapter 3 with the story of Elizabeth Hayrick, the 18th-century British campaigner against slave sugar. We argued that in the future, there could be a Hayrick in every household, ready to switch brands at the drop of an ethical clanger. But who's to say what constitutes an ethical clanger? The pressure groups? Their attacks on big business are often inaccurate and always unrepresentative.

Readers of Anita Roddick's *Take it Personally* are advised to "make ethical consumer choices," and to "avoid multinationals,"[9] but elsewhere in the book[10] there's a plug for Reebok trainers, thanks to the company's human rights record. Who says Reebok has a better human rights record than other multinationals? Anita Roddick? Actually, no: she refers to "a Jakarta based independent research and consulting firm" who monitored factory conditions inside the plants that Reebok uses to make most of its shoes. But who knows anything about this firm and its ethics? After all, it was "hired" by Reebok. Roddick cites other organizations that consumers can turn to to find out about the standards of multinationals, including The National Labor Consortium, the Worker Rights Commission and Sweatshop Watch. But however impartial and accurate their work, consumers can't possibly have confidence in their judgments

BISHOP BURTON COLLEGE
LIBRARY

unless they're part of an independent, universally adopted and properly policed framework of standards. What's the use of knowing about the odd company that happens to have been investigated? OK, we may accept that Reebok is squeaky clean, but that's not much help if we're choosing between Puma and Fila.

Independently verified social auditing, freely entered into by corporations, offers a truly democratic solution, and one that provides another synthesis. If you're suspicious of big business, you'll want to know the objective facts about a company's social and environmental record. If you're part of big business, and you're proud of your record, you'll want people to know the objective facts too, because you're confident they'll work to your commercial advantage. Over the years, as more and better information is provided about corporate activity, it won't just be an ethical clanger that can cause people to switch brands: it will be ethical successes too. But corporations will need to find new and compelling ways of communicating the information. Leaflets in a rack won't do. It could eventually involve new technology – smart bar codes that consumers can quickly scan to find out about a product's origins and its producer's corporate record. Already, the bar code on a Marks & Spencer beef sandwich in Britain can be used to trace the family history of the cow that provides the beef. In the meantime, it could involve conventional vehicles like packaging, websites, customer databases, and direct mail. Again, there are signs of this happening: in the UK, McDonald's only uses free-range eggs in its products, a fact which is now communicated on the products' packaging. There will be an obligation on the media, too, to treat this area more seriously. Too often, the one-sided and inaccurate claims of pressure groups are faithfully recycled. Knowledge that there is independently verified social audit information around will give journalists confidence that if they present a corporation's side of the story, they're not just falling for expensive spin.

This is all to the good and thoroughly democratic. Corporations are the most accountable institutions on the planet. No-one else is subject to the same degree of scrutiny, nor required to be as transparent in their operations. No politician has to seek re-election every day, every week, every month like most businesses do. As social and environmental concerns become more closely associated with the workings of capitalism; as social responsibility becomes a business prerequisite; as corporations realize that through social leadership they can help make the world a better place and help their business too, it's a reasonable bet that in ten years' time we'll be saying that shopping is the new voting.

So the question is, how should a company draw up its manifesto to attract the new electorate?

5

Anatomy

In *The Communist Manifesto*, Marx and Engels noted dismissively that "a part of the bourgeoisie is desirous of redressing social grievances, in order to secure the continued existence of bourgeois society. To this section belong economists, philanthropists, humanitarians, improvers of the condition of the working class, organizers of charity, members of societies for the prevention of cruelty to animals, temperance fanatics, hole-and-corner reformers of every imaginable kind."[1] One hundred and fifty years on, we would like to invite corporations to join this rogue's gallery; but only on condition that they behave, in Engels' words, like "the manifold types of social quacks who want to eliminate social abuses through their various universal panaceas and all kinds of patchwork, without hurting capital and profit in the least."[2] Now there's a mission statement for you; and here's a new rule of thumb that corporations can apply as they're drawing up their own manifestoes, developing their ideas about social responsibility and social leadership. What are the qualities and resources within their businesses that could have a dual purpose, social as well as commercial? By spotting these opportunities, corporations can indeed help "eliminate social abuses," not only "without hurting capital and profit in the least," but positively helping it.

The easiest way to go about identifying such opportunities is to have a close look at the anatomy of a corporation. What are its constituent parts? What are the individual items that could have a dual purpose? How to judge what kind of social purpose would make the most sense, and produce the most commercial benefit? These are the questions we try to answer in this chapter. We've dissected the corporate anatomy into eight little pieces, and for each one, supplied stories which illustrate how a dual purpose can be created. Regrettably, there seems to be no trite mnemonic available to encapsulate this approach: "Ten Commandments"; "Seven Deadly Sins"; "Top Six" – OK, we've had that, but "Eight ... what?" You'll just have to make do with "eight pieces of the corporate anatomy that can have a dual purpose, social as well as commercial." Stephen Covey can rest easy in his bed.

The first piece, for most corporations, is their most famous one: their brand. We've talked about the cultural power of brands, and how this could be harnessed for social benefit. Here, you will see what we mean. The second piece is nothing tangible, nothing you could point to or measure, but is nevertheless one of the unique strengths of businesses: the ability to get things done, to make things happen. Quickly. The third item on our list couldn't be more tangible. It's corporations' grass roots presence, a presence that in many cases reaches further and deeper than most other institutions on earth. Fourth, human insight. Corporations, or at least the best ones, possess exceptional knowledge and insights into human attitudes and behavior. Surely they could do something good with that? The fifth piece of corporate anatomy, as you'll see, has to be stated three times. Location, location, location. The sixth is probably the most predictable – people. We'll look at the best and most profitable ways for companies to find a dual purpose for the people who work for them. Piece number seven is the one that all the charity fundraising managers have been waiting for: money. Yes, it's that age-old question, how should businesses spend their money? (We'd hate to give anything away, but the charity fundraisers are in for a shock.) And finally, the eighth piece, the big bugbear of the anti-capitalists. Marketing. Is there anything good to be derived from this wretched profession? Funnily enough, yes.

Most of the stories used to illustrate the dual purpose arguments are projects that we've been involved with. Where the organization concerned is or has been a client of our company, we make that clear, so you can discount the whole thing as sleazy puffery – sorry, so that there is complete transparency in the author–reader stakeholder partnership.

So it's piece number one, brands. We've talked about brands already, but rather defensively as we tried to bring a sense of balance to the way that consumer brands' cultural influence is presented in the anti-capitalist literature and in the media generally. Everyone agrees that brands are powerful. But it seems a little dull to leave it at that.

Brands can represent something bigger than a product or service for sale, and there's one group of people that already understands this very well: marketing and advertising people. Advertising, despite its image in some quarters as nothing but a bunch of jumped-up, overpaid, vacuous, cocaine-snorting nancy boys prancing around trying to figure out new ways of extorting money from hard-pressed housewives, is actually rather a thoughtful business. The late Roger Opie, an economics Fellow at Oxford University, was fond of setting his students the brilliant – if rather eccentric – essay title: "advertising is such a waste of money and an insult to everyone's intelligence that it ought to be banned." But far from insulting consumers' intelligence, marketing professionals tend to treat them with the greatest respect, often going to extraordinary lengths to understand their needs and desires. More relevantly here, they often seek to imbue brands with a sense of meaning that conveys more than just the functional benefits of whatever is being promoted. Brands lay claim to a social role too. However, it's rare to see these claims backed up by concrete social action. More usually, they are artificial constructs designed solely to identify with consumers' social concerns, rather than to actually do anything about them. This doesn't make brands a bad thing, but it does help explain why some anti-corporate critics profess to hate them so much. In fact, the evolution of brands is nowhere near complete, and the next stage in their development will be the realization on the part of marketing people that brands can have a dual purpose, social as well as commercial. But it's worth reminding ourselves why they're useful just as they are.

The Economist magazine explained the background to the branding phenomenon in an editorial comment in September 2001: "[Brands] began as a form ... of consumer protection. In pre-industrial days, people knew exactly what went into their meat pies and which butchers were trustworthy; once they moved to cities, they no longer did. A brand provided a guarantee of reliability and quality. Its owner had a powerful incentive to ensure that each pie was as good as the previous one, because that would persuade people to come back for more. Just as distance created a need for brands in the 19th century, so in the age of globalization and the Internet it reinforces their value. A book-buyer might not entrust a company based in Seattle with his credit-card number had experience not taught him to trust the Amazon brand ... because consumer trust is the basis of all brand values, companies that own the brands have an immense incentive to work to retain that trust."[3]

A similarly robust defence of brands has been mounted by advertising guru and marketing commentator Winston Fletcher: "Brands exist because consumers want them. Every successful brand provides consumers with a trolley basket full of benefits ... in a world of massive choice and complexity, brands are quickly and easily identified. It is almost impossible to overemphasize how important this is for consumers today. Supermarket shoppers are now besieged by 30,000 or so [product] lines, and will select a couple of dozen of them. How could this be achieved without branding? Shopping would take forever. In a world without choice, brands would be unnecessary – but who wants a world without choice? ... Shysters sell you something once and then run off with your money. Brands want to sell themselves again and again, so they take care not to disappoint ... brands and branding encourage economic development and innovation because they make it possible for consumers to associate product improvements with names and logos. Without branding, how could the public recognize new products? Only at the end of the chain do imagery and glamour – the facets of branding that so bemuse outsiders – come into play. As a shorthand, we say people buy images. But they do not. They buy products. You can't put an image in a shopping trolley. And in many markets – household goods, medicines, most foods, retailing itself – imagery (of the glamour kind) is relatively unimportant. Taste, functionality, value and effectiveness are what matter, and those are the unglamorous things brands in those markets provide. None of the brand benefits I have mentioned primarily benefit corporations. They benefit the public."[4]

The consistency, reliability, and useful service that brands deliver to the public, in the various ways outlined above, are what makes them trusted. But it's not just that they're trusted: they're trusted more than anything else in society. Surveys[5] show that the most famous consumer brands are respected more than political parties, individual political leaders, teachers, the police, the church, the United Nations – you name it, the brands come out on top in the trust stakes. This applies in all age groups, and amongst brands in all sectors.

Interestingly, this does not translate into support for corporations themselves, or into approval of business in general. The same surveys that show massive trust in brands also reveal huge distrust of "multinational corporations." People can hold two apparently contradictory opinions at the same time: a love of brands and a hatred of companies. But this is not as contradictory as it seems. Remember the earlier discussion about the backlash against business. Think about the representation of business in popular culture – Mr Burns from *The Simpsons, et al.* Consider the messages that people normally receive about corporations: stories in the media about job losses, huge pay rises for bosses, sweatshops, financial scandals – it's not a pretty picture. But when it comes to brands, what do people see? Positive, often extremely entertaining and creative advertising, associations with popular artistic and sporting events through sponsorship, and then trumping all of this, actual experience day in, day out of a decent quality, good value product or service. When communicating with the public, companies invest far more time, effort, and money in building a positive image for their brands than they do in promoting their reputation as a corporation. Indeed, one of the primary aims of the anti-globalization campaigners is to expose what they see as the vast gulf between the wholesome, upbeat images that companies develop for their brands, and the destructive, irresponsible behavior of the brands' corporate parents. They're starting to succeed, hence the commercial need for corporate social responsibility. But so far, and no doubt much to the activists' irritation, the brands retain higher levels of trust than anything else that's around in our society – and this gives corporations a ready-made tool for social leadership.

There are two ways of looking at the cultural power of brands. You could shake your head in despair and consternation, bemoaning the fact that our world has come to this sorry state; that the species which produced Shakespeare, Confucius, Michelangelo and Mozart has ended up with people who pay more attention to a Nike commercial than to a speech by the President. Or you could be a little more constructive about it. You could say: if these brands have such a strong influence, and are so trusted, then why can't we use them to change things for the better? Public trust in brands could become a priceless asset in campaigns for social change. And campaigning for social change could become a priceless asset in making money for the corporations behind the brands.

This is emphatically not the same as brands linking up with charities or good causes for mutually beneficial promotional campaigns. Rather, it's about a corporation using its brand's ability to change consumer behavior as a way of changing social behavior at the same time, thereby strengthening that brand's reputation. Frankly, if brands can persuade people to pay extra for toilet paper with aloe vera in it, is there anything that's beyond them? And equally, wouldn't the aloe vera toilet paper people feel a bit more inspired if they got home at night having used their lavatorial influence for an additional and more directly social purpose? But for once, bathroom tissue is just the beginning ...

If a brand can sell a child a dream, then why can't it persuade that child to read? In fact, you could argue that because that child pays more attention to brands than to many other social influences, brands are actually more likely to have an impact on his or her desire to read books than any of the conventional instruments of social policy. Look at the Coca-Cola literacy campaign which was the backbone of its sponsorship of the first *Harry Potter* movie.[6] (We should at this point declare an interest since Coca-Cola is a client of our company.) The aspect of the campaign that attracted the most media coverage was the headline deal which involved Coca-Cola distributing millions of books to communities around the world. Some commentators, predictably enough, derided the entire exercise as a vaguely sinister attempt by a huge American (and therefore bad) corporation to "buy" socially responsible credentials. In fairness, most acknowledged it for what it was: an interesting and positive development in both movie and soft drink marketing. But in the UK, there was a radically progressive extension to the campaign which demonstrated genuine social leadership, albeit on a small and local scale. This involved not just the Coca-Cola *company* giving away books – something which any big corporation could do – but the company using the Coca-Cola *brand* for social change. Through its Valued Youth initiative, developed in partnership with local education boards, British 14-year-olds who are on the brink of being excluded from school (for example because of truancy or anti-social behavior) are matched with four younger children. They meet once a week, and the older, at-risk child helps teach literacy and numeracy skills to the younger children. It has a phenomenal success rate, with parents and teachers reporting transformed attitudes among the 14-year-olds as they learn a sense of responsibility. The essence of the project is that it works precisely because the Coca-Cola brand is involved; because it's a brand that teenagers know and trust. It works, not to put too fine a point on it, where the best efforts of teachers and parents have not. It's a small project, and it's not going to change the world. But it *is* changing some people's worlds, and it's a good example of a brand's dual purpose being put to use, a good example of corporate social leadership.

It's also interesting to think about the other part of the Valued Youth equation, the connection with *Harry Potter*. The film industry, and indeed the entertainment industry generally, also possesses powerful and valuable brands – whether it's movie stars and the characters they play, so-called movie franchises like the James Bond series (and indeed *Harry Potter*), or successful TV shows and their characters. Like the early industrial philanthropists, the generally wealthy individuals in the entertainment industry take their philanthropic activities seriously, often making a huge difference to charities and good causes by lending their glamour and pulling power to them for fundraising and awareness campaigns. But just as the early industrialists separated social responsibility from their day jobs, so does much of the entertainment industry. Movies, actors, TV shows could themselves develop powerful social leadership campaigns. They have just as much cultural influence as consumer brands. And just like consumer brands, with a bit of creative thinking, the entertainment industry's cultural power could have a dual purpose.

So this theory can apply to every social issue, and in every business sector. In the previous chapter, we compared two BT advertisements to illustrate the difference between the right and the wrong way for corporations to talk about their social responsibility programs. Here's another such comparison. Around ten years ago, BT ran a corporate commercial which dramatized the social value of its core business, communication. Featuring the wheelchair-bound scientist Stephen Hawking, it was a beautifully crafted, emotional and uplifting piece of film. But it served only one purpose: to promote BT. A few years later, the company's advertising switched to a much more down-to-earth style under the slogan "It's good to talk." This point was made by reference to everyday situations in which communication was shown to be making life better, and the advertising was supported by BT Talkworks, a practical guide to communicating that was mailed to millions of households. BT Talkworks gave step-by-step advice on a huge range of scenarios, from how to tell people bad news, to how to ask for a pay rise. It's a fair assumption that the kind of people who will read this book could manage perfectly well in their everyday lives without recourse to such a manual. But our smart readers are also smart enough to recognize that significant social problems stem from many people's inability to communicate properly, and BT's brand marketing campaign might well have changed many such people's lives.

Take another social issue: smoking. You want to encourage an eight-year-old boy not to smoke. What do you think is most likely to work? A lecture from his parents? A message from his teacher? A message from the government? Or a message from a youth brand, say adidas? Now flip the question on its head to see how it would be in adidas' commercial interests to play such a role. You're the parent of that eight-year-old boy. He comes along and asks for a new pair of shoes. Will you feel better or worse about adidas if you know that it's helping to tackle an issue that you care about – like stopping your son smoking?

MTV, a company which stands head and shoulders above most others in the world in the extent to which it has recognized and acted upon its ability to influence social attitudes and behavior, has copious research findings which comprehensively demonstrate the failure of traditional public service campaigns carried out by governments or charities, and the effectiveness of such campaigns if carried out by trusted consumer brands.

And up with MTV sits another brand that lives and breathes social leadership: the Mates condoms brand that Virgin boss Richard Branson created as a way for business to respond creatively to the looming AIDS crisis of the 1980s. The key social change that was required in order to limit the spread of HIV infections was to encourage people to use condoms – something of a snigger-inducing taboo at the time. Government campaigns could bang on about the need to use condoms, but if wearing a condom is about as culturally acceptable as wearing school uniform to a garage club, it's not going to have much effect. Mates condoms, in the UK at least, changed all that with its up-front and credible branding, packaging and advertising. It was the full social leadership package, with sales of Mates funding a new medical foundation, and every aspect of the brand performing an important social role. It contributed to the UK's dramatically lower HIV infections rate than that in other European countries.

Think about the range of social policy problems that governments all over the world wrestle with on a daily basis. Many of the toughest ones are issues that are hard for the public authorities to deal with using the normal tools at their disposal: passing laws and spending taxpayers' money. Issues like literacy, where in rich societies the greatest single change that needs to happen is not for more books to be provided, but for more parents to read with their children from an early age. Issues like health, where the real prize is not finding more efficient and affordable systems to cure sick people, but to prevent people from becoming sick in the first place by living more healthily, taking exercise, and so on. Issues like crime, racism, cultural tolerance, respect for senior citizens, responsible car use, changing attitudes towards people with disabilities, care for the environment, using energy and other resources more efficiently, giving young people a sense of purpose, looking after the local neighborhood, self-esteem and confidence, rediscovering a sense of community spirit, drug abuse ... For all these issues and more, the social policy requirement is for a change of attitude and a change of behavior. It's the same in the developing world: governments and aid agencies can pump billions into disease-eradication programs, but these will only work if attitudes and behavior also change. On our planet today, who's best at changing people's attitudes and behavior? The answer is consumer brands, and this is why corporations' cultural power, not their often overstated economic power, should be the aspect of globalization that we pay most attention to. Not by criticizing it, but by harnessing it for social ends.

This dual purpose for brands is an asset that you won't find valued on any balance sheet. Instead, over the past few years, companies have been valuing their brands in a different way, by calculating their commercial value. Nothing wrong with that in an age where brands play such a powerful part in commercial success – think about the value of Heinz as a company without the Heinz brand name and all that goes with it. In many cases, rigorous actuarial skills are applied to calculating the financial value of brands, a technique pioneered by Interbrand, the world's leading brand consultancy. In other cases, the process is not so much rigorous as risible. One of our friends in a famous advertising agency was asked by his client, the Finance Director of one of the UK's leading corporations, to "have a look at" the valuation of his company's brand that had been produced, at considerable cost, by experts in the field. "I think it's a little high," our friend was told. What could he do? He didn't know the first thing about how to value a brand. He consulted his boss, who was less than helpful. "Just make it up," he said. "That's what all these brand consultants do." Our friend proceeded to make it up, throwing in the odd fact about market share here and there in an attempt to give a hint of brow-furrowing intellectual endeavor. He faxed it over to the Finance Director. Having cleared up a slight inconsistency – our friend had multiplied two figures instead of dividing them, or some such footling error – the great man accepted the new, lower "valuation," which was duly recorded in the company's accounts. Who says all this brand stuff is a load of hot air?

The true value of brands, however, lies not just in their contribution to commercial success, but in their potential contribution to social progress. This is the one aspect of the debate about business and society that is least well understood, even amongst those who are experts in corporate social responsibility (and certainly amongst the anti-capitalist movement). It's also the quickest and most high-profile way for corporations to move from social responsibility to social leadership, thereby gaining the commercial benefits of the social investments they have already made, and presenting a more persuasive case to their anti-corporate critics. And the use of a brand for a social purpose would accomplish through a single initiative every one of a modern corporation's communication goals: engaging on an emotional level with customers; inspiring current workers; recruiting new workers; becoming desirable business partners; establishing better relationships with local communities, NGOs, suppliers, local and national government; gaining positive media coverage. The beauty of using a brand for social leadership is that it's so efficient.

The story that we've chosen to illustrate this particular dimension of social leadership involves one of the UK's best known companies. BSkyB is Britain's leading provider of multi-channel television, under the Sky brand. A few years ago, Sky began developing a new community investment project. The aim was to do more than just the traditional corporate "do-gooding," more than just donating money to charities. Sky's business is built on innovation: it wanted to be similarly innovative in the way it approached its social role. As before, we should declare an interest, since Good Business was involved; as well as this, it's worth acknowledging at the outset the friskiness of anti-capitalists when a brand like Sky is mentioned. You can write the script by now: Sky's social role is wholly negative, beaming non-stop (American) garbage into millions of households, turning children into couch potatoes and husbands into uncommunicative sports-junkies. Worse still, Sky is part of the evil empire of Rupert Murdoch, so by definition cannot possibly do anything good.

The Murdoch point can be quite rapidly dispatched by pointing out that *No Logo* is published by HarperCollins in the UK, also part of the "evil empire." If he's good enough for Naomi Klein, he's good enough for us. The couch potato/garbage point is a classic case of shooting the messenger. If millions of consumers choose to purchase Sky TV, who is anyone else to tell them that they're wrong? And if children are allowed to watch television all day and husbands end up not talking to their wives, then it might be more in order to think about parenting and relationship issues than to blame a corporation; but of course, it's so much easier to blame a corporation, and what's more, you're likely to get a cheap cheer every time you do it. The fact that Sky is a popular and successful brand should be seen as an *opportunity* for anyone genuinely interested in social policy. The people at Sky are obviously doing something right, something that has mass appeal. So how could the Sky brand be used for a social, as well as a commercial purpose?

That was the question Sky asked as it sought to develop its new community initiative in Britain. Its own market research showed that of all age groups, teenagers felt most positively about Sky, judging it to be a "cool" brand that spoke to them in a language they could relate to. Sensing that this might be fertile territory, Sky commissioned a nationwide research study of teenagers' attitudes and experiences, talked in more depth to teenagers from schools close to its west London headquarters, and consulted widely with individual experts and organizations working closely with young people – teachers, academics, charities, government officials, and of course, parents. Over and over again there was one specific gap in social provision for teenagers that stood out: careers advice. A disturbingly high proportion of teenagers reported a lack of drive and ambition, no sense of purpose, and no faith in the ability of school, family or the Government's careers service to help them. 81 percent of British teenagers said that they'd had help from school or college careers teachers, but only 37 percent found this advice helpful. 70 percent had had help from other teachers, but only 27 percent rated this advice as being helpful. And even though 85 percent of young people said they'd received guidance from their parents, nearly as many thought it was as unhelpful as helpful. The worst performing sources of careers advice, ironically enough, were specialist careers advisors, whom only 15 percent of teenagers thought gave helpful advice.[7]

This was a significant finding. Academic studies show that careers exploration skills are the most important factor in helping young people make the transition to adult life successfully.[8] But we don't need academics to tell us this: it's common sense. If young people have a sense of purpose and ambition, it's a reasonable bet that they're more likely to take their studies seriously, channel their energies into productive activities, and avoid the temptations of drugs and crime.

The importance of this issue is clear once you think about the consequences of not getting it right. Sky's research revealed a stark divide in the attitudes of British teenagers. Around half were happy, confident and motivated; the other half were anything but. The attitudes of this "problem" 50 percent could be further subdivided. For most, the indications were that they would drift through school, play truant occasionally, do OK at their exams (but not as well as they could). They might end up falling into a job they didn't particularly care about, or take a place on a government training or employment scheme of some kind, maybe even make it into college – but more because they couldn't think of anything else to do than because of a burning desire to complete the particular course they chose. And they might well not complete the course anyway, becoming one of the 20 percent of students who currently drop out of higher education in the UK.[9] This type of teenager, without effective intervention, could easily pass through life as one of the millions who are in some way dependent on government social assistance, whether through welfare benefits, or less directly through targeted campaigns and initiatives focusing on specific aspects of their life. They'd be fine: but they wouldn't have fulfilled their promise, and they wouldn't have made the most of the modern world's opportunities.

But there was a second, far smaller category of "problem" teenager. These young people could start going off the rails at an early age, becoming persistent truants, being excluded from school for violent and disruptive behavior. They could start hanging out with other youngsters in the same situation, becoming regular drug users, and starting to steal. First just small items from shops, then cell phones, and then moving onto cars and breaking into people's homes. They could end up falling off the radar of state social programs, and become a statistic in the appalling number of teenagers who go missing each year. Alternatively, they could end up as career criminals, in and out of prison and unable to fashion a positive, constructive life for themselves. They could easily have children and abandon them, helping to perpetuate many of the problems that they themselves suffer from. Worst of all, they may not even make it that far: they could become one of the fast-growing number of teenagers that commit suicide every year.

Both types of young person – the low-achieving drifter, and the high-risk waster, were just as likely as any other teenager in Britain to live in a household with Sky TV.

From a social policy perspective, there are two sides to this coin: economic, and emotional. Economically, it's crazy to tolerate a situation where young people's potential is wasted: they are the most valuable asset of any modern nation. It's a cliché – but like most clichés it happens to be true. The costs of wasting this asset are huge. Not just the opportunity costs arising from an individual's failure to maximize their potential contribution to the economy and the nation's welfare, but the actual costs of failure: social security, crime, government programs to try and improve their lives … The emotional side of the coin is equally galvanizing. It's a question of happiness: the happiness of the teenagers who are about to become adults, and the happiness of those of us who already are. The fact that many young people are limited in their aspirations, and will therefore be limited in what they do with their lives, should make all of us plain sad. The fact that some young people are on the brink of a life of crime should make us worried.

Looking at all the evidence it gathered, Sky believed it could help. Most experts agreed about the changes that needed to take place in the support available to teenagers. In a 1999 report by The Industrial Society[10] the policy experts identified a range of priorities, from more and better careers information to the need to focus much more on teenagers' own personal skills and passions rather than offering them a limited number of pre-determined options from which to choose. This was backed up by Sky's own research: a constant complaint from teenagers was that those who tried to give them careers advice totally failed to understand what made them tick, what got them excited. There was one particular interview that everyone remembered.

A 15-year-old boy in Liverpool told Sky that his first love was football, and that that's what he wanted to do for a living. But all he knew about was playing football: basically, he wanted to be Michael Owen. Crushingly, he'd already been told that his skills wouldn't allow him to become a professional footballer. When it came to his careers "chat," he'd been too embarrassed to reveal his ambition to the teacher. He thought he'd be called "stupid." Instead, he was given quite a few suggestions about what he could do with his life; one of them was to join a supermarket chain with the aim of becoming the local store manager. None of the suggestions appealed, which was hardly surprising. After comparing notes with his mates, he realized that they'd all been given precisely the same suggestions, exactly the same advice. He was gloomy, bored, unmotivated, surly. (Your average teenager, in fact.)

But what if someone had actually asked him what he loved, and then told him about careers that matched his passion? What if someone had told him about the hundreds of different jobs connected with football? He could design football boots, be a sports writer, become a groundsman or a physiotherapist, work for a sports marketing company, start up a football website ... (OK, maybe not. But this was 1998.) There are plenty of football-related careers to choose from – if only he knew about them, that 15-year-old could get excited, develop a sense of purpose, start finding out what would be involved in getting one of those jobs, and then work towards his goal. If in five years he changed his mind and decided to become a tree surgeon, so what? At least he would have made a successful transition to adult life, and most importantly of all, he would have developed a sense of self: the realization that he could shape his own destiny. As pompous as it may sound, this would actually be the greatest practical benefit that any careers guidance service could deliver. By starting with who he was and what he was like, as the experts recommended.

Another specific need they identified was the absolutely crucial importance of making careers guidance fun, and speaking to teenagers in a language that would excite and inspire them, rather than terrifying them or turning them off. Furthermore, Sky's research showed that the effectiveness of help was influenced by the context and environment in which it was offered. Thinking about your future is a deeply personal activity. It's hard to do this in front of other people, whether it's your classmates and friends, your teachers, or sometimes even your parents. Because of a persistent "anti-swot" culture in schools, and because of the unintentionally patronizing response of many adults in the "official" careers guidance system, teenagers seemed to be put off from expressing their true desires and dreams – just like the 15-year-old in Liverpool. They wanted a safe environment to explore potential careers; they wanted to know that any advice they received was impartial and anonymous.

All this was meat and drink to Sky in its hunt for a suitable social initiative. The reason Sky could be confident that its commercial skills could be applied to tackling this problem was that many of the drawbacks of existing approaches to careers advice were cultural: guidance and support which is seen by young people as boring, not tailored to their needs, too didactic and too mechanistic. The Sky brand, however, represented a strong and positive appeal for teenagers, and it was precisely that excitement which had been missing. There had been no shortage of worthy careers schemes by government, schools, charities and others: but more and more teenagers were being left unmotivated and lacking a sense of purpose. As the Falklands War hero Simon Weston, founder of the inner city youth charity Weston Spirit (and a partner in the Sky project) said subsequently: "if you say the words 'careers programme' no-one is interested, but the minute you say 'Sky', everyone wants to get involved – it has the appeal we need to reach the young people in our area who most need advice and inspiration about the future."[11] The trick would be to identify the specific areas where Sky's brand could help.

There was no point in Sky being diffident about its role. It shouldn't just give money to an existing, traditional careers organization or charity in exchange for sticking the Sky logo on a leaflet. To really make a difference, the initiative should feel as much a part of Sky as any of its channels, since those were precisely the things that attracted teenagers.

After many months of research and planning, the project was launched in May 1999. Called Reach For The Sky, its central message was "see what you can be." The aim was to inspire teenagers to discover their hidden talents and passions, and then provide them with practical guidance about how those talents and passions could be turned into careers. It wouldn't be a "dream factory," dangling the suggestion that every teenager in Britain could become a pop star. In that specific area, for example, it would show young people interested in music that there are many different careers in the music industry which they could realistically aim for.

The project had a number of components, each presented in a "cool" and professionally-branded way to make sure teenagers found it attractive, and distinctive from the existing forms of careers advice that they had said was unappealing. Reach For The Sky advertising campaigns featuring teenagers thinking about their future choices told teenagers about the various new things on offer. There was a free 64-page magazine, developed with the help of an Editorial Board of teenagers, which opened with a questionnaire to help readers work out their talents and aspirations. The rest of the magazine contained inspiration and information about future career choices, including details on next steps, and job profiles provided by people in a diverse range of sectors.

A new website featured thousands more job profiles and the chance for teenagers to get straight talking and anonymous advice from an Agony Aunt panel of experts. The website was hot-linked to other relevant information sites and its bulletin board gave young people the chance to swap advice and tips with others, and access information on work experience placements. The final component was a series of grass-roots careers development workshops held in various locations around the country – the Reach For The Sky Awards. These three-day courses were as much about giving teenagers confidence and inspiration as about guiding them in particular directions, although each one had a specific theme, like music, entertainment, journalism, the community, sport, or science and technology. These courses were developed with the close involvement of Sky employees; for example Sky News helped create the workshop on journalism. Hundreds more Sky employees volunteered to be mentors, talking to teenagers about the world of work and offering practical advice on how to get started down the right path.

An evaluation of Reach For The Sky by Oxford University[12] showed a dramatic improvement in career choice skills amongst those teenagers who had participated, compared to those of their peers who hadn't. It confirmed Sky's hunch that its brand would be an effective hook to get teenagers interested, and that by talking about careers in the same language as the rest of the Sky brand did every day, teenagers would be inspired. Commercial purposes were served too: research showed a positive change in perceptions of Sky, among customers and the general public alike. Sky workers that took part in Reach For The Sky reported a huge boost from their involvement, and the project enabled Sky to create a whole range of new and productive partnerships. It's now being developed in a range of ways, using the Sky brand to inspire young people not just about careers, but about many other aspects of their lives.

It's a good example of the potential dual purposes of a consumer brand, and for policy makers the world over, it's an indication of what can be achieved by tackling youth development issues from the perspective of an organization whose particular commercial talents lie in speaking persuasively to young people.

Boris Becker also speaks persuasively to young people. So does Pele. And Bobby Charlton. And Ed Moses. And Martina Navratilova. And Michael Jordan. And Katarina Witt. And Sugar Ray Leonard. And another forty or so all-time legends of sport who have been brought together by two corporations in a social leadership initiative that illustrates the second piece of the corporate anatomy that can play a useful role in society: the ability to get things done; quickly, professionally, and globally.

In the summer of 1999, two global corporations began planning something that could safely have been described as ambitious. Within just over a year, it would see Ed Moses visiting a project in a run-down US inner city, observing that "For people who live in communities like this, it's never been a secret that if you can give them something to do that is positive, you can distract them away from negative things and in fact you can be feeding them positive information at the same time. And sport has always been one of these types of activities where if you can get kids interested then you can feed them other information and correct things that are wrong and re-program them and that's what is happening here."[13]

Boris Becker, fresh from playing in a basketball game with a group of teenage tearaways, was similarly enthusiastic about this new initiative: "To be believable, this project had to be hands on, meaning the members who speak in public about it actually have to do something for it, as Sir Bobby Charlton went to Kenya. It's our duty to give back."[14] Sir Bobby Charlton in Kenya?

Yes indeed, and he "had a brilliant day – I've been round the community, I've seen the work they've been doing. We've been into the slums and seen them getting rid of the rubbish and piling it onto their own wagons which they've raised the money for through sponsorship and they're going somewhere now. There's no despair here, they know that they've done something really worthwhile, I think they will be an inspiration to everyone in every other community like this. There is hope and I've felt great all day because you meet people who feel that they're going somewhere and it's absolutely sensational, there's no feeling like it."[15]

Sir Bobby was speaking in the Mathare slum outside Nairobi, which is a long way from the plush office in Mayfair, London, where the plan was hatched a year or so previously. We'd been asked to a meeting to hear about a new idea being developed jointly by the global car giant DaimlerChrysler and Richemont, the luxury goods firm that owns brands like Cartier and Alfred Dunhill. The two companies had decided to create an annual event that would celebrate global sporting achievement worldwide. The logic was pretty straightforward: both companies sponsored a wide range of sports around the world, sport is a fantastically positive cultural force with a universal appeal, and yet there exists no international annual sporting celebration as there is for example in the movie world, in the shape of the Oscars. By joining forces to create an annual "Oscars of sport," with all the glitz and media appeal of the movie Oscars, DaimlerChrsyler and Richemont could not only develop a powerful and valuable media showcase for their consumer brands, but they could make a significant contribution to sport itself – by rewarding and highlighting success, and by emphasizing sport's unique and positive qualities. They also had a dual purpose in mind. To find a new way of using sport as a vehicle for social change.

A new brand was created for the "sporting Oscars" celebration, the Laureus World Sports Awards. Plans for the inaugural event began to be realized. First, recruits were found for something called the World Sports Academy. But these recruits were pretty special, comprising around forty sporting legends who had retired from active competition. This Academy would award "Oscars" to the world's top sportsmen and women on an annual basis in categories such as Sportsman of the Year, Team of the Year and Comeback of the Year. Hundreds of the world's top sports journalists were invited to draw up nomination shortlists from which the Academy would chose the Laureus winners. Nelson Mandela agreed to be the guest of honour at the first ceremony. The event itself was to be a three-day extravaganza held in Monaco immediately before the Grand Prix, including a fashion show with Naomi Campbell and assorted supermodels; Samuel L Jackson and Sylvester Stallone playing in a celebrity golf challenge, and the prospect of a "Race of Kings," in which six real, live kings would race yachts across the waters of the Côte d'Azur.

Our role was to develop a social dimension to the project. This was needed for a few reasons: to make a tangible reality of DaimlerChrysler and Richemont's desire to use sport as a vehicle for social change; to provide a real sense of purpose for the event, and to help secure the participation of the sporting legends who would make up the World Sports Academy, and whose involvement was crucial in establishing the credibility and value of a Laureus Award. It was important for winners to feel that they had been judged the best in the world by their peers, rather than by an anonymous or second-rate committee. Of course, legendary sporting greats are rarely short of things to do. They would not be paid for their participation, and so it was felt that giving them a way to use their talents and reputation for a good cause, combined with the prestige of the event itself, would be the combination most likely to secure their involvement.

The central theme of the entire Laureus project was the cultural power of sport; its ability to bring people together, to excite them, to inspire them. Surely the same was true in the social arena – so why not do something about it? Why not use Laureus to see if sport could have an impact on social problems? Why not create a new organization that explicitly promotes sport as a tool for social change? It could be funded by a proportion of TV proceeds from the Awards event, and it would be an accurate and inspiring way to bring alive the mission and purpose of the entire Laureus project. There it was: Sport for Good.

Sport for Good is based on a fundamental truth about social action. In our work with a wide range of community projects, we're always struck by the repeated success of those initiatives that use a creative, lateral approach to tackling problems. If you want to get teenagers to care about the local environment, the last thing you should do is lecture them about neighborhood renewal. Far better to engage them with something that appeals to them, whether it's an activity they enjoy, like music, or a brand they aspire to. Time and again we've seen the success of this approach where traditional methods have failed. Sport falls directly into this category. As Nelson Mandela said at the inaugural Laureus World Sports Awards: "Sport has the power to change the world. It has the power to unite people in a way little else does. Sport can create hope where once there was only despair."

That was not just rhetoric.

The year is 1987 and in the slums of Mathare, outside Nairobi, sewage and refuse clog the sweltering streets. Conditioned by lifelong poverty and neglect, the area's half a million residents seem oblivious to these breeding-grounds of disease, and resistant to all attempts to educate them. One in five people has AIDS. At the same time on another continent, the young men and women of Richmond, Virginia, seem equally inured to the violence that surrounds them, and equally unreachable. Shootings, many of them drug-related, are a nightly occurrence. Meanwhile, on the borders of Northern Ireland, successive generations of children are being raised against a background of almost routine violence and segregation. But what unites these three beleaguered communities today is not defeatism and division; it's a spirit of hope and reconciliation. And in each case, this transformation has been brought about by the same unlikely catalyst: sport.

The Mathare Youth Sports Association (MYSA) was formed with the intention of using football as a magnet to draw out disaffected young people from their slums. From these humble beginnings, it's had an amazing impact. Over 600 teams now compete in the MYSA football league, and the first team were recently crowned Kenyan champions. But the successes of the league off the field – from clearing the streets of infected garbage, to running AIDS education programs – have been even more inspirational, as Sir

Bobby Charlton found on his visit. The way it works is simple: teams that play in the league are encouraged to do things together that benefit the local community. For every project they finish, they get extra points which boost their league standing. Sport for Good is now enabling the construction of proper office facilities and playing fields, the supply of up-to-date equipment, and the creation of a mobile AIDS workshop.

In Richmond, the Midnight Basketball League has also had an amazing effect on its local community. The idea was to give young people something positive to do between 10 pm and 2 am, when the temptations of drugs and crime are greatest. The League doesn't just give young men something to do: in order to be able to play, they have to attend workshops on a range of topics, from job interview skills to parenting. After its first year, reported crime dropped by 60 percent. More than half of the participants go on to college or new employment. Sport for Good is now helping to transform the reach and scope of the project within the USA.

Youth Sport Foyle in the border country of Northern Ireland is a genuine beacon of hope in a part of the world that's long been resistant to reconciliation. A recent research project undertaken by the University of Ulster (and reported in *The Belfast Telegraph* on 4th January 2002) found that 68 percent of young people in Northern Ireland had never had a meaningful conversation with someone on the other side of the religious divide. Through the attraction of playing sports, Youth Sport Foyle has helped to overcome prejudice and bring together young people of different religious backgrounds for the first time in their lives. Local schools from either side of the border are linked together, with Catholic and Protestant children playing each others' traditional sports in mixed teams. What a contrast to the scenes in Belfast during the summer of 2001, when the world looked on, sickened, as young Catholic children endured a daily routine of spitting, jeering, jostling – and on one occasion bombing – while walking to their school through a Protestant neighborhood. Youth Sport Foyle is using sport to try and help as many children as possible in the north of Ireland grow up knowing that people from a different religion can still be your friend. Sport for Good is helping to make it more widely accessible.

As these three projects show, the basic idea behind Sport for Good is nothing particularly new or radical: there are countless schemes around the world that use sport to tackle social and community problems: indeed, one of the main objectives of Sport for Good is to identify the very best of these, and provide them with funding that enables them to expand the scope of their activities. But there's another objective which harnesses the particular qualities of fast-acting, decisive global corporations, and their ability to get things done.

This is the aspect of Sport for Good which is truly distinctive: it takes something that works in one place and then sets up new projects which use the same techniques to tackle the same social problems, but in a completely different part of the world. So in September 2001, the Laureus Sport for Good Foundation organized a training camp in Northern Ireland for sports coaches from Israel and Palestine, aimed at passing on the knowledge of sports peace and reconciliation programs that had been built up by Youth Sport Foyle. Working with the Peres Centre for Peace, a new Sport for Good project has been established in the Middle East. Training for Peace will develop and promote sports training activity for Palestinian and Israeli sports instructors and young people. It will also improve community sporting facilities around the region, and facilitate co-operative sporting activities that bring opposing sides in local conflict together.

With the secure backing of DaimlerChrysler and Richemont (in itself a valuable commodity for the organizers of community projects, who complain constantly that public sector funding is unreliable and often time-limited), and the pulling power of a host of global sports celebrities that only corporations such as these – with their powerful brands – attract, plus their ability to make it happen globally, Sport for Good is set to grow into the most effective worldwide resource for the tackling of social issues through sport. Already, its projects stretch across the globe. In

BISHOP BURTON COLLEGE
LIBRARY

Argentina, the newly established Futbol Futur supports projects in Buenos Aires and Mendoza that tackle crime, delinquency, and drugs amongst disadvantaged young people, and involve them in community regeneration. In Australia, the indigenous Sports Program runs sport-related cross-cultural awareness activities which broaden the understanding of Aboriginal culture among main-stream sports providers in Australia, and increase the opportunities available to indigenous people through sport. In eight of the most deprived districts of Berlin, KICK is working with police and sports clubs to help juvenile delinquents by getting them off the streets and into organized sporting activities. In Uganda, the Nakalubye Community AIDS project runs football and netball matches with healthcare workshops at half-time, making use of a captive audience: local people had previously been resistant to any attempts to provide AIDS awareness and safe sex education. In Cape Town, South Africa, Street Universe helps relocate and re-train street children through a program of sporting and educa-tional activities, giving them the chance to start a normal life. In the Czech Republic, the Special Olympics Unified Sports Program brings together people with and without mental handicaps on the same teams for training and friendly competition. By playing sports together, those without mental handicaps learn that their teammates with mental handicaps are energetic, social, motivated, and capable. It's an incredibly powerful way of changing attitudes, breaking down barriers, and promoting integration. Sport for Good is now taking it to China, starting similar projects in a dozen cities.

Sport for Good[16] shows how corporations can multiply the beneficial impact of a cultural force like sport, and take it in new directions and to new places. But it needn't just apply to sport. Music, like sport, speaks to people all over the world in a way that no politician or NGO ever could. Over the years, we've seen examples of this in action, Bob Geldof's Live Aid being the most famous. And on an individual basis, record companies have excellent records (sorry) on social responsibility, investing in community and school music activities, music therapy and other associated good causes. But there are no sustained, long-term social leadership projects which use music creatively as a way of tackling social issues, and involving recording artists in the process. The Sport for Good model could just as easily apply in the world of music.

Clearly, an individual initiative like Sport for Good is not in itself going to make much of a dent in the world's social problems overnight. But it's a start, and by backing innovative solutions and spreading the learning around the world, it shows that corporations can play a useful part in social policy development. Along the way, it is transforming many thousands of individual lives, as one of the organizers of the Midnight Basketball League in Virginia reminds us: "There was a player in here tonight – I mean he was on a total road to destruction, he was out there selling drugs, and you know carrying around guns and all that type of thing. He hadn't killed anybody yet, but I mean he was really on his way downhill. But once he started coming here instead of hanging out with gangs, he's here every other night, working on his game and he would get in and he was tired. So he went home and went to sleep, like you should and didn't kill anybody."[17]

As we saw in Chapter 2, one of the most common complaints about big corporations is that they're everywhere – you just can't get away from them wherever you go on the planet. But might not this piece of the corporate anatomy, companies' pervasive grass roots presence, actually be able to help campaigners achieve their aims? This is particularly worth thinking about in the context of another point that's often made by the same people: that the scale of global problems means we need effective global institutions to deal with them. Some have proposed a World Parliament; others talk about giving more power to the United Nations. This is not the place for a discussion of the merits of these proposals, but the reality is that we already have global institutions with the power and the presence to help tackle global problems: they're called multinational corporations. You can imagine the howls of outrage that might greet this observation in certain circles, but before coming to a judgment, consider this story.

One of the world's greatest health challenges is the AIDS crisis in Africa. Zackie Achmat, chair of South Africa's Treatment Action Campaign (TAC) is a passionate critic of those he sees as standing in the way of effective treatment for the millions affected by AIDS, including global pharmaceutical companies and currently, the South African government, which TAC has taken to court over its refusal to issue treatment that would prevent the transmission of HIV infections from mothers to their children. Achmat argues that "The most effective way to prevent the spread of HIV/AIDS is to offer people the chance to be tested, treated and counselled about how they can change their behavior."[18] That's easier said than done given the state of the continent's distribution infrastructure, lack of resources for effective AIDS education, and the logistical and cultural problems of co-ordinating action across countries. But an unlikely ally has recently appeared on the scene.

In June 2001, the Joint United Nations Programme on HIV/AIDS, UNAIDS, announced a partnership with the one organization with the best distribution network on the continent: Coca-Cola. The partnership is designed to help co-ordinate local support for AIDS programs in Africa by making the most of the unrivalled Coca-Cola distribution and marketing system which reaches into practically every nook and cranny of nearly every country.

This is not about Coca-Cola setting itself up as a provider of healthcare, it's just an eminently practical way of finding a social purpose for a corporation's existing commercial activities, in this case its widespread grass roots presence. Coca-Cola is not developing new health initiatives; it's simply providing logistical support to the large number of ongoing initiatives that are being run by other organizations in the public and non-profit sectors. It's not Coca-Cola taking over the job of public servants, it's Coca-Cola helping public servants do their job better. The priorities and objectives are identified by UNAIDS, and Coca-Cola helps where it can.

For example, Coca-Cola in Zambia will store education materials at its facilities in Lusaka and then help to distribute them to 72 district AIDS education officers around the country. Representatives of the Coca-Cola company and the local Coca-Cola bottler will work with the Family Health Trust, an education project that works with young people in more than 2,500 anti-AIDS clubs. In Nigeria, the company is providing expertise in logistics, and helping to distribute testing kits in all of the Nigerian states. It's also supporting the work of Nigeria's National HIV Sero-Prevalence Sentinel Surveillance Survey for women attending antenatal clinics, and offering marketing assistance in the development of awareness materials on the sentinel sero-surveillance program. Across Africa, Coca-Cola will help create public awareness and information campaigns for UNAIDS and local campaigning organizations. Since the company already has a system geared up for producing campaigns that are effective in each part of Africa, it makes sense for Coca-Cola to be involved. The AIDS education messages will be tailored to suit local cultural and language needs, and will promote open communication about sexuality, and support for the inclusion in community life of people living with HIV/AIDS.

As the largest private sector employer in Africa, Coca-Cola is also taking a lead in developing policies for its workers that can serve as a model for other employers. It has introduced minimum standards for its regional offices which require the formation of local AIDS committees that include representatives from management, human resources, labor organizations and medical staff.

Why is Coca-Cola doing all this? Not for some sinister payback, as some anti-corporate critics might suspect. The short answer is, Coca-Cola is doing this because it can. Robert Lindsay, the company's Africa Vice-President, puts the point graphically. "Every day as I used to take my children to school, we would see coffins on the streets, and they would ask me why? What is happening? You can't live and work in Africa without being affected by AIDS. If it's possible for us to do something about it by using our presence across the continent, then how can we not?"[19]

There are other instances of corporations finding practical social purposes for their grass roots global presence. Mobile phone maker Ericsson is building up a considerable body of expertise in global disaster relief through its Ericsson Response program.[20] This tackles one of the most immediate problems aid agencies and others face when responding to disasters, which is that in emergency conditions, communications networks are often the first vital systems to be damaged, making it much harder for rescue missions and relief operations to work effectively. Ericsson Response provides immediate help: on the ground volunteers to help repair basic communications infrastructure and to train local people, and donated mobile phones and other communications equipment. It's been tested in many of the biggest recent humanitarian and natural disasters, including the Kosovo refugee crisis and the Turkish earthquake in 1999, and the Gujarat earthquake and Algerian floods in 2001. The lessons learned are providing valuable research for the continuous improvement of disaster relief strategies, and Ericsson is taking an active leadership role in campaigning for a better understanding of how communications can help.

It's easy to lambast business for being big and global. But so are many social problems, and very often what makes the most difference in tackling them is a reliable grass roots operation, something which many corporations have in abundance.

———————————

They also know a lot about people. Corporations, to do their job properly, need to be in touch with people. They have insights into human attitudes and behavior that are often just as sophisticated as the best social research organizations. Adair Turner, the former Director-General of the Confederation of British Industry, has warned against corporations getting too closely sucked in to the priorities of government: "It all sounds rather attractive. But as a guide to practical policy it is at best a cul-de-sac, at worst dangerous ... The good society is delivered by a robust tension between politically defined constraints and the self-interest and animal spirits of businesses and entrepreneurs, and it is not always wise to muddy that division of roles."[21] Respectfully, we disagree. The good society will be delivered by finding the best solutions to social problems, and the sources of those solutions are surely less important than whether or not they work.

Through their extensive and in-depth market research, and their observations of how people behave, corporations have unrivalled knowledge of *why* people think and act as they do. They gather this information for commercial purposes, but in many cases, it could be put at the disposal of policy makers in order to accomplish a social purpose. We worked recently with a company on a project whose target audience was mothers with young children. At the initial briefing session, we were staggered by the level of knowledge this company had about this particular group. The knowledge covered not just, as you might think, purely business issues like why they buy this product rather than that one, but every conceivable aspect of their lives. What does it feel like to be a parent in today's society? What are the pressures of balancing family and work life? What are the support mechanisms out there? What effect does government policy – on education, on crime, on tax, on welfare services – have on their family? What's missing? What would they like to see change? It felt less like attending a briefing at a consumer goods company than being present at a high-level think-tank's social policy seminar. Anti-capitalist critics might react to this with horror: "You see! We told you they were manipulative bastards and all they want to do is get inside people's heads so they can sell things!" Well, yes: that is after all their job, and we've already described the ways in which selling things is a socially beneficial function in itself (creating jobs, profit, etc.). But corporations' human insights could be transformed into a more explicit social benefit so easily, as the following story shows.

There's a school playground in Stockwell, South London, that's the location of a fascinating experiment in social policy. It involves the British government, a leading sports charity, and one of the most famous brands on the planet. The playground makes an arresting sight, covered as it is with red, blue and yellow paint. All sorts of odd things go on there, like seven-year-olds handing over tokens that look like credit cards, and eleven-year-olds wearing caps that identify them as supervisors. It's an experiment that's trying to tackle a serious – but often hidden – issue facing the education systems of developed countries. It's got nothing to do with academic studies or exam results. It concerns the *behavior* of children at school, how this affects their academic performance, and how it affects them – and society – in later life.

Study after study[22] has shown a worrying rise in anti-social behavior at school: fighting, bullying, and racism. And most of it goes on in the school playground. As one researcher put it: "children spend approximately one-fifth of their school life in the playground. It is a time when they can interact freely with one another, gain social skills, and be active and inventive in their play. It is the most unstructured part of the school day and the place where children are most left to their own devices. For many children it is also a time of extreme stress and the experience of school which overrides all else ... Much of what occurs in the playground may be felt to be out of line with (or even undermining) school policy. There is a powerful 'hidden curriculum' in the playground where issues of race, gender, class, sexuality, disability, and culture can come together in raw power dynamics and an ethic of might is right."[23] Wow. And you thought kids were just popping out to swap Pokemon cards or have a sly smoke behind the bike sheds.

Free play time is a chance for children to learn about social behavior, and to establish rules and conventions about how to deal with other people. What they learn – or don't learn – at school about these things has a marked effect on how they behave in later life. Playground experiences can have an impact on a whole range of life scenarios, from whether or not children turn into obese and unhealthy couch potatoes and computer game addicts, to their ability to form relationships, to their skill in dealing with and resolving difficult situations. Children's success or failure in learning social skills at school can affect many social policy problems that might at first glance be considered separately.

For example, there's a link between anti-social behavior at school and juvenile and adult crime. One researcher who has studied this connection reports that: "the impression given by young offenders of their schools is a very distinct one. It is of a culture that encourages disruption, a culture of disobedience, and a culture that nourishes fighting. The symbolic centrepiece of this culture is the playground, those spaces where pupils are left for the most part on their own and where they pursue their personal social lives through their interactions with others. The culture of the playground is set up in primary schools, so that long before there are serious signs of truancy, let alone exclusion, certain norms of behavior are already imbibed … the schools that the young offenders attended all seem to have developed a culture of fighting."[24]

Over recent years, prompted by a number of high-profile, and sometimes tragic examples, bullying has gained considerably in prominence as a social issue. It's high time it did: look at this vivid description of the horrific impact of bullying behavior highlighted by Cherie Booth, wife of British Prime Minister Tony Blair: "Last week I received a letter from the mother of a teenage girl in the south-west of England. She wanted my help. Her 15-year-old daughter was the sort of girl we might all feel proud to be the parent of. She didn't smoke, drink, go out late at night and was motivated and hard-working at school. But her mother wanted my help. It is hard to imagine what the problem could be with a child like that, isn't it? But this girl had recently tried to commit suicide. Why? Because she was being bullied at school to such an extent that she felt worthless enough to want to take her own life and was too scared to tell her parents until it was almost too late. Unfortunately, stories like this are all too common … "[25]

And then there's racism. An expert in the area found that "racist name calling is common (if not endemic) in the joking, teasing and bullying vocabulary of children … Above all, it is in the playground that pupils learn and enact the verbal and social vocabulary of racism and anti-racism, replaying the elaborate games of domination; handling the visibility factor of skin color; discussing or acting out television games and stories. There is a host of rituals which state and restate the social order into which pupils are inducting one another … the most detailed studies to date … emphasize the contradictory and sometimes conflicting elements which are being developed by primary school pupils and how confused they can become if deprived of reinforcement of what is just and fair … "[26]

Hardly a safe place for children it would seem. "Now hang on a second," you may be thinking. "Surely playground games are just youthful 'larking around.' OK, they can be cruel and painful but at the end of the day that's how children are. There's no point in getting too hung up about it, any more than we should get hung up about other cruel, painful but unstoppable phenomena like, say, Anne Robinson on The Weakest Link." But there's a world of difference between natural boisterousness that passes with age, and systematic anti-social activity that ruins children's school lives and passes into unhealthy and destructive patterns of behavior in adult life.

So what's all this got to do with corporations? Potentially, a lot. For years, there have been attempts to tackle the problem of anti-social behavior in the school playground: partnerships between parents and schools, between charities and schools, and of course between government and schools. But the problem is getting worse, not better; certainly in the UK, if recent reports are anything to go by. It's not for want of support from the private sector: many companies around the world have donated equipment to playgrounds and helped raise money for playground refurbishments.

But it's not just a question of physical resources, of giving playgrounds a makeover. It's about behavior. Physical environments certainly make a difference to behavior, but if that's all it took, the problem wouldn't take much fixing. Isn't it possible that corporations could try to help tackle the behavioral issues too? They have insights into people's behavior. Could they find a dual purpose for these insights? What about a company that understands the youth market? A brand that knows how to speak to young people in their own language. A brand that's associated with sport and play. A brand that could help provide the resources – not just physical but motivational – to try and change social behavior at school for the better.

For anti-globalizers, the famous Nike swoosh logo is a symbol of all that is wrong in the world. They would argue that the Nike brand is probably the *cause* of anti-social behavior in schools as kids attack each other to get their hands on a pair of Nike shoes. But this is simplistic and superficial. First of all, it's important to see it in perspective: such incidents have occurred, and they've attracted widespread publicity. But they're hardly an everyday occurrence. More importantly, the reason such incidents take place at all is not *because* of Nike. Far deeper and more complex factors are at work: a lack of understanding of the difference between right and wrong, failure to develop self-control and discipline, and so on. Imagine if we applied such anti-Nike arguments to crime in general: the police wouldn't be pursuing criminals, but the people who make things for them to steal.

The fact is that Nike *is* widely admired by young people; it has the power to excite and inspire them. It's got the power to influence social behavior as effectively as it can influence consumer behavior. Furthermore, Nike understands, perhaps better than most organizations on the planet, exactly what makes young people tick – not in every aspect of their lives, but certainly in those aspects of life that are connected with sport, with achievement, and with ambition. Nike knows – because it's Nike's business to know – how to communicate with young people in a way that will provoke a positive reaction, an enthusiastic response. For billions of young people around the world, the Nike swoosh is an attractive and aspirational symbol. So the choice is either to recognize that fact, and to see if Nike's knowledge of young people can be put to an additional social purpose, or to simply ignore that fact and thereby forgo the good that Nike could do by working with young people in a social context.

A further objection might be presented on the grounds that it's morally dubious for a company to use its know-how to make life better for young people in one part of the world while using its manufacturing systems to make life worse for young people elsewhere on the planet. We would share this concern, but we don't believe that it applies to Nike. Nike is a client of our company, so you may discount our views in any case, but there's ample objective evidence that Nike has responded with considerable energy and determination to the criticisms that have been levelled at it regarding its employment practices.

Nike has opened up the factories of its subcontractors to impartial inspection, and such observers report that wages and working conditions in Nike factories are substantially better than what is available in alternative local employment. Linda Lim, from the University of Michigan, found that in Vietnam, where the minimum wage was $134, Nike workers were getting $670. In Indonesia, where the minimum wage was $241, Nike's suppliers were paying $720.[27] The Global Alliance for Workers and Communities report from anonymous interviews with employees that while there are complaints, most Nike workers are pleased with their working conditions and consider their jobs good ones to have.[28] In Indonesia, 70 percent had travelled long distances to get to work, and three quarters were happy with their bosses and felt able to make suggestions about workplace conditions. In Vietnam, 85 percent wanted to carry on working for at least three years and said they were happy with working conditions and equipment. In Thailand, only 3 percent said they were on poor terms with their bosses and 72 percent considered themselves to be well paid. The particular aspects of working for Nike that were singled out for praise included free medicine, healthcare, clothing, food, and transport. In general, the International Labor Organization has shown that multinationals like Nike are leading the way towards better working conditions in the developing world, and this point of view has been backed up, amongst others, by Zhou Latai, one of China's leading employment lawyers who specializes in representing injured workers.[29]

Of course it will always be possible to highlight individual instances of abuse, but these give not just a distorted picture: they actually communicate the opposite of the truth, which is that as we argued in Chapter 2, the presence of corporations like Nike in Third World countries is generally a force for raising local employment standards, not lowering them.

However, even those who from a distance would question these assessments would surely accept that socially harmful activity in one aspect of a company's business does not rule out the possibility that other activities of that company could be socially beneficial. The aim of everyone who wants to see business improve its social impact must surely be to change what's bad, and keep what's good. It makes no sense to condemn everything, good and bad. Could Nike help tackle anti-social behavior in schools? In fact, it's already trying to do just that as part of its British community investment program: Nike is the brand participating in the south London playground experiment that is the focus of this story.

For a number of years, Nike in the UK has worked with the Youth Sport Trust,[30] a charity whose aim is to increase the quality and quantity of physical education and sports programs for young people in Britain. A few years ago, Sue Campbell, Chief Executive of the Youth Sport Trust, proposed a new collaborative project to Nike. The focus would be on school break times, and the need to create more positive playground environments and more constructive activities for children to get involved in.

Sue had come across an amazing, inspiring teacher at a primary school in the Midlands town of Derby, who had transformed the academic performance of his school by tackling playground behavior problems through sport and play. Ian McMahon's system included an aerobics class for all pupils first thing in the morning; a set of structured and collaborative games that children could play in break time; new equipment which could be used for creative group and individual play; the transfer of responsibility for that equipment to the pupils themselves, and the training of older pupils to act as teachers and supervisors for the younger ones. Sue Campbell's idea was to take the example of what had been achieved in that one school, and turn it into a template that could be replicated in all schools. Nike agreed to get involved, and there was a promise of match-funding for the initiative from the government.

So it's easy then: Nike would just stump up some cash from its charity budget, pat itself on the back and leave it at that: a nice bit of corporate social responsibility, stepping in to fund a community project just like any charity foundation or government organization with some spare grant to give away. But this scheme aimed to tackle playground behavior; Nike's money couldn't help with that. The critical requirement here was to replicate the all-round success of the project in Derby. The trouble was, much of that success was down to the sheer drive and inspiration of the teacher who designed and ran the system. Ian McMahon's determination to promote positive physical and behavioral change in the playground, and his enthusiasm for its benefits, was instantly infectious and attracted the support of pupils throughout the school. But there isn't an Ian McMahon in every school. To achieve similar results elsewhere, it would be necessary to replicate not only the actual system Ian used, but the inspirational qualities that excited the pupils at his school. This is where Nike could step in and make a telling difference.

Stockwell school in Brixton, south London, was chosen to pilot the project. Its playground is in three sections around the outside of the school buildings, and before the project began fitted the description used by one academic researcher to describe such facilities: "Most school playgrounds are bleak sites – empty spaces between buildings and perimeter walls which do not invite or encourage creative play and which lower the spirits …"[31] Changing the physical environment was an essential starting point, not least because one of the key problems in playgrounds, and one of the main factors leading to anti-social behavior, is the dominance of the physical space in the playground by one game: usually played by boys, usually football, and often aggressively excluding all the children not involved in that game. The solution found was to create three distinct zones, physically distinguished by painting the ground in each zone a different color: the red Sports Zone, the blue Skill Zone, and the Yellow Chill-out zone.

The next step was to provide new equipment so the pupils could play new collaborative games, designed by the Youth Sport Trust to promote positive social interaction. To make sure the equipment would be used properly, a set of activity posters were created, and to teach pupils a sense of responsibility for the equipment, a credit-card token system was introduced. The problem of supervision is a huge one in school playgrounds: teachers need break time too, and financial constraints mean that schools often rely on parents to supervise playground activity. Inevitably they struggle to keep order, and have no chance at all of paying attention to individual children's needs. So a mentoring system was set up, which saw the older pupils volunteering to supervise the younger ones, teaching them a sense of responsibility and leadership. To signal change, and to make the pupils feel special, the entire playground at Stockwell was given a new identity – no longer the "playground," but the "zoneparc."

Since the project has been up and running, Janet Mulholland, Stockwell school's Head Teacher, reports a transformation.[32] There is less bullying and racism in the playground, and most significantly of all in her eyes, the most difficult children (the ones that used to cause the most trouble and victimize others), are the ones that have volunteered to be supervisors. Why? In her view, it's because they get to be called "zoneparc players," and think the whole thing is "cool" rather than "sad," because it's something to do with Nike.

It's worth looking in detail at the anatomy of this experimental private–public partnership. There are countless projects around the world which involve corporations in some kind of social action. As we saw in the previous chapter, it is an accepted part of corporate social responsibility. Why is the Nike zoneparc project different? It's different because the brand is not just sticking its logo on someone else's project. That old-fashioned approach fails to get the most out of corporate involvement. In this case, Nike was involved at every stage of the project's design and specification, passing on its expertise in understanding what would appeal to pupils. However trivial the details may seem, issues like the right visual identity, the right tone of voice, the right judgment as to what age to pitch things, were essential in ensuring the enthusiastic take-up of the scheme by Stockwell's pupils. These skills, the skills involved in creating youth appeal, are not widely present in the public sector or the voluntary sector: why should they be? But they are present in abundance in a youth brand like Nike. By finding a social purpose for these skills, Nike was able to make a unique contribution to the success of the three-way partnership.

Nike does not have a monopoly of wisdom about young people. There is no shortage of ideas in government, in academia and in the voluntary sector, about how to deal with anti-social behavior in schools. But the involvement of Nike in this project unquestionably made it better – more likely to succeed, more likely to capture the imagination of children, more likely to be replicated elsewhere. This is what we mean by social leadership. Nike could not have done it on its own. It took the expertise of the Youth Sport Trust, and the backing of the government, to make this project work. But it's the inclusion of Nike as a partner that lifts this project out of the realm of tried and tested initiatives that never quite manage to crack the problem, into something that genuinely feels as if it could be part of a long-term solution.

The truth is, the problems of fighting, bullying, and racism will need to be tackled school by school, community by community. That's why we described in such detail the way in which the zoneparc project has come to life in one school in south London. But if it can work there, it can work anywhere. It's not a theoretical argument, not an academic study, not a broad statement of government policy: it's a real, practical demonstration of how to make life better in schools. There's absolutely no reason why in ten years' time it shouldn't be the conventional way to run a school playground in any country.

Of course, there will still be objections (although in the case of Stockwell there have been none from the people who really count: pupils, parents, and teachers). George Monbiot has already publicly criticized[33] this particular project as an unwelcome intrusion by private corporations into the public realm. Others might raise fears that Nike is trying to buy its way into every school playground. But these objections are wide of the mark. Brands are already in the playground, children wear them, consume them, and talk about them. This is not a marketing exercise for Nike, it's a community investment project, but one that's a good example of corporate social leadership. Nike employees see that their expertise can have a dual purpose, and that makes them feel good. It's the sort of thing that the most progressive corporations increasingly want to do because it chimes with the personal values of the people who run those corporations. It is not some kind of school branding exercise of the type that Naomi Klein rightly condemns: that would have just meant sticking swooshes everywhere. That type of crass commercialism certainly goes on in schools all over the world, but it's not what we mean by social leadership: it gives corporations a bad name, and they should stop doing it. Instead, they should think creatively about how their business know-how and their insights into human behavior could have a positive social purpose as well as a commercial one.

In his book, *Marketing Social Change*,[34] the US academic Alan Andreasen brilliantly describes how governments and social change agents can learn from the expertise of private sector marketers when designing programs to effectively tackle social policy problems, from health education to crime. But it needn't just be a question of the public sector *learning from* the private sector;

it could and should be the case that the public sector *works with* the private sector to deliver social change.

Location, location, location – the fifth piece of the corporate anatomy under review. The decision about where to locate can be one of the most important social levers at a company's disposal. Traditionally, it has been purely financial and commercial factors that have influenced this type of decision – rents, transport links, incentives from local authorities, and so on. But very often, the difference between alternative locations can be marginal. Imagine if companies could incorporate a social element in their decision making. By locating in a deprived area, for example one with high unemployment, a company could become a powerful agent for regeneration, and moreover, do this in a sustainable way. Government grants for regeneration are quickly spent: but a business that puts down roots in an area would be providing a social benefit for years to come. Companies that are social leaders have the imagination to see the commercial value in such an approach.

While at Saatchi & Saatchi we realized its potential in a very direct way. Susan Angoy was Chief Executive of Deptford City Challenge, an initiative set up in response to an imaginative plan for inner city regeneration developed by Michael Heseltine, who was then the Environment Secretary in the Conservative Government. The idea was to stimulate local communities in deprived areas to get together, develop their own local plans for regeneration, and then bid for money from central government to help make their plans a reality. A key element of City Challenge was the role of the bids in stimulating investment in the area, to provide jobs and services for local people in some of the poorest parts of Britain.

Susan had a difficult task at Deptford. Deptford is in the south-east corner of London, geographically close to the huge wealth represented by the City of London financial district, but culturally and economically on a different planet. She wanted to use advertising to attract businesses to the area, and we thought that Saatchi & Saatchi should be able to help. An idea came about by chance while we were in Deptford for a meeting. We saw a sign above a piece of derelict land next to the railway station – it was a real estate company's "Sold" sign. Out of curiosity, we made enquiries as to who had bought the land. It turned out that the purchaser was the supermarket chain Sainsbury's. They were planning to build a new superstore in this deprived London neighborhood.

This prompted an idea: what more powerful testament could there be to the potential of the area and the opportunities to regenerate it than the fact that a big business was planning a development there? A TV commercial was duly produced which encouraged other business leaders to think about investing in Deptford using the tag-line: "What do Sainsbury's know that you don't?" We thought Sainsbury's would welcome the ad, since it highlighted their contribution to inner city regeneration and commitment to local communities. Susan was confident that the ad would have a powerful impact in changing perceptions of Deptford from being a god-forsaken, poverty-stricken backwater to a place that potential investors should consider seriously.

For months, meetings were held with various Sainsbury's executives: their permission was needed if the ad was to go ahead. But they didn't make a decision until just four days before the commercial was first due to be aired; and the decision was no. We needed to get something on air, and an alternative was quickly produced, but the original message was infinitely stronger, since it used a real-life example to highlight the potential of business to regenerate a deprived neighborhood. Years later, we were to debate precisely this issue on a radio program with George Monbiot. It's a debate that's relevant to every deprived community in the world: George argued that when big business enters a poor location, it drives out local businesses and impoverishes the area. In fact, the opposite is true: the arrival of a new business development certainly changes the character of an area, but infinitely for the better. If you want proof, go to Leeds.

Leeds is one of Britain's largest cities, in its heyday a center of the world textile trade. Like many formerly industrialized cities in Britain, Leeds has entered the twenty-first century with booming new businesses springing up in some parts of town – but with areas of extreme poverty and urban deprivation in others. One of these is the giant Seacroft social housing project. Tesco, another major British supermarket chain, was planning a new store development in the Leeds area. Before deciding where to locate its new store, Tesco engaged in a wide round of discussions – stakeholder dialogue if you prefer the jargon – with various key players locally, including county employment services, Leeds City Council, local building firms and local charity and community groups. Based on these discussions, the decision was made to locate the store in the Seacroft estate – hardly the place anyone would have predicted a profit-conscious business to go. But Tesco understood that if it had the confidence to make the investment, the investment would deliver a commercial return as well as serving a social purpose too.

What happened was a model of corporate social leadership. Tesco worked with local training providers and the employment service to identify skills gaps in the area that might normally prevent it from hiring local people. Instead of recruiting from outside the area, Tesco set up training programs so that it could provide new jobs for local people – and it has: 320 local jobs have been created, 243 of them filled by previously unemployed people. On an ongoing basis, Tesco provides literacy and numeracy training for those staff who need it, and the company worked with local community groups to provide childcare facilities too. It's even set up a free bus service so that people who live on the Seacroft estate, many of whom can't afford cars, can easily visit the new store. It's no exaggeration to say that Tesco's decision to locate in Seacroft, and the meticulous way it went about meeting local needs, has given new life – and new heart – to the area. Tesco is now planning at least another ten similar developments in the UK.[35]

When a company invests in a previously run-down neighborhood, it's doing more than providing a new local service and creating local jobs: it's a vote of confidence in the community, and one which attracts further investment, helping to revitalize the area to everyone's benefit. This is a perfect example of how a company's location decision can have a powerful social impact without in any way compromising commercial imperatives: quite the reverse, it's good for business.

The reality is that all around the world, governments have ploughed money into urban regeneration projects with mixed success. The reason is that they're not sustainable: government money is usually allocated on a short-term basis; in Britain, for example, the standard funding period is three years. Businesses, on the other hand, think for the long term. If they make an investment in an area by setting up a shop, office or factory, they'll want to make it pay, and as the Tesco example shows, can put in place creative ways of ensuring that the local community can benefit from the investment. Community leaders who actually live and work in deprived areas recognize that business is the key to their regeneration, not a threat to it.

Business location decisions can do more than assist economic regeneration. Ever since he signed the Oslo Peace Accord, Shimon Peres considered it an essential part of the Middle East peace process to encourage overseas corporations to locate commercial facilities in the Palestine Authority. The creation of local jobs and the establishment of wealth-creating activities would give Palestinian people both a genuine stake in their society, and an incentive to support the peace process. Corporations with no sectional agenda, motivated by commercial rather than religious or political forces, would be able to foster economic co-operation between Israelis and Palestinians, helping to build trust and security. At least that was the plan: and for many years, it worked.

The Peace Technology Fund, the first international venture capital fund of its kind, was initiated in 1998 by Shimon Peres, Yasser Arafat, and the President of the World Bank, James Wolfensohn. The idea was to make equity investments in companies and joint ventures to build links between Palestinian,

Israeli and international companies: the fund has been a powerful catalyst promoting private-sector economic development in the West Bank and Gaza. The Peres Centre for Peace has facilitated a number of corporate investments which have led to businesses setting up in Palestinian areas. Timex has established a sophisticated research and development facility in El-Bireh in the Palestinian Authority. A new technology park was located in Tulkarem in the West Bank, close to the center of the Israeli hi-tech industry, in order to attract Israeli-Palestinian joint ventures. A joint venture involving Sivan, Israel's leading computer training company, trains students in centers across the West Bank in professional software development. Barilla, the Italian pasta company, has invested in the development of new methods for the higher-yield cultivation of desert varieties of durum wheat at several sites in Israel, Jericho, and Egypt.[36]

In October 2001, we addressed a conference held by MAALA, Israel's leading corporate social responsibility organization. Two hours before the conference began, Israeli Cabinet Minister Rehavam Ze'evi was assassinated. Despite – or perhaps because of – the shock caused by that news, there was a palpable determination on the part of the leading Israeli business figures present to increase their efforts to establish commercial relationships in the Palestinian Authority. Later that day, in East Jerusalem, a leading figure in the Palestinian business community told us of his belief that the location of foreign businesses in the West Bank, which had been proceeding apace until the renewal of the Palestinian intifada in 2000, was the single most important factor in creating the conditions for lasting peace. And the negative impact of the intifada on that process, in his view, was its single most damaging consequence.

The conventional wisdom is that it requires the leadership of politicians to create environments in which corporations are happy to invest. But by their location decisions, corporations can demonstrate leadership of their own. Whether it's regenerating the poor parts of rich countries, creating new wealth in poor countries, or laying the foundations for peace in countries in conflict, there's no doubt that businesses can, if they choose, take the initiative. By doing so, they will help create the conditions for their own commercial success, and the community's social benefit.

An important aspect of many of the more traditional "good cause" campaigns that companies embark on is the volunteer involvement of the company's staff. Flick through any piece of corporate literature, and you can safely bet a year's profits that somewhere in there you'll find the phrase, "our people are our greatest asset." Unlike some of the stuff you read in such publications, this is actually true. People are the sixth piece of the corporate anatomy that we'll take a look at, and in a way that moves beyond the traditional and familiar corporate social activity, staff volunteering.

It's true that staff volunteering is an increasingly significant aspect of corporate community involvement. The idea is that companies allow their staff some paid time, during work hours, to volunteer for work with a local charity or good cause of some kind. This could be anything from reading with kids at the local school, to helping to redecorate a run-down community center or senior citizens' home. Some firms actively help organize volunteering opportunities for their workers by posting times and places on an Intranet; others, particularly the smaller firms, encourage (or simply allow) volunteering by their staff on a more informal basis. A number of organizations have sprung up around the world to perform a brokerage service, telling companies and their employees about volunteering opportunities in their area. The pioneer was the US-based City Cares program, which now operates in most major American cities and has been successfully exported to the UK (as Cares Incorporated) under the aegis of Business in the Community.[37] The BBC's Timebank is another version of the brokerage technique: it's a web-based service where you can enter your details, including the particular skills you have to offer, and be put in touch with a community organization that could make use of them.[38] It's fair to say that the concept of employee volunteering has taken a firm hold in the corporate world, and is set to grow – indeed some companies have embraced the concept so enthusiastically that employees are expected to participate in such programs, leading to a kind of "compulsory volunteering" which, if you think about it, slightly defeats the object.

But we don't actually want to talk about volunteering at all, at least not in the conventional sense. When we talk about employees as assets, we're talking about more than a couple of hours a week as unpaid labour in the name of a good cause – praiseworthy though that may be. Obviously, the more volunteering the better, no matter what form it takes. But it's worth looking at it a bit more carefully than that. The main reason companies support volunteering schemes for their workers is the impact of such schemes on staff morale and loyalty – people enjoy the fact that they've been able to help out someone less fortunate than themselves, and they're grateful to their employers for giving them the opportunity. In the words of the one-time marketing slogan of BBC Timebank: "you get more out than you put in." Social and community projects are also featuring more prominently on the agendas of the people who organize corporate team-building exercises of the sort we used to read about in the newspapers, mostly when they went tragically wrong. Stressed out executives would be sent off to shoot paint at each other in the woods and build bridges over roaring torrents, carrying out such offbeat and faintly alarming activities in the name of inter-departmental bonding and camaraderie. Nowadays, you're as likely to find teams of said stressed-out executives renovating an inner-city playground or turning some urban wasteland into an organic vegetable patch. Undoubtedly this is preferable to seeing a bunch of renegade military types, thrown out of their obscure army regiment for some unspeakable disciplinary dereliction being paid a fortune to play out their frustrated martial fantasies on a shivering group of unsuspecting suits. But it does beg the question: isn't it a bit odd for companies to try and make their workers feel better about their jobs by encouraging them to do something entirely different, like deliver meals to old people?

If you really want to make someone proud of their job, give them a chance to show how their everyday skills can have an extraordinary impact when applied to a social setting. Think how much schools could benefit from some of the pioneering and progressive work being done in the field of pedagogy by corporate training experts. The Media Trust in London is a good example: it's an organization that offers media professionals the chance to lend their skills to charities that need them. For example, ad agency creatives are matched with charities that need posters and marketing materials; PR managers are introduced to charities that want to raise their profile, and commercial or film directors help NGOs produce videos about the issues they're campaigning on. The Media Trust has even managed to persuade the UK's digital TV companies to collaborate in the creation of the Community Channel, a dedicated TV service for the voluntary sector that's carried free of charge on the main digital television platforms.[39]

It's one thing to fit individual people's job skills to social need: but companies can go a step further. They can bring into play the collective creativity and expertise of their organization to try and crack a social problem. There's every chance they could do better than policy makers, government officials or charity workers. Every company on earth has skills and creativity within its business, and there'll be unmet social needs right there on every company's doorstep that it could play a part in meeting. It's just a question of finding out what the needs are, then applying some imaginative thinking to make the connection between what the community needs and what the company's people can offer. Cisco Systems, the leading US technology corporation, provides a good example.[40]

In the early days of its existence, Cisco's community involvement program involved not much more than donating equipment free of charge to community groups that could make good use of it – for example, giving away network routers. But it soon became apparent that the charities that received these types of corporate gift actually weren't in a position to make the best use of them, since they had no experience of, or training in, how to use the equipment. At the same time, the people that worked in Cisco's sales force were realizing that schools which purchased network routers didn't have the know-how to install and service them successfully, placing additional cost burdens on the company through the ongoing need to provide maintenance. Cisco saw an opportunity to design a program to train students to service the computers in their schools. This would help the students with training, enable schools to fully utilize the potential of the company's information technology, and of course, reduce Cisco's costs in having to service the equipment. It would also register the Cisco name with the next breed of users in a positive light. The result was the creation of the Cisco Networking Academy Program, through which Cisco employees give their time to train community and school users of Cisco IT equipment.

Based on its initial success, Cisco expanded the Networking Academy Program to serve even more ambitious objectives. It became the centerpiece of the company's efforts to play a major part in tackling a growing social problem that policy-makers are having to deal with: the so-called digital divide, the gap in IT skills between the information haves and have-nots. As information technology skills become increasingly essential for participation not just in work, but in society in general, bridging the digital divide is a key policy objective. Cisco's contribution is an eminently practical one: its workers now train students and low-income individuals in IT skills. This is a great example of the business benefit from socially-focused activity: Cisco is helping to build a skilled workforce for the future, but is also enhancing the company's network of trained, third-party service providers, meeting a core business need. And Cisco workers see the social benefit of their commercial skills. There are now over 8,000 academies around the world, in more than 130 countries. Microsoft runs similar initiatives; for example, it trains unemployed graduates in IT skills throughout North Africa, and uses the proceeds of anti-piracy suits to fund a

European Scholar Program which trains the long-term unemployed in 12 European countries.

One of our very first client projects at Good Business was in this area: not using a company's brand for social change, because it was not a company that dealt with consumers. Although as you'll see when we tell you the name of the company, it's not exactly an anonymous shrinking violet either. GTECH is a US firm that specializes in running lotteries. To British readers, it's a company made notorious by its Chief Executive's unsuccessful attempt to sue Richard Branson, founder of the Virgin empire, for libel. In the UK, GTECH was looking to develop a project with a social dimension: the idea was to highlight its technological skills by putting them to use for a social purpose. Through Business in the Community GTECH had been made aware of the growing interest in the concept of social entrepreneurship – a new and more businesslike approach to tackling social problems (which will be explained in more detail in the next section, dealing with money). With GTECH, we met some of these social entrepreneurs, and were frankly blown away by their energetic, optimistic, and creative attitude. Leading writers and social policy experts had argued for a while that there was a need for some kind of networked organization to enable the quality and quantity of British social entrepreneurs' work to increase. Such a network would enable social entrepreneurs to talk to each other, share ideas, and learn how to harness technology to make their projects more effective. This was particularly important since by nature, people who can be described as social entrepreneurs are neither interested in technology, nor aware of its potential benefits. With no formal business training, these people tend to have an attitude of "who needs these fancy computers – I'll just get on and do it."

This was a perfect match for GTECH: the company's expertise lay in creating networks and systems, and that's exactly what the social entrepreneurs needed. With some seed-corn funding, a lot of technical advice, and access to GTECH employees for training, the Community Action Network (CAN) was born – now the focus for social entrepreneurial activity in the UK.[41] CAN is both a physical organization, based in London and with a growing network of regional hubs around the UK, and a virtual one: exciting projects are identified around the country, the people that run them are then provided with IT equipment, teamed up in groups of 10 "buddies" and then given intensive training in how to make the most of IT. The real excitement about CAN, however, lies not in the network itself, but in the many individual projects that have flourished as a result of its existence. An IT learning center has been set up in a soccer ground in Macclesfield in the north of England. Aimed at the poorest members of the community, who would be reluctant, for cultural reasons, to attend formal training provided by the government or education establishments, they are perfectly happy to visit this particular learning center since it's based in the unthreatening environment of their local sports club, which many of them visit anyway. Another project in Newcastle, also in the north of England, gets heroin addicts back into mainstream society by creating entry-level jobs for them in partnership with local businesses, combined with training in life skills such as the importance of getting up in the morning, showing up for work on time, and having a tidy appearance – all things which are taken for granted by most of us, but which are huge obstacles for people who've lived a life of drug addiction and crime. There are countless other projects springing up the whole time, each making a big difference in the local community and each learning from the experience of the others. It wouldn't have happened without the initial input from GTECH – less their money, but the volunteer time of their staff, their technical expertise, and their creativity in helping to make the concept a reality.

At last, the piece of the corporate anatomy that many people might think should be the first one to be used for a social purpose: money. Corporations have a lot of money. So it's obvious then, that they should give away more and more of that money to social causes. After all, it's their responsibility to put something back, isn't it? Stop right there. Nothing characterizes the old-fashioned, unproductive, uncreative, well-intentioned but intellectually lazy attitude to corporate social responsibility so much as the notion that corporations should simply dole out crumbs from the boardroom table to supplicant charities in exchange for honors for the Chairman and Chief Executive and the chance to have their photo taken with the First Lady or Prince Charles.

First of all – and let's not labor the point all over again but still, it's worth repeating – companies already "donate" to social causes through the taxes they pay. Second, they need to provide their shareholders with a decent return – that's also in a good cause as it pays for our pensions and insurance claims. It's unrealistic and misguided to expect companies to cut deeply into the profits they earn for shareholders in order to bankroll charities: take away profits and you damage social welfare. Britain's Business in the Community runs something called the Per Cent Club. In order to qualify for membership, companies have to commit to donating at least half a percent of pre-tax profits to charity. (Why isn't it called the Half A Per Cent Club – typical corporate hype, eh?) Two hundred or so of Britain's leading companies are members, and this is seen as the decent, acceptable benchmark for corporate giving.[42] But even at today's level, corporate contributions are tiny in comparison to the overall size of the UK charitable sector – accounting for just 4.7 percent of charities' income.[43] *The Guardian* newspaper's first annual "Giving List" in 2001 made this point with force, establishing that the top 100 British companies gave on average 0.4 percent of their pre-tax profits to charity. The "Giving List" was a valuable attempt to assess and publicize, for the first time, the scale and nature of the UK corporate sector's social contribution. It makes an excellent template for any newspaper anywhere in the world to adopt. But as the *The Guardian* acknowledged, developing a reliable benchmark for corporate giving is problematic: "A company's contribution to good causes is often far and above the cash donations it makes to charity. If it allows staff time off to volunteer, provides free professional services, opens up its meeting rooms or in-house training courses, or gives away used office equipment or computers to charities, this support can all be justifiably classified as a corporate's community contribution."[44]

The truth is, the amount of money companies give to charity is peanuts: not for them, but in relation to the overall size of the charity sector. This is true even in the US where there is a higher level of corporate giving than elsewhere, with companies donating on average 1.2 percent of their pre-tax profits to social causes. Double the size of corporate donations, and you'd just be left with more peanuts.[45] The proposition that by urging companies to give away more of their money to good causes you'd help to tackle social problems in a serious way is a non-starter. Of course, many worthy causes would benefit if companies gave more. But just giving more money is not the best way for companies to help worthy causes, even if the worthy causes say that that's what they most want from companies (wouldn't you?). Furthermore, the idea that by upping their donations, corporations would gain any business benefits, in terms of improved image for example, is pretty unlikely. The minute a company announces a huge gift to a good cause, what's the reaction? "You've given ten million bucks to charity? Gee, we love you now." Hardly. A more likely response would be: "Ten million? Is that all? What's the matter with you, you stingy bastards, can't you see we've got issues here? You're as rich as Rockefeller and all we get is a pathetic ten million – and you're only doing it for the tax relief anyway."

Doubts about the social value, or indeed the commercial value of corporate charitable donations should not be interpreted as a Scrooge's Charter, a mean-spirited bid to starve the voluntary sector of funds. Money is without doubt one of the key ways in which companies can, and should, help tackle social issues. Money can have a dual purpose. But not if companies just give it away to charities. The modern and progressive approach is for companies to find ways to integrate social objectives within their mainstream business, and to do this only where there is a clear business case for action. This will lead to better outcomes for business and for society: it stands to reason that if something helps a company make more money, then it will do more of it. This may be a harsh lesson for those who dream wistfully of an explosion of corporate altruism and philanthropy, but the truth is that if a company's social contribution is dependent on the good intentions – or often more accurately, the whims – of its senior executives or owners, then that social contribution is far more susceptible to the vagaries of the business cycle, fashion and mood than if it is made a core part of doing business. The best news for social causes would be the death of altruism, for where there is self-interest, there is commitment, and what social causes need more than anything else is commitment.

So, if it's wrong for companies to just write checks to charities, what should they do with their money? They should use it to do what they do best – invest and take risks. As the Sport for Good examples show, there are countless fantastic social initiatives out there which need just small amounts of money to get off the ground and prove their worth. Often, these projects are set up to tackle the most intractable social problems, in areas where state intervention, and state funding, have comprehensively failed. Such projects are run not by traditional charity workers but by a new breed of individuals who apply the energy, determination, and flair of commercial behavior to their work in the social sector. We referred to them earlier: they're known as social entrepreneurs, and if you're interested in finding out more about the kind of work they do, you should visit newprofit.com, or search the web for "Venture Philanthropy" (in the US),[46] or for a European perspective, read Charles Leadbeater's report, *The Rise of the Social Entrepreneur*,[47] visit the website of Britain's Community Action Network at www.can-online.org, or the School for Social Entrepreneurs at sse.org.uk.

The key here is that projects run by social entrepreneurs tend to have difficulty in attracting funding from the state or from private benefactors because they're more risky. Here's an example of one that we came across in Manchester, England that struck us as a brilliant, if unconventional idea. We were there to take part in a workshop the Co-Operative Bank was running, designed to explore ways in which it could enhance its famous "ethical policy"[48] by helping its customers to participate in social and environmental campaigns. During the course of the evening, a chance remark by Jack Middleton, the Co-Operative Bank's social campaigning manager, caught our imagination.

Jack mentioned that she (yes, she) had met a community worker with an innovative idea for which he was struggling to find backing. It was a great piece of lateral thinking. The idea was aimed at reining in the delinquent activities of teenage tearaways. One of the biggest problems in one particular part of town was the high incidence of car theft and joyriding. This local community worker had a crucial insight. He realized that while many of the teenagers who got involved in this type of crime were persistent truants, often excluded from school and completely uninterested in gaining academic qualifications, there was one exam that they all wanted to pass: their driving test.

This insight was the origin of a program that we then worked up in partnership with Weston Spirit, a British charity with expertise in working with inner city teenagers. It's called Driving Ambition, and the aim is to provide teenagers with a structured route out of crime by using the cultural hook of helping them pass their driving test. There are various components: teaching literacy so that the youngsters can pass the written part of the test (compulsory in the UK) – and since this is now administered on PCs, it provides an opportunity to give participants IT training as well. Another element gives the teenagers the chance to learn advanced driving skills on the local police driving track. To the participants, it's a chance to zoom around and have fun. But there's an underlying social and community benefit from the time they spend with police officers, realizing that they're not the enemy. The program also requires attendance at weekly courses, teaching discipline and commitment, and training in how to cope with road rage – a neat way of teaching anger management. The teenagers would need to make presentations to the rest of the group about their progress, giving them self-confidence, and at the end of it all, they get to pass their driving test, giving a further boost to their self-esteem. Along the way, they will have learnt a whole range of practical and social skills.

This is exactly the type of initiative that's worth trying; exactly the type of creative solution that policy-makers could look at in cities all over the world, where delinquency is a common problem. But ideas like this nearly always fail to attract government funding – they're far too risky. When spending taxpayers' money, governments are notoriously reluctant to experiment. Furthermore, the requirements of accountability deter many smaller, often one-man band organizations from seeking government funding in the first place. Recipients of state funds have to spend so much time filling out forms, providing feedback and evaluation that they just can't cope. One charity we know has stopped applying for funding from the European Union for precisely this reason – on one particular occasion when they were bidding for funds, they would have needed to employ an extra person just to comply with the EU's administrative requirements.

Levi Strauss provides a good example[49] of the more risk-taking approach to corporate giving, using its money to tackle an issue that had long been avoided by other groups. The issue is the widespread racist victimization of gypsies in Eastern Europe.[50] In the late 1990s, the company began supporting gypsy communities in Hungary and the Czech Republic, where it has significant business operations. Among a number of projects it has provided financial support for is Hungary's Autonomia Foundation, a gypsy organization that tries to counter high unemployment rates among Romanies by providing training, set-up advice, grants, and low interest loans to would-be entrepreneurs. It's given money to a gypsy high school in Hungary and helped set up the Center for Independent Journalism in Budapest, which trains 15 young

Romanies each year to work in the media, where Romanies are under-represented. Levi's has also begun to support debating societies across Eastern Europe run by the US-based International Debate Education Association, which brings together gypsies and others to talk about racism. Most recently, the company has decided to support Radio C, the first Romany radio station in the region with a grant of $10,000.

Zoltan Valcsicsak, Levi's community affairs manager for the region, understands precisely how important it can be for corporations to get involved in more edgy projects of this kind. Talking about Levi's investment in Radio C, he said: "In some ways, given the level of prejudice against the Romany population, it's a risky strategy, but it's also the right thing to do. We have basically been the only corporate to fund Romany projects and because we are often operating in countries where good corporate citizenship is not common, we are acting as ground breakers to some extent. It's not really about the money we have provided, but rather about the visible support and approval that we have given to the venture."[51] Levi's will advertise on the radio station to encourage other businesses to view the gypsy population – which makes up 10 percent of Hungary's population – as an important market.

This is how companies can make the most difference, and it's the small-scale, risky social projects that companies should support, rather than topping up the bank accounts of big national charities that increasingly resemble corporations themselves with their fancy logos, business plans, and advertising campaigns. Not because the big, national charities aren't worthy of support – far from it, they perform a vital function in society. But the truth is, they'll always be OK – they're well-known enough to attract donations from individuals, and they're increasingly well-funded by governments in order to deliver state welfare programs. The appropriate role for companies is to use any funds earmarked for charitable giving – and often very small sums will do – to provide the investment to back innovative, creative projects that could lead to genuine breakthroughs in social policy. Diageo, the corporate owner of world-famous brands like Burger King, Johnnie Walker and Guinness, has been one of the leaders in this field: for years, its Diageo Foundation has led the way in spotting creative ideas in the social sector that deserve backing. For example its UDV drinks business in India provides start-up loans for 18–30-year-old entrepreneurs and business advice to help them make the most of the money. In the UK, its long-running Tomorrow's People project has helped more than 350,000 disadvantaged young people find a job, and it was acknowledged by the UK government to have influenced the design of its flagship welfare to work program.[52]

The British government, more than most, is recognizing the potential of this new, more progressive role for corporate funds and know-how. It has recently championed the ideas proposed by the Social Investment Taskforce,[53] which include tax incentives to encourage companies to make loans to fledgling social enterprise projects. A whole range of creative mechanisms are suggested, all of them designed to increase the scope and effectiveness of community development finance. This is a brilliant way to ensure more corporate funding for high-quality projects that give people in disadvantaged neighborhoods a real incentive to improve their own lives, rather than to rely on hand-outs. There are some companies, like Barclays Bank, who have a track record of investing some of their corporate giving budgets in such projects. But inevitably, there will be a limit to the amount of money available. With the government stepping in to provide tax credits and other incentives, there's every chance that more and more companies will be motivated to participate, that the infrastructure for community development finance will become more sophisticated, and that the overall amount of lending to the social enterprise sector will increase dramatically.

Corporate social leadership is not about companies giving away ever increasing sums of money to prove how generous they are. The sums that even the most generous companies give are dwarfed by the size of government budgets. But equally, the potential of companies to mobilize support for social causes, or new social policy solutions, dwarfs the capacity of the public sector to act in this way. As we've seen, a company's social contribution can and should come from any and every part of its business, not just its bank account. Where companies do earmark money for donation, the best way for them to spend it is on backing risky social projects that have difficulty getting funding from other sources.

And so the final piece of our dissected corporate anatomy, the last one we'll look at. Suitably enough, this is often the aspect of business activity that anti-capitalists most love to demonize. What social purpose could there possibly be for marketing?

We've already looked at the potential of consumer brands to change social behavior. This type of marketing technique is known as cause-related marketing, or sometimes social marketing. But there's another aspect of cause-related marketing that's better known, because to date, more of it has been done. This is the use of a sales promotion campaign to benefit a social cause. In the United States, where it is pretty much a commonplace activity for major corporations, it began with a partnership between American Express and the Statue of Liberty restoration fund in the 1980s, where every time customers used their card, money would be donated to the fund. Amex built on this with its Charge Against Hunger campaign, which raised over $21 million in four years to tackle the problem of hunger in the USA. American Express' rival VISA developed its own version. Through its Read Me A Story campaign, a donation was made to Reading is Fundamental, a leading literacy organization, every time VISA customers used their credit card.

Cause-related marketing is less common in other countries, although in the UK in recent years, prompted to a considerable degree by the energy of Sue Adkins who leads the Cause Related Marketing campaign at Business in the Community, the phenomenon has truly taken off. Half of the UK's top brands have now carried out a cause-related marketing campaign, 67 percent of British consumers say they've participated in one, and 96 percent of marketing and community affairs directors say they support the concept.[54] The Business in the Community definition of cause-related marketing is "a commercial activity by which businesses and charities or causes form a partnership with each other to market an image, product or service for mutual benefit." The best known UK scheme is probably Tesco's Computers for Schools campaign, which has been running since the early 1990s. During a two-month promotional period Tesco customers receive vouchers at the supermarket checkout which they then hand in to their local school. The school exchanges the vouchers for free items of computer hardware and software. Another successful cause-related marketing campaign has been Kellogg's Kids Help Line in Australia, a fundraising and promotional initiative supporting the country's only free, 24-hour confidential and anonymous telephone counseling service for 5–18-year-olds.

But there are hundreds more examples: to understand the area, and to see how to put such partnerships together, there are two excellent books worth looking at: Sue Adkins' *Cause Related Marketing: Who Cares Wins*, and *Brand Spirit: How Cause Related Marketing Builds Brands*, by Marjorie Thompson and Hamish Pringle. Alternatively, the Business in the Community website, crm.org.uk, has many varied case studies.

Cause-related or social marketing, however, is not the same as socially responsible marketing, and this is an area that deserves far more attention from corporations. The marketing function is one of the most important within modern business. Marketing is not just designing ad campaigns and logos; it's the entire process of developing new products and services and finding a way to sell them. For many people working in marketing (and there's a lot of them these days), social and environmental issues might at first glance seem entirely irrelevant. Except on those occasions when a specific social or environmental message is involved, or when a cause-related marketing campaign is being run, social and environmental issues would normally be left in the hands of the corporate affairs department, or the production managers, or the social responsibility people – someone else. But many of the decisions made by marketing people have a powerful dual impact: not just a commercial one, but a social one too. Look at Procter & Gamble's Sunny Delight drink. After a spectacularly successful launch in the UK, it had an equally dramatic fall from grace as media reports of its high chemical content (and the lurid tale of a girl in the US who turned orange as a result of drinking too much of it) turned consumers away. One aspect of the Sunny Delight marketing campaign was given particular prominence in the media – the requirement for retailers to place Sunny Delight bottles in chiller cabinets to give the impression that it was a perishable – and therefore fresh – juice drink, even though it could perfectly well have sat on regular supermarket shelves. This was taken as evidence of sinister manipulation by Procter & Gamble, but there's an environmental aspect that passed unnoticed: the unnecessary use of energy that was the consequence of the decision to market the product as a "fresh" drink.

This is a small example of how a decision made for purely marketing reasons can have consequences far beyond the immediate success or failure of the product. Other examples include the environmental impact of encouraging people to wash their hair more frequently, or the impact of an airline's decision to upgrade its seats – what happens to the old ones? The mobile phone market is a classic example – manufacturers and retailers, for sound commercial reasons, develop marketing campaigns promoting the desire to have the latest handset, even though the old one would serve the purpose perfectly well. How is the impact of such a marketing decision evaluated? On the one hand, there's clearly an environmental and resource use cost, but on the other, there are social gains from the jobs secured through increased sales and the financial success of the corporations involved.

What about advertising to children, the famous "pester-power" argument? Swedish authorities ban advertising aimed at children under 12 in order to reduce the pressure on parents to buy the latest product. A recent UK study found that "in one three hour period of commercial television there were 127 adverts for products – ranging from food to toys – aimed at children aged 11 and under."[55] As the report went on to note, however, "what the study didn't prove was that children ended up wanting the particular products they had seen in the advertisements. At six, the researchers said, children had little resistance to ads, but little brand awareness. By 11 or 12 they had developed a 'healthy scepticism'". Is this good news or bad?

There are no straightforward ways to resolve these debates, and they'll go on for as long as we live in a market economy. It's fair to say, however, that not everyone in the mainstream global marketing profession has given these issues as much thought as they might. When attacked by anti-capitalists for "creating false needs," or for promoting reckless and debilitating consumerism, most marketing people tend to adopt a posture of either hand-wringing angst or fist-waving defensiveness. There's a perfectly valid defence of consumerism – that it creates wealth, generates funds for social welfare, fosters product and service innovation that makes people's lives easier and more comfortable (yes, even the aloe vera bathroom tissue), and that in any case consumers choose to consume; no-one's forcing them to do it. But at the same time, it would be in all our interests for some of the creativity that abounds in the marketing industry to be more rigorously applied to the task of combining marketing innovation with social and environmental concern.

The most progressive companies have always done this. The carpet tile company, Interface, revolutionized the office carpet market, incorporating environmental priorities into its new product development.[56] Even more dramatic are developments such as the Ford Motor Company re-examining its role from being that of a car manufacturer to a provider of sustainable mobility. This would create the possibility, for example, that Ford would end up leasing cars rather than selling them – no longer persuading families constantly to buy new cars even though the old ones are perfectly good.[57] A pioneering project exploring these complex issues has been set up by a British expert in socially responsible marketing, Chris Seely, in collaboration with the UK's Chartered Institute of Marketing.[58] It's already establishing a wealth of thought-provoking research and new thinking.

Just as corporate social responsibility generally can be seen as either a challenge or an opportunity, depending on your point of view, so too can social responsibility in marketing. It needn't be seen as a negative, defensive concept – it can be embraced as the chance to demonstrate social leadership. Our final story illustrates this perfectly, but oddly enough, it's a story that starts with a charity.

Too often, charities ask how they can "get more money out of companies." That's the wrong question. The question should be, "How can companies help us achieve our mission?" We work with the British disability charity Leonard Cheshire, and a project it developed a few years ago provides a great example of the more progressive approach. Leonard Cheshire is the biggest pan-disability charity in the country, dealing with every type of disabled person's needs, from wheelchair users to the visually impaired. It has a broad remit: providing a national network of support services, campaigning for changes in legislation that would benefit disabled people, and as in the case of this particular story, trying to change attitudes towards disabled people, helping them to lead a fuller and happier life.[59]

Leonard Cheshire's aim is to transform the way the general public sees disability. At the moment, people see it as a medical problem – almost as if a disabled person is sick and unwell. But it's actually more of a social problem. The real issue is how society is organized with respect to disabled people, and how they are treated on a day-to-day basis. So Leonard Cheshire wanted to promote a different view of disability. The way it chose to do it is a brilliant example of the potential social purpose of marketing. It also shows how corporate action can often be more effective than action by the state.

If you heard the words "a campaign to change attitudes towards disability" you'd probably think of the TV commercials and billboards pretty easily. Worthy messages urging people to "see the person, not the disability." Indeed, this was precisely the slogan used by the British government in a recent campaign along those lines. But Leonard Cheshire took a more creative approach, realising that it could recruit corporations as its allies in the battle to change attitudes.

The charity's insight was to recognize the powerful and regular cultural impact of advertising and other marketing communications, like in-store leaflets and direct mail. It noted that while commercials have moved beyond the portrayal of women in purely domestic roles, and that increasingly commercials portray a fair representation of ethnic minorities, disabled people are nowhere to be seen. Even though there are around 8 million disabled people in the UK, they never seem to crop up in ads. No wonder many people view disabled people with a certain wariness and lack of understanding: they're mainly invisible. When it investigated the reasons for this, Leonard Cheshire realized that they were mainly based on practical issues rather than any kind of prejudice. The fact was, there were not many disabled actors and models around. Furthermore, corporations and their ad agencies, when casting the commercials, had no particular tendency to exclude disabled people; it just didn't occur to them that they should be included.

So the charity developed a simple and practical way to start changing the situation. Rather than running its own expensive and inevitably rather didactic campaign, it encouraged leading British advertisers to include disabled actors and models in their marketing communications; not in a preaching manner that made a big deal out of the fact that a disabled person was present, but in a "slice-of-life" format where one of the characters on display just happened to be disabled. The campaign was called VisABLE, and ten major corporations including McDonald's, British Gas, the Co-Operative Bank and B&Q signed up. Their commitment was twofold: to include at least one disabled actor or model in one of their commercials, and to contribute a small amount of money to a fund set up to launch a new competition for disabled models, so that they would be more likely to come to the attention of casting directors. It worked brilliantly, and companies found it an easy way of making a difference. Within weeks of joining the initiative, for example, cell phone company One2One produced a TV ad with a love story theme, where the "leading man" just happened to be a wheelchair user. The VisABLE campaign shows how simple it can be to find a dual purpose for commercial activity – participating corporations instantly won 8 million new friends, many of whom could end up as new customers, and the goal of persuading the public to see disabled people differently began to be achieved in a subtle way, with the message reaching far more people on far more occasions than if Leonard Cheshire had tried to run its own social marketing campaign. It's a lesson for other charities whose objectives involve changing public attitudes, and it's a good example of social leadership through marketing.

It's easy for skeptics to say that a few tales of good deeds hardly add up to a revolution. And we'd be the last people to be complacent about the extent to which business has woken up to its opportunities for combining commercialism with an active desire to change the world. There is a long, long way to go. But the various projects and approaches that we've just described show that it *can be done*. What's more, it can be done in an imaginative and creative way. Companies not just doing the bare minimum to be considered socially responsible, but actually doing more than is strictly necessary, playing a leadership role in society, and consequently getting more back in return – whether it's in the form of more loyal customers, more motivated workers, or a better reputation overall (which in turn makes it easier for companies to do the things they want to do).

You could look at the stories and say: "Well, it's all fine, but it's hardly going to change the world, is it?" And you'd be right. You could also look at them and say "Fair enough, they may be doing some useful things here and there – but what about the rest of their business, the main part? All this stuff is just marginal." And in the grand scheme of things, you'd be right there too. But that's missing the central point.

We're not arguing that companies should stop doing what they do and turn themselves into social workers. We're arguing that by finding a dual purpose for things they're already doing, they could play a more positive social role, and that this would translate into commercial benefits in the long term. For detractors and critics of big business to ignore or belittle these efforts would be to shoot themselves in the foot. You only have to look at stories like Coca-Cola's work on AIDS in Africa, Nike's attempts to tackle bullying and racism in schools, and Sky TV's application of its brand values to try and give teenagers a sense of purpose and ambition, to see how short-sighted it would be to ignore the potential contribution that companies could make to solving difficult social problems. Not on their own: there's no suggestion that the task of delivering social progress should just be handed over to profit-making businesses. That would clearly be absurd. All we are saying is that within companies, there are many specific resources and skills that could be used in a different way; that could have a dual purpose, social as well as commercial. In partnership with the traditional mechanisms for bringing about social change – governments, NGOs, charities, international bodies like the UN – companies could therefore make a big difference, and help their business at the same time. To exclude this possibility would be the ultimate triumph of dogma over common sense.

The type of stories profiled in this chapter, even though they may be surprising to some readers, are actually becoming more and more familiar in the business world. There are millions of other projects of this type going on, and most people working in the world's leading companies today will instantly be able to supply their own, equally powerful examples. But there's still a valid objection, the first one we listed. It's hardly going to change the world, is it?

As it stands, that's perfectly true. But it doesn't have to be like that. If we're serious about tackling social problems, and if we feel that corporations could help, then why not help corporations to change even more, to do even more? Not just because it's the right thing to do, but because it will help their business too. We need to lift the sights of business leaders, to get them excited about the potential they have to change the world for the better. We can't expect them to do it on their own, because it will be difficult. Those that do it first will be daring and courageous. So we have to help them through the process, and we have to support them in the process, rather than criticizing them or ridiculing them in a way that sends them scurrying back into the corporate bunker. And collectively, we have to know what we're aiming for. We have to imagine the possibilities, and that is what we try to do in the next chapter.

6

Possibility

The reason Einstein was interested in wrestling with the problems of physics, he once said, was their simplicity. If they weren't simple, he wouldn't be interested in them. This is the same reason business leaders should wrestle with the concept of corporate social leadership. It's actually quite a simple idea, and it comes down to a single word: focus.

We believe that by focusing the efforts of their businesses on a single social issue, companies really *can* change the world. We believe that they can turn excellent, but piecemeal, community involvement projects into inspiring and substantial contributions to global social progress. But this requires a leap of imagination – not just on their part, but on everyone's part.

One of the most common feelings people have about big business is a sense of dull resignation. People are concerned about corporate behavior, and they're worried about a wide range of social issues; but they can't see what on earth they can do about these things. So they go on protests, take part in boycotts, express their criticisms – and leave it at that. Which is hardly very satisfying. Wouldn't it be more constructive, and personally rewarding, to channel the energies of protest into positive solutions for social change? Some of this happens already – as we noted earlier, anti-globalization activists and writers should take much of the credit for prompting the growth in corporate responsibility. But there's so much more that could be done.

So what we're going to ask you to do now is imagine some of

the possibilities. Imagine what could happen if corporations decided to focus in a single-minded way on tackling the social issues that citizens care about. This would be a chance for all of us – consumers, bosses, workers, campaigners – to actually do something positive about changing the world for the better, rather than just worrying and complaining all the time. In Chapter 5, we described the various components of the corporate anatomy that could usefully be applied to social problems. In each case, it was just one component being applied – often in a small, though effective way. What we're going to do in this chapter is to dramatize what might happen if many or all of those components were *simultaneously* focused on a social issue.

The other crucial difference between the stories you've seen so far and the four stories you're about to see is that the ones in this chapter are imaginary. They don't involve real brands – we've left it open to you to decide which brands and companies would be best suited to the tasks we describe. The four ideas may seem fanciful or over-ambitious to some, but after you've read them, you'll realize that they're perfectly achievable – because they're actually quite simple ideas. And there are a thousand and one other possibilities: these four are intended solely to whet your appetite, to stimulate your imagination. There are as many opportunities as there are problems in the world. The crucial thing is to have an open mind, and to accept that while the four ideas presented here would not on their own change the world; if every company thought and behaved like this, we really would be getting somewhere.

The first story is the most ambitious – but in many ways, it's the easiest one to imagine happening. There's a ready made plan on the table, and all that's needed is for a global corporation to pick it up and make it work. The story shows how the extraordinary combination of resources that a big global business has at its disposal enables it to make a unique contribution to tackling big global problems. It shows the anti-capitalist campaigners in the most dramatic way possible how business can be their ally, not their enemy. The story concerns the small matter of world peace.

It was announced in the aftermath of September 11th that Charlotte Beers, former Chairman of ad agencies J Walter Thompson and Ogilvy & Mather and recently appointed the US State Department's under-secretary for "public diplomacy," was considering a campaign to take America's message directly to the Arab world in a series of advertisements that would run on the newly-famous TV channel, Al-Jazeera.[1] As the British magazine *Marketing Week* rather acidly noted, "the idea of running ads proclaiming that America is not the 'devil' some perceive it to be, while at the same time carrying out carpet-bombing in Afghanistan, sounds strange to many people."[2] Most observers interviewed in connection with the news were warily skeptical of the idea that an advertising campaign could make much of a contribution to reducing global tensions, although some actually thought that using marketing techniques in this way could be a useful way of promoting a new world order. However, *Marketing Week* concluded that "if it were seen to fail, it would be a message to the ad industry the world over to stay in their offices and concentrate on selling products and services rather than making forays into the realm of global politics."

Perhaps: but the real problem with the idea is not the principle of business people getting involved in global politics. You only have to read *The Business of Peace*, a brilliant survey of opportunities for "the private sector as a partner in conflict prevention and resolution," produced by Jane Nelson of the Prince of Wales Business Leaders Forum, to see that corporations can indeed play an important role – direct and indirect – in tackling security issues around the world.[3] The reasons for skepticism about the ad industry initiative mooted by Charlotte Beers are that first, an advertising message with no substance behind it is unlikely to be taken seriously by anyone, and second that the "brand" that would be doing the advertising – the US Government – is perhaps not the most universally trusted global messenger at the moment. However, there *is* a substantive and credible way for business to promote world peace, and it's an idea with an impeccable pedigree.

In Ancient Greece, Ifitos, King of Elis, went to address the Oracle at Delphi. It was the 8th century before Christ was born. The embattled King wanted to know how to end the wars that were at that time devastating the Peloponnese. According to the myth, the god Apollo responded with a clear instruction: "Ifitos and the Elians should restore the sports contests" in Olympia, as a mechanism to achieve and celebrate peace. Dutifully taking heed, King Ifitos established the very first Olympic Games, and went on to sign, with rival Kings Lycourgos of Sparta and Cleosthenes of Pisa, the longest-standing peace accord in history: the Olympic Truce.

The Olympic Truce turned into the sacred Greek tradition of "Ekecheiria," and went on to serve as the cornerstone of the Olympic Games for twelve centuries. Throughout the duration of the Olympic Truce, from the seventh day prior to the opening of the Games to the seventh day following their closing, all conflicts ceased, allowing athletes, artists, and spectators to travel to Olympia, participate in the Games and then return home in safety.

But that was Ancient Greece. What we need now is the globalization of this simple and practical idea. Fast forward to 1992. The International Olympic Committee began the process of resurrecting Ekecheiria by calling on all nations to observe the Olympic Truce. Never slow to muscle in on an opportunity for global grandstanding, the United Nations embraced the Truce idea in 1993, passing a resolution that called on all member states to cease hostilities during the Olympic Games. And on a few isolated occasions, it has actually worked. During the 1994 Winter Olympics in Lillehammer the Truce was observed in war-torn Sarajevo; during the Nagano Winter Olympics in 1998 (why can't there be a Truce in the summer?) Kofi Annan intervened with the US to seek a diplomatic solution to the growing tensions in the Persian Gulf, citing the Olympic Truce as a reason for President Clinton to hold back from bombing Iraq.

In its successful bid for the 2004 Olympics, the city of Athens pledged to promote the Truce concept as part of its hosting duties, and in December 1999, the IOC announced the establishment of an International Olympic Truce Foundation and Center in partnership with Greece. Since then, the Truce Foundation has been working with organizations like the UN, and a wide network of NGOs and individuals, to turn the idea of the Olympic Truce into reality. The aim is to promote peace through sport in places around the world facing armed conflict. The International Truce Foundation and Center provide, in collaboration with various partners, humanitarian aid to countries in conflict; they activate support for the observance of the Truce, and they organize sporting events, youth camps and round table discussions based on sport and creating a culture of peace. On November 27th 2001, Jacques Rogge, the President of the IOC, went to visit President Bush and asked him if he would call a Truce in the war on terror during the 2002 Winter Olympics in Salt Lake City. (The President said no, incidentally, although he did promise to fund extra security to enable participants to travel to and from the Games in safety.)[4]

The Truce Foundation has a board comprising all the usual suspects from the international great and good, and it expresses its mission as follows: "An ancient tradition for a new millennium. Challenging our times, through a vision set in motion by the citizens of the world. Building a global culture of peace through sport and the Olympic ideal. The International Olympic Truce Foundation and the International Olympic Truce Center, new instruments for peace in our time. Experience the days of Truce. If we can stop fighting for sixteen days, maybe we can do it forever [!] Create an eternal legacy in value. Bring humanity together for a common goal. Work for peace and reconciliation. Assist those in need. Join the effort. Celebrate humanity."[5]

Well, OK. That's all fine: exactly the kind of well-intentioned, unexceptionable guff that you expect from people who spend too much time in five star hotels. But honestly. Does anyone think that the IOC, the Truce Foundation, even the UN are going to make it happen? Not on their own, they're not. But that doesn't make it a bad idea. In fact, shorn of pompous rhetoric, a global Truce, even for a few days – and even if it was only observed in a few places – remains a beautiful and noble idea. It's also a very practical idea: a seven-day truce was US Senator George Mitchell's starting point for his Middle East peace plan. The fact that even this has so far been impossible to achieve doesn't mean that the idea of a truce is bad. A truce can't resolve all conflicts, but no conflict can be resolved without one. This is what makes the idea of the global truce, under the aegis of the Olympics, such a tantalizing prospect. But it's an idea that not enough people know about. And if people don't know about the Olympic Truce, there's not much chance of it happening. What's needed is a mechanism to capture the world's imagination, to get everyone in every country behind the idea, whether it's people who are causing conflict, people who are the victims of conflict, or people unaffected by conflict who want to stop it. We need something to lift the idea of the Olympic Truce from a noble mission statement to a real world event. We need a global communications campaign. We need events, activities, excitement, all over the planet. We need muscle and momentum, organization and inspiration. Who could possibly achieve something like that?

Step forward, a global brand.

It's a simple enough idea: let's make the Truce Project happen during the next Olympic Games. There's no better time to have a shot, given that the Games will be held in Athens: it would be a fitting tribute to the origins and history of the Truce idea. And we've got every chance of delivering it since there's plenty of time to get things organized between now and August 2004. Here's how it could work, and here's where you can start to imagine a new social role for big business.

Imagine if the Truce Project teamed up with a major global business partner – say a consumer brand that's one of the best known cultural icons on the planet, a brand which has a presence in more places around the world than many other institutions, whether in the private, public or non-profit sectors. An announcement is made that together, the Olympic movement and this global brand are going to try and make the dream of the Truce Project a reality. This brand would also have the commercial clout to get a global media company, or a number of companies, on board as partners. The mechanism would be exactly in line with the ideals of the original Olympic Truce: for seven days before, during, and seven days after the Olympics, a clear and inspiring call would go out asking the opposing sides in conflicts to lay down their weapons in order to participate in sport. Only this time, it wouldn't just be in the Peloponnesian peninsula, but everywhere in the world. Think of it as the globalization of Ekecheiria. Even if you loathe brands, viewing them as grisly abominations, you'd have to be pretty damn churlish to object to this.

With its considerable marketing resources, this global brand, assisted by media partners donating airtime and ad space, could make sure that the Olympic Truce message gets out to every community in conflict. The message could be incorporated in ad campaigns, printed on the packaging of this brand's products, and communicated by leaflets and word of mouth through its distribution network which reaches into the far corners of the planet. But the communications campaign is just the tip of the iceberg. The real work would be done at grass roots level, and who better to do it than a brand which is practically ubiquitous? The brand you're thinking of (if you've got the hang of this) is likely, as most global consumer brands are, to be heavily involved in the sponsorship of sport. So it could work with local organizations to create sporting events during the Truce Period that bring together, for a few days, the opposing sides in local conflicts. We know this *can* work: think of the First World War soccer game between

German and British soldiers, or some of the Laureus Sport for Good projects featured in Chapter 5.

During the days that the Olympic Truce Project would be up and running, imagine a global program of soccer matches, basketball tournaments, whatever sports you like – all with the same mission, to bring traditional enemies together on the sports field rather than the battlefield. People who work for the corporation backing the Truce could team up with local voluntary organizations to help organize community-building events around the sports contests, and a few flagship initiatives could be given sponsorship money to make them special and to create awareness.

To give focus to the project, the first day of the Truce could be declared World Truce Day, when there would be at least one high-profile sports event of a specific kind – say a soccer match – played in every country in the world in aid of the project. Traditional enemies would be brought together to play with each other on the same side, and it would create instant global awareness of the aims of the Olympic Truce. Global sports celebrities would be involved, and it would be televised around the world, like Live Aid all those years ago, or more recent events organized by Cisco's NetAid. All proceeds from the event could go towards the Truce Project fund, which would support grass roots conflict resolution efforts on an ongoing basis. A worldwide cause-related marketing campaign could see a donation made to the Truce fund for every product sold.

For the remainder of the Truce Period, until seven days after the Olympic torch has been extinguished, the aim would be to get as many as possible of those groups engaged in armed or violent conflict around the world to agree to a ceasefire. At the last count, there were 72 countries with security risks arising from conflict[6] – even if the Truce was observed in only a handful of these, it would be a major step forward. And of course, there's no guarantee that fighting wouldn't start again immediately afterwards: but imagine the opprobrium that would fall upon the first group to break the Truce. Since a key part of the Truce plan is to use the period of the

Truce to get grass roots dialogue going between traditional opponents, who knows where that dialogue might lead? At the very least, by participating in joint sporting events during the Truce period, people currently in conflict might start to see their opponents as human beings with shared interests and values.

It needn't be a one-off for the Athens Games, nor even limited to the Olympics every four years. The Truce project could be given a renewed focus every year with an annual Global Truce Day featuring linked sports events around the world. Alternatively, it could be adopted by the organizers of other sporting tournaments, like the soccer World Cup or the World Athletics Championships, who could participate in the Truce project in their own way. The full Olympic Truce itself would be repeated around each subsequent Olympic Games. Over time, lessons would be learned about how best to organize it; what works and what doesn't. The other brands sponsoring major sports events, often criticized for doing nothing but over-commercializing sport without making any practical social contribution, could get involved too. They could follow the lead of the brand that becomes the founding corporate partner of the Truce project and build support for conflict resolution activities into their sports sponsorship agreements. Such action would transform the reputation of the Olympic movement and other international sports bodies, and it would go a long way towards alleviating concerns about the over-commercialization of global sport. Commercialization would be shown to deliver tangible social benefits. Just as importantly, thanks to the sporting and community projects around the world linked to the Truce Project and annual Global Truce Day, this idea would give sponsors lasting and genuine benefits in terms of brand exposure: not just associating their logo with a global sporting event, but taking the unifying message of sport to communities all around the world at a grass roots level.

A little ambitious for a corporation that makes consumer products? Starry-eyed romantic nonsense? Well, it's certainly romantic, but if you put aside conventional ways of thinking about the problems of war and conflict, you'll see that it's far from being nonsense. For decades, countless peace initiatives run by the UN, national governments, statesmen, conflict resolution experts, trained negotiators and mediators have had patchy results. Some have ended in heroic success; more have ended in honorable failure. No-one can argue that conflict resolution isn't an urgent global problem which tests the limits of mankind's ingenuity. There are still too many violent conflicts around the world, and many of them have dragged on for years, decades. It's precisely because of the relative failure of the traditional approaches that it's worth trying a new way. It's exactly because a sport-sponsoring consumer brand is an "outsider," an apolitical cultural force rather than a partisan political force, that makes it not just *able* to make something like this happen: it's the *only possible type of organization* which could make something like this happen. Never mind that the kind of brand with the power to do this will probably be an American one. As we argued earlier, real people in real communities, from Kabul to Kinshasa, from Grozny to Gaza, don't muddle up American brands with the American government like the smart commentators sometimes do.

The critics of globalization miss their target when they argue that because of their economic muscle, brands are more powerful than governments. It's not that global brands are more powerful economically; the real point is that they're more powerful culturally. And the question for the brands is: what to do with that global cultural clout? Use it to sell more of their products? For sure; that's their job. But the Truce Project shows how they could use that cultural power for a social purpose too. Because the resolution of conflict is an example of a global problem to which the solution, at least in part, involves cultural and emotional change. A global brand is just as well equipped to communicate on a human level to individuals around the world who are fighting as a UN official is, or a peacemaker flown in from the other side of the planet. Why not try both? Who knows, a global brand just might get through where the traditional methods of communication have failed. Linked to the indisputable global and universal appeal of sport, the Olympic Truce Project has as much chance of successfully delivering world peace as anything else that's been tried. If anything, it's got more chance.

So why not? Why not, exactly? You can see it now – the global ad campaign, World Truce Day, the grass roots events happening in each place around the world where violence is tearing communities apart. Who else could make this happen, other than a global brand? Could the UN make it happen? Not likely. Through no fault of its own, since it has a very different job, the UN doesn't have the emotional appeal, the grass roots presence, the insights into people's behavior, the ability to get things done quickly and all over the world at once. Is the Truce a good idea? Yes. Is it physically possible? Yes. So come on then! Let's have a go – imagine if it worked. Talk about job satisfaction – "What did you do at the office today?" "Well, I hired a great new divisional director, approved some new cost reduction plans, and helped bring peace to the world." Someone, somewhere in business could be saying that in a few years' time.

There's no practical reason why this idea couldn't be tried, just our own preconceptions about the social role of business. This applies both inside and outside companies. You can hear the corporate Doubting Thomases already: "What if we do it, and it doesn't work? What if we don't create world peace for a few days? We'll look like fools." Really? If it doesn't work, you'll be in pretty good company – in other words, the UN, the League of Nations, Gandhi, and every great statesman that's ever walked the face of the earth. It would be interesting to meet the person who thinks that world peace is an easy one to crack: that's about the only type of person who would criticize anyone for trying and failing.

Or try this objection: "Why should we bother with this, it's too much effort to organize." Rubbish: if you can organize a global network to get your product in the hands of consumers on every continent, even in some of the most remote corners of the planet, you can certainly organize a global communications campaign, a few sporting events and a global telecast on one day every year.

How about this: "We'd just be giving ammunition to our critics. The hordes in Seattle and all those other places already think we're too powerful. We're trying to show how local we are. This would make us look incredibly arrogant, claiming we could help bring world peace." First of all, it wouldn't be you on your own: it would be your brand in partnership with the Olympic movement and the power of sport. Second, you'll never be able to pretend that you're not a global corporation: you are; you always will be; that's your business. So instead of running away from the globalization argument, take it head on and demonstrate the positive aspects of globalization. Show how you can do good precisely because you're big and global, and that if you weren't so big and global, you wouldn't be able to do as much good. Third (and this may be painful for some big corporations to hear) your corporate mission statement, if it's like that of most global businesses, is hardly a model of humility. You're happy to make big claims in a corporate brochure: by supporting the Truce Project, all you'd be doing is practicing what you preach.

There's another angle. "What if people say we're just trying to look good by doing something like this. We'll be needlessly putting our head above the parapet; people will accuse us of trying to cover up our anti-social activities." Well, if that's how you see it, yes, they probably will. But as we argued earlier, a social leadership campaign of this kind is not a substitute for a corporate social responsibility program, it's an extension of it. Of course it's important to make sure your own house is in order, and no brand should contemplate getting involved in a project on the scale of the Olympic Truce unless it's doing just that. But being responsible within your business is just the starting point. The truth is that the actual commercial activities of even the biggest corporations only directly affect a tiny proportion of what goes on in the world. The impact of their brands on global culture, on the other hand, is enormous. If you really want to make a name for yourself as a good citizen, you'll have to go much further than running your business responsibly; you'll have to actively use your business for social change. Backing a big idea like this will be less likely to give ammunition to your critics than to take the wind right out of their sails.

And then the final objection, the killer argument: "Is this actually going to help me sell more of my product? Is it a good use of my resources?" In all honesty, there's no definite answer to this. But none of the sponsorships that corporations currently undertake can guarantee a sales increase: that's not what they're for. Companies have different commercial weapons at their disposal that they use to increase sales: price cuts, distribution arrangements, one-off sales promotions and so on. Brands sponsor a huge diversity of projects in sport, in the arts and in the community not because they're guaranteed to increase sales, but because they believe the association with the activity being sponsored will be good for their overall brand reputation, will increase their visibility, will bring them closer to their customers, and will motivate their employees. The Truce Project ticks all those boxes: it's unquestionably a good cause, and so will be good for brand reputation; it could hardly provide more visibility given the media interest it would generate, and it would undoubtedly provide a compelling new way of engaging with customers around the world. As for the employee benefit: it's difficult to imagine an activity that would foster as much loyalty as knowing that your company is involved in reducing global tension and conflict. These things may not translate into an instant sales increase, but they'll make a business more successful in the long term. Just because this idea is in the social arena, why should more be expected of it than from a conventional type of sponsorship activity?

So there you are. Any ideas for a suitable brand? If you can think of a corporation that could help make the Truce Project happen, tell them. Just imagine what that business could do.

The second idea is a bit more complicated. This time, there's no ready-made plan on the table for a corporation to support. The challenge is to imagine a company that could use various pieces of its anatomy to create a new and progressive social leadership program from scratch. Its role will be to help tackle a social problem that's turning into a bit of an obsession for policy-makers in democracies all around the world. And as you try to imagine which brand could make this work, remember to think commercially as well as socially: the aim here is for the brand (or brands – it doesn't just have to be one) to use its conventional commercial activities in order to reach out to its target customers in a new way, thereby increasing its hold on those customers' loyalty. You have to make sure that the social issue matches the corporation's marketing objectives.

The aim of the story is to show how social leadership works, from both sides of the table. On the one hand, it will take you through the process that policy-makers and non-profit organizations might follow when thinking creatively about how to bring about social change by using business as their ally. How to identify the right corporate partner. How to structure a campaign. How to achieve the social purpose by harnessing the most appropriate qualities of a corporation. On the other hand, it will describe how a company could think about its marketing plans in a new way. How it might develop a social campaign instead of a traditional one. How to make sure there's a bigger commercial benefit than if it was just an old-fashioned corporate social responsibility project.

The social issue is democracy itself. The specific democratic problem is disengagement: political apathy in young people.

In Australia, voting is compulsory. But elsewhere, voter turnout is falling.[7] Pick up any newspaper, listen to any current affairs discussion, and you'll hear a familiar mantra – people are losing faith in political institutions, all politicians are regarded with contempt and loathing, democracy is losing its meaning, single-issue pressure groups are exerting a growing appeal … something must be done. The commentators who whistle this despairing tune nearly always include a special blast at young people: it's even worse amongst the "youth of today" they argue. Young people *really* couldn't care less about politics (while the rest of us, we must presume, are just mildly disenchanted). It's perhaps predictable that the political and media establishment should get in a state about the "anti-politics" phenomenon: after all, if no-one's interested in what you're doing, you're bound to feel a little aggrieved. And what, they cry, can we do about all these hooligans demonstrating on the streets about economics, globalization and political matters when none of them bother to voice their opinions at the ballot box? (The anti-capitalists, of course, have an answer to this – it's the politicians' alleged sell-out to corporate interests that is disenfranchizing citizens.) But opting-out is just a counsel of despair. There ought to be a way to channel the energy of protest constructively within the system.

Of course, you could argue that this is all a fuss over nothing: if people don't vote, then it means they're reasonably happy with the way things are – they'll get down to the polling station quick enough if they've got a real beef with their government. And what kind of utopian dreamer is surprised that young people think politicians are a joke – isn't that what young people are supposed to think? And anyway, is it really getting worse? Or has it always been like this, but because contemporary media culture is so prone to hysterical, alarmist, navel-gazing introspection, a perfectly normal historical tradition is turned into an urgent crisis demanding instant solutions.

So the solutions are proposed, one wrong-headed gimmick after another: post your vote by e-mail, voting booths at supermarkets, voting at weekends – you name it, some think tank or other has proposed it, and some poor benighted voting district has been forced to trial it. Instead of trying to make voting popular, they're only thinking about making it easier. These "solutions" totally miss the point. They're nothing but a creeping infantilization of electorates. It doesn't matter how much ketchup they try to put on the cabbage, if you're not interested in eating vegetables, you won't do it.

The politicians themselves don't really get it either. Any time you see them debating this issue, they prostrate themselves before the public and whine on and on about how they're going to have to talk to people in a different way, cut out the spin, change the language of politics, blah blah blah. But again, this misses the point. It's not that they've got the talking part wrong. As President Bush (partly), and Prime Minister Blair and Mayor Giuliani (convincingly) demonstrated in their immediate response to September 11th, the public actually likes politicians to speak and act in a statesmanlike way. They don't want their political leaders to talk like them: they want them to talk like leaders. No, the bit that the politicians get wrong is not the talking, it's the listening – or rather, the non-listening.

It's quite wrong to assume that young people aren't interested in politics just because they don't vote. Young people are interested in political issues all right: eavesdrop in any bar or pub populated by "youths" and you'll be convinced. The problem is, they just don't believe politicians ever listen to them. Whether you think that voter apathy is a serious and worrying issue or not, you have to agree that an improved dialogue between the governed and the governing would be a good thing. So the question is, how can the dialogue best be improved?

To the extent that young people feel alienated from society's mainstream institutions – not just politics, but the police, the media, the legal system, and so on – it's because they don't trust those institutions. They perceive them as being uninterested in their views and unresponsive to their demands. So this is a problem that politicians, the police, whomever – can't fix all on their own. These institutions can and should aim to find ways for young people to express their views and concerns about society, and to feel that they're being listened to. But a politician is not the best initiator of such a process because the politician is already distrusted. What *could* help is for those institutions that young people *do* trust to play a part. Like brands, for example. They could get the dialogue going, help melt the ice a bit. This is a story which shows how it could be done: you just have to pick the corporation that plays the starring role.

Imagine a brand with youth appeal and a high proportion of young customers. It could be a fashion brand, or a fast food chain, or a technology brand, or even a record label. This brand is constantly looking for ways to connect with the youth market. It sponsors cool and funky sporting activities like snowboarding or surfing, it supports music events, it creates interactive websites that feature competitions and celebrity gossip. On the side, and in a relatively minor way, it may do the odd bit of community activity – giving money to youth education charities or breast cancer research, for example. But isn't it missing a trick? If this brand carries out intelligent market research amongst its youth target audience, it would know that young people, at a time in their lives when they don't have family responsibilities to worry about, have extremely strongly held views about social and political issues. And these views are not just about the issues that are conventionally labelled "youth" subjects – drugs, the environment, and human rights – they're also about mainstream issues like healthcare and the economy. But when it comes to talking about these things, young people feel negative and constrained – no-one ever asks their opinion, and if they do, they tend not to be taken seriously; they feel patronized.

Think about the occasions when youth brands have engaged in these issues before: examples like MTV's Rock the Vote campaign, or a similar initiative organized by the Ministry of Sound clubbing empire in the UK. Imagine such a campaign not just as a one-off, temporary idea aimed at increasing young voter turn-out at elections every four or five years, but as an ongoing, brand-building strategy which acts as a permanent inspiration and mechanism for young people to become active citizens.

Here's a fantastic opportunity for whichever youth brand you've picked. By connecting with young people's social concerns, it could establish a far deeper and ongoing loyalty than by finding a succession of other people's youth culture events to sponsor. The brand could actually play a new and more central role in youth culture. It could help young people to express their social and political beliefs through a thoughtful and progressive social leadership program. The corporation involved in such a program would win far greater approval from its target audience this way than by irritatingly plastering its logo all over a dance music festival. The social benefit is equally clear: if the younger generation feels that it's being listened to, that its social concerns are being taken seriously, then it's more likely to play an active part in society. Creating a culture in which young people feel they can express their social concerns is the best way to make sure citizenship classes in schools have a real impact. But it's a brand that could play the crucial inspirational and facilitating role. Because it's already trusted by young people, it's able to perform this role far more credibly than any politician could.

So what exactly could it do? The reality is that there are a multitude of projects going on around the world that are explicitly aimed at tackling this problem. Projects run by non-profit organizations, projects run by academic institutions, projects funded and run by local and national governments, and projects run by international bodies. There's no shortage of ideas. What's needed is an idea that really takes off and engages young people on a mass scale. Here's ours: the youth brand that decides to use its cultural influence in this way could link citizenship issues with an area that it's already likely to be involved with, for very good reasons – music.

Music is the most powerful cross-cultural unifier around; it appeals to just about every young person. It symbolizes freedom, self-expression and empowerment. It doesn't divide along gender lines or tribal sub-groups, for example like sport, fashion or computer games, the other staples of today's youth culture. As Madonna so rightly said, "Music. Makes the people. Come together." And you don't have to take her word for it: Dr John Baily, a reader in – wait for it – "ethnomusicology" at Goldsmiths College, London, has even identified music as the promoter of racial harmony in, of all places, Afghanistan.[8] The two principal ethnic groups in Afghanistan are the Pashtuns ("true Afghans," who dominate the south of the country and share a culture with the Pashto speakers of northern Pakistan), and the Persian speaking Tajiks. "One of the few areas where a pan-Afghan identity has emerged," says Baily, "is through popular music, which is a hybrid of the Pashtun musical style with a lot of Tajik language. This music, particularly as broadcast by the radio, brought together these two groups." No wonder the Taliban banned it.

Here, then, is a potentially powerful combination: music; a brand with youth appeal, and an important social issue – the need for young people to become more active citizens. The resources and creativity of business could be the ideal catalyst to bring these things together in an inspiring way. The mechanisms would be determined by the brand's commercial activities and objectives, but the basic idea would be to find a social purpose for some of the things it does anyway. Advertising, sponsorship, public relations, employee volunteering websites, text messaging, discounts, and special offers: all could play their part in creating awareness of the citizenship program and encouraging youth participation in it.

In our particular idea, the central vehicle would be the organization of grass roots activities that enable young people to express their social concerns through music. Using the tried and trusted format of a song-writing contest, but one with a social and political dimension, our youth brand could engage young people in a way that politicians could never manage. Bob Dylan invented the protest song, showing that music could speak powerfully about things other than love and relationships. Why not encourage young people to write their own songs about the social issues they care about today? At first glance, some might view the prospect of creating a generation of budding Bob Dylans as a truly horrific one, but think about the fundamental point: we know that young people are into music. We know that young people are into certain brands. We say we want to get young people to be less apathetic about politics and social issues – so let's use those cultural hooks that work for young people in order to achieve our social objective.

The precise details of how it would work would vary from country to country, and according to whichever brand was involved. But it would only work if it was done in a big way, in a way that got everyone talking and in a way that permeated youth culture. That means a combination of national awareness activities and local grass roots events. Not every young person would participate, not by a long way. But that's not the point. The point would be to prompt young people to think and talk about social issues, and to make them feel that someone is listening. A youth brand could easily achieve that. It could get the songwriting contest going, working with local schools to organize local performances and judging. It could work with local councils to put on music events in the community where budding musicians could perform their songs. It could create a website, or a magazine, which talked about politics in a fresh and engaging way – partly to stimulate ideas for songs, and partly so that those young people who wouldn't actually write a song would still have an ongoing way of being involved.

The end result of the songwriting competition could be for the winning songs to be turned into a CD, either for sale or distributed free on the Internet. The brand could organize a national music event at which the winning songs were performed to an audience of politicians, newspaper editors, police chiefs, business leaders, doctors, teachers … It would be a tangible demonstration to young people that they were being listened to. The brand could take the issues that young people chose to talk about in their music and launch campaigns based on those subjects. The brand could arrange local meetings at which young people could talk face-to-face with community leaders and relevant decision-makers, and hear the other side of the story. It could organize a "Use Your Vote" campaign along the lines proposed by Britain's Citizenship Foundation, showing that voting is important not just in political elections, but in many other spheres of life.

The most important outcome would be that young people would no longer see politics as a remote, dull occupation, but something that's relevant to them and welcomes their participation. Frankly, such a campaign would serve its purpose if it did nothing other than to make politics "cool." Endless worthy academic and media projects have talked about the need to "re-brand" politics. But rather than trying to artificially create a new brand for politics, isn't it easier to use an existing, successful and attractive brand to draw young people in? Once they'd been drawn in, there would be no limit to what the youth brand could achieve in this area. For a start, it could repeat the songwriting competition every year, allowing it to grow in stature and appeal. But on an ongoing basis, it could use its knowledge of youth culture and its understanding of how to communicate effectively with young people as a way of introducing them to the complexities of policy-making.

It would be relevant and attractive in any country; indeed it could be run in every country simultaneously by a global brand. To have a big social impact, it needs a big brand to get involved, and it needs the brand to think big about its involvement. This story shows that corporations can achieve far more when they engage directly in an issue rather than just handing over cash to a charity. In this case, the whole point is for the corporation to find a dual purpose for its commercial activities, because it's those commercial activities that have mass youth appeal. And by doing so, it would strengthen its connection with its customers, as well as inspiring employees and transforming its corporate reputation.

Our third idea shows how social leadership could be a far more inclusive doctrine than the conventional thinking about corporate social responsibility allows. Social leadership can be extended to tackle problems that at first glance might seem to be no-go areas for business. In reading this story, try to imagine which brand could realistically set out to tackle modern society's biggest taboo.

The World Health Organization's World Health Report 2001[9] focused entirely on mental health. It found that at some point in their lives, up to one in four Europeans will be affected by mental health problems, and more than 10 percent of children will suffer from one or more mental and behavioral problems. Depression is now the fourth biggest cause of disease and disability worldwide (after respiratory infection, infant deaths and HIV/AIDS). But the problem is much worse in Europe and North America than in the developing world.

A chink of light for the anti-capitalists? "We told you so: the countries with the worst mental health problems are the ones with the most 'advanced' capitalist economies. Now will you believe us when we tell you that the entire system is shallow, corrupt, and destructive?" Let's think about it … no. All societies have problems; different societies have problems of different kinds. You've got to weigh up the negatives against the positives. So while more people are suffering from mental health problems, fewer are suffering from physical health problems. The answer is to mobilize resources to tackle the mental health problems just as we've been doing to tackle the other kind. And this is where a corporation comes in.

Look at the problem in more specific detail. Suicide rates are alarmingly high – between 11 to 36 per 100,000 people, depending on the country. (East European males are at particular risk, although adolescents and women in the West are becoming increasingly vulnerable.)[10] What's the main issue? People don't talk about their problems until it's too late for them to be helped. Many people with mental health problems don't get the care they need: WHO's survey found that out of an estimated 33 million people who suffer from severe depression each year (that's 58 out of every thousand adults in the world), only 18 percent get the right treatment. 66 percent of the 41 million adults thought to misuse – or to be dependent on – alcohol don't get any treatment at all. And in any case, it's estimated that one to two thirds of men who are alcoholics use drink to cope with an untreated depressive condition. They don't talk about their mental health problems, they turn to alcohol, they don't talk about their alcohol problems … The report found that 15 million people in Europe will have epilepsy at some point in their lives, but that 56 percent of people with epilepsy don't get any help. The report also cites a study showing that 57 percent of young people with a psychiatric disorder go untreated.

The key issue in tackling these issues is communication. As another investigation, by *The Observer* newspaper, commented:

"awareness of the problem remains low – the whole subject wrapped in a Dickensian aura of ignorance, secrecy and fear."[11] We have stereotyped and extreme perceptions of mental health problems: the crazy schizophrenic, the manic depressive, the danger to society. Because of these stereotyped views, and because of the aura of dark and unpleasant mystery that surrounds the issue, people simply don't acknowledge their problems. If you have a physical ailment, you don't hesitate to visit the doctor. But all too often, if you have mental health problems, you suffer in silence. Tragically, many people suffer until it's too late for effective treatment. The list of mental health symptoms encompasses all ages and all sections of society: eating disorders, depression, stress, addiction, the balance between work and family life – and as the WHO report shows, vast numbers of people around the world are affected every single day.

The taboo that surrounds mental health problems is the single biggest barrier to their effective treatment, and this is particularly true in the workplace, where it is simply "not done" to admit problems of this type. (Apart from anything else, this is bad for business: stress-related absences account for about half of all sickness, according to a British campaigner.)[12] A survey by the Mental Health Foundation found that 47 percent of people with mental health problems had suffered discrimination at work; while 55 percent felt they couldn't tell their colleagues about the problem.[13] A famous study in 1998[14] sent two very similar CVs to 200 company personnel managers. They were asked to evaluate the job prospects of the two "applicants"; one suffered from diabetes, the other had recovered from a period of depression. The "applicant" with the history of depression was judged "significantly less employable" than the one with diabetes. This type of discrimination simply reinforces the feeling among sufferers that they can't reveal their suffering.

The tragedy of this is that mental health problems can be treated. Suicides can be prevented. Alcoholics can recover. The World Health Report pointed out that 60 percent of people with depression can recover if they have the right combination of antidepressants and psychotherapy. There are many practical recommendations for what governments can do about mental health problems: they can provide treatment in primary care, organize community care services, make psychotropic drugs available, increase the proportion of health budgets spent on mental health (in some countries, it's as low as 3 percent). But even if care services are dramatically improved, they won't be much use if sufferers won't talk about their problems, and won't seek care in the first place.

This social taboo has translated into a corporate taboo, too. Mental health is exactly the type of issue that critics of cause-related marketing cite when they complain that by taking a marketing approach to corporate social investment, companies sound the death-knell for charities working in "unpopular" or "unfashionable" areas. Such critics have a point: but it doesn't always have to be like that. There's no reason why a brand couldn't tackle a risky, edgy issue like mental health. Indeed, you could look at it a different way, and argue that the marketing involvement of a mainstream brand is exactly what difficult social issues need if they're to move into the center ground of mass public awareness. And mental health makes sense for a corporate initiative because although it commands little public attention, it affects people on a mass scale – and not just directly. It affects partners, parents, friends of sufferers too. In other words, customers and employees of big corporations.

But which brand could tackle this complex subject sensitively? That's down to you. As for what a company could do, here are some ideas.

The key focus has to be on communication. It's about changing perceptions of mental health problems. Bringing them out into the open, telling people that mental health problems are nothing to be ashamed of, any more than a broken leg or a brain tumor is something to be ashamed of. So this might be a suitable challenge for a media company, or an entertainment company. After all, this is about helping people to be happy – which is their business. There could be a number of components. You could imagine storylines in drama programs or features in popular newspapers that highlight the issues in a sensitive way. A website could be established and promoted – it would provide information and real-life stories to show sufferers that they weren't alone. Directories of local care facilities could be created. People could be put in touch with peer support groups and charities dealing with the problem. Employees could be supported in raising money for such organizations. A corporation could develop best practice in dealing with mental health issues in the workplace, and share the learnings with other companies; it could become a public advocate for openness on mental health.

There could be a combination of public and personal activities. Part of the objective is to change society's attitudes, so an awareness campaign seen by all would serve an important purpose. But equally, mental health is an intensely private problem. It would be important to give people information in a format that they could use at home, on their own. Brands are in people's homes all the time – maybe there's a role here for a mass market consumer brand? A cause-related marketing campaign in partnership with a mental health charity could deal with both aspects at once.

Or it might be possible for different brands to tackle different aspects of the problem. A company whose expertise lies in communicating with women could develop projects centered on the aspects of mental health that have a female bias, like post-natal depression or eating disorders. A company in the leisure industry might want to tackle the problem of stress, and of balancing work and home life. It might be able to prompt people into recognizing that something is wrong in their lives by producing simple self-diagnostic questionnaires in a non-threatening style, distributed through leisure or entertainment venues.

Whatever the chosen brand, and the chosen methods of communication and assistance, it's important to remember the specific role that a corporation could play. Not providing care, but directing people to the providers of care. Not solving problems, but giving people the confidence to acknowledge them – the first stage of effective treatment. By changing society's attitudes towards this growing, but hidden problem, a brand could change society. That would indeed be an example of social leadership.

And now for the final idea, where we not only look at matching a brand to a social issue, but we also look at the process a company might follow in articulating its basic business purpose. It's a chance to imagine social leadership as the solution to a corporate, as well as a social, problem.

Picture a specific type of company. In this story our company manufactures white goods – that is, refrigerators, cookers, and other similar domestic appliances. Imagine that this company is looking for a way to differentiate itself from its competitors. It wants to describe its various activities with a simple and catchy theme. You may ask, why? If a company makes domestic appliances, why not just say, "we're a domestic appliance manufacturer"? What is there to think about? For those uninitiated in the rituals of the branding and marketing professions, what follows may sound suspiciously like money for old rope. But in business reality, there are indeed a number of reasons why brands may want to go further than a purely functional description of their activities.

The first is to stand out from the competition. In every business sector, there will be a range of companies doing pretty much the same thing. Each company needs to make itself attractive – to customers, to investors, to potential employees, and so on. You don't make yourself attractive by saying "we're exactly the same as all the others": you need to find a distinctive quality which you can make your own in the marketplace, whether it's as simple as saying: "we're the biggest, so we're the best," or "we're German, so we're the best"; or something less tangible like "we're the brand for families," whereas a competing brand may position itself as being the "choice of go-getting individuals."

A second reason that corporations decide to identify and lay claim to the "ownership" of a quality over and above their functional definition is because this can help determine future business strategy, thereby helping to attract investment. For example, a company that describes itself as "an airline" is pretty much limited to flying planes around. But by describing itself as "a tailor-made travel solutions company," it would open the door to new business activities and income streams – selling holiday packages, insurance, car hire and all the other activities involved in travel. This is good news for investors who want to put their money into companies that offer the prospect of ever-increasing returns. Finally, and perhaps least tangibly, companies often want to, in their jargon, "capture the high ground" – to express what they do in terms of the ultimate benefit to society, rather than the more mundane and humdrum day-to-day reality of their operations. So a credit card company may choose to say that it "makes dreams come true" rather than saying that it simply facilitates electronic transfers of cash, a prosaic definition which may not exactly get the workers leaping out of bed every morning raring to go.

When companies choose to describe themselves in terms of their social role, rather than their functional attributes, a social leadership initiative of some kind is the best way to communicate it. You can write "we make dreams come true" as many times as you like on annual reports, corporate brochures and mission statements; you can even stick the phrase up in huge letters in the front lobby of your glamorous corporate headquarters. But if it's just words, it's unlikely to be persuasive. However, if you put in place a social campaign which literally makes people's dreams come true, then the corporate aspiration will be manifested in a tangible – and more persuasive – way.

So imagine that for a combination of such reasons, our domestic appliance company was looking for a theme that it could own; and having decided what that theme was, that it was looking for a social initiative, something to bring its dual purpose alive. To get the process going, the company tries to identify the real social benefit of its products, and to express this in a way than none of its competitors is doing. OK, the thinking might go, we make fridges and so on – but so do all our rivals. What can we say that will make us distinctive – what's the social benefit of domestic appliances, what's the high ground in this sector? The first thought might be a simple one: health. Fridges, freezers, cookers, washing machines – they all contribute to better health, through enabling people to live more hygienically. What's more, this is true everywhere – from the hi-tech home in California to the remote village in Africa. Having settled on this theme, the challenge would be to develop a worldwide campaign that explicitly helps deliver health improvements over and above the company's core business activities – a simple and a clear dual purpose.

But is health the right idea? Is it the best possible issue on which to lead? It's clearly not an irrelevant theme – it's undeniable that modern domestic equipment contributes to better hygiene in the home. But is it a theme that rings true for outside audiences? Say the word "health" and wouldn't people immediately think of global healthcare or drug companies? Imagine the presentation of the new strategy to a group of major investors: "here's our corporate mission – we promote better health." If you heard that, you might be mystified. Where's the business going next – building hospitals? Finding a cure for AIDS? Would the theme just create confusion? Hardly the ideal outcome of a corporate strategy.

Perhaps another idea might be worth considering. What's the fundamental truth about this company's role in society? What do its activities represent? What do its products collectively mean to people beyond their immediate utility? Maybe it's something to do with technology. It's a company that's renowned for technological innovation – would that make a suitable theme? No. Again, while it's certainly a true and accurate expression of one aspect of this company's work, it's not particularly distinctive: there are plenty of corporations that market themselves on the basis of their technological know-how. Is there something else that the company could credibly say – something that really captured the essence of this brand's worth to society …

When governments and statisticians compile rankings of poverty and deprivation, one of the things they look at is ownership of white goods like cookers and fridges. They are literally a symbol of social progress and development. By making its products available to more and more people around the world, this company contributes to social development. So what about selecting that word as the preferred expression of the company's mission: the word "development"?

The next step would be to construct a social leadership program that instantly communicates this brand's commitment to "development." In social and economic policy terms, development refers to tackling poverty and deprivation in the world's poorest countries. How could this brand really make a difference in that area, given the huge efforts being applied to tackling development problems by national governments, aid agencies and international organizations like UNICEF and the World Bank? There's no point in thinking that some kind of charitable donation would be the answer: any money that this company could donate to an organization like, say, OXFAM, would be a drop in the ocean and, while undoubtedly welcome, would barely make a difference. And in any case, it would not capture any specific sense of this brand contributing to development. It would just be writing a check to a charity. The company needs to do something innovative, something that would make a real and practical contribution to development, and something with which its brand could uniquely be identified.

Something like micro-finance.

Micro-finance is acknowledged by governments, economists, aid agencies – yes, even by anti-globalization campaigners – to be a more progressive approach to development than the simple distribution of aid. It works on the basis of the old adage: give a man a fish and he'll eat for a day; teach him how to fish and he'll never starve again. Micro-finance is a way of helping some of the poorest people on the planet to develop their own sources of income, so they're not reliant on hand-outs from others. It also happens to support our central proposition in this book: that business is the best way to tackle social problems.

In 1974, Professor Muhammad Yunus, a Bangladeshi economist from Chittagong University, led his students on a field trip to a poor village. They interviewed a woman who made bamboo stools, and learnt that she had to borrow money at such a high rate that all she had left was a one cent profit margin. Had she been able to borrow at more advantageous rates, she would have been able to amass an economic cushion and raise herself above subsistence level. Yunus took matters into his own hands and from his own pocket lent the equivalent of $25 to 42 basket weavers. He found that it was possible with even this tiny amount not only to help them survive, but also to create the spark of personal initiative and enterprise necessary for the basket weavers to pull themselves out of poverty. Against the advice of established banks and the government, Yunus carried on giving out micro loans and in 1983 formed the Grameen Bank (meaning village bank). In Bangladesh today Grameen has over a thousand branches with 12,500 staff serving 2.1 million borrowers in 37,000 villages. On any working day, Grameen collects an average of $1.5 million in weekly instalments. Of the borrowers, 94 percent are women, and 98 percent of the loans are paid back – a recovery rate higher than in any other banking system.[15]

So the purpose of micro-finance is to help people start their own micro-level businesses as a route out of poverty and deprivation. It is a practical and sustainable contribution to solving a global problem, and it's as relevant in deprived neighborhoods in rich societies as it is in developing countries with widespread poverty. Grameen methods are applied in projects in over 60 countries, including the USA, France, the Netherlands and Norway.[16] Micro-finance has already attracted the support of corporations – for example the Ford Motor Company has been a major player in the area – but no corporation has used micro-finance in a high-profile, social leadership campaign. No corporation has used it to help define its own corporate purpose. As a result, micro-finance has not yet captured the public's imagination on a grand scale. But a corporation could change that. A public campaign on micro-finance could engage Western consumers in development issues, in many different circumstances.

For example, it could help tackle the sex trade in Eastern European countries. In Moldova it is not unusual for entire villages to have no women in them between the ages of 16 and 40. Promised better lives by unscrupulous and exploitative criminal organizations, they've been sold as prostitutes to work in Turkey, Russia, Italy or even to service the carnal needs of the international peacekeeping forces in former Yugoslavia. How to stop this vile practice? There's no point anyone telling the young women not to go – they're desperate for money, and there are no prospects for work in their home towns or villages. The only sustainable solution is to find them work. But it's not easy to create businesses from scratch that will employ local women. Imagine if a young woman wanted to set up a bakery business in a village. She wouldn't need much, but she'd need something – an oven, a start-up stock of cash to buy raw materials. Where's she going to get the money? Conventional banks aren't geared up to granting start-up business loans on such a small scale. The answer is micro-finance, also known as micro-credit or grameen lending in honor of its founder.

The way it works is simple in conceptual terms, but involves a complex network of participating organizations. Many of them are the leading international aid organizations, some are conventional banks who have developed divisions servicing the credit needs of micro-enterprises, but just as many are tiny start-up non-profit organizations. A micro-finance lender will visit a village, and talk to the local people about potential business ideas. When a realistic idea is identified (and very often, it doesn't take long, as people have plenty of ideas about what they want to do, they just don't have the wherewithal to get started), the lender will agree terms for a loan – say $100 dollars, to be repaid over two years at a nominal interest rate. There are a variety of models used: for example, loans are sometimes given to groups of four people only, so that a co-operative business is started; but the principle is the same, giving people the bare minimum to start their own micro-business on accessible terms.

A real individual's story profiled by one of the world's leading micro-finance organizations[17] brings home in an immediate and practical way how micro-finance can help people in even the most unpromising circumstances. The story is about Jane, a woman who survived the horrors of the Rwandan genocide – her husband was killed, her home was pillaged and her life uprooted. After she returned home with her children from a refugee camp, Jane took a small loan from World Relief and started a business washing and ironing clothes for taxi drivers. She now pays another woman to help her wash and has hired a teenager to repair and shine shoes. Before embarking on her own business, Jane carefully planned what she would do and how she could target customers. "I used to pass by this corner and saw that I could have a good business. Most of the drivers are single and don't have wives or house boys to do their laundry and shoes." She received four loans and repaid each before assuming the next one. "The loans empowered me because I could buy a flat iron, washing basins, all sorts of polish colours and needles and thread for shoe repair. I used to operate my business in the open. Now I have a kiosk. It really has a good future." With her earnings, Jane continues to expand and improve her business. She also manages to save $3 a week for both her and her family's future. Thanks to micro-credit Jane is rebuilding both her home and her life.

Jane's story shows how micro-credit can be a crucial factor in increasing economic opportunities, particularly for women. When it's done well, it gives people the chance to make a living on a sustainable basis. Micro-credit could unleash the economic potential of hundreds of millions of the world's poorest people: and there are stories from countries on every continent showing how micro-credit, having enabled the birth of small businesses, has led to further development. For example, once enough people in a village are running a business, they can club together to pay for electricity supply for the first time. Micro-credit is no instant solution to global poverty, not by any means. It's not a substitute for a solidly-based economy of small, medium and larger businesses, an economy with entrenched property rights and a thriving enterprise culture. But micro-credit is a real and practical way of helping individuals and families quickly. It can be the first step on the road to development and prosperity.

There are now hundreds of thousands of micro-credit organizations operating all over the world. It's a fantastic example of business principles helping to deliver social progress, as Kofi Annan has explained: "Micro-credit is a critical anti-poverty tool – a wise investment in human capital. When the poorest, especially women, receive credit, they become economic actors with power. Power to improve not only their own lives but, in a widening circle of impact, the lives of their families, their communities, and their nations."[18] But micro-credit needs a number of things if the concept is to continue helping more and more people around the world. It needs more investment money, to provide the initial small loans. It needs champions, to encourage more people to see it as a way to alleviate poverty, and to mobilize support among rich nations and wealthy people. And it needs ongoing advice and support to help turn micro-businesses into sustainable small- and medium-sized companies. Isn't it more effective for corporations to support business development in this way, rather than simply handing over money for aid? And wouldn't anti-globalization campaigners welcome such an approach, and want to be part of it?

So here is a suitable social issue for our global white goods brand. If the corporate strategy is expressed as "development," what better way to illustrate that than becoming the global corporate champion of micro-credit? It would be truly distinctive branding territory, and a practical way to make a positive difference. It would immediately communicate the social dimension of the corporation's commercial purpose. What's more, constructing an effective campaign would be straightforward: there's a ready-made infrastructure which the company could work with. An organization based in Washington DC, the Micro-Credit Summit Campaign, acts as an umbrella organization for thousands of micro-finance lenders in the developing world. At a conference in 1998, with Hillary Rodham Clinton as the keynote speaker, it set itself the goal of reaching 100 million of the world's poorest families by 2005. As Mrs Clinton said: "Although it is called 'micro-credit', this is a macro idea ... with vast potential. Whether we are talking about a rural area in South Asia or an inner city in the United States, micro-credit is an invaluable tool in alleviating poverty, promoting self-sufficiency and stimulating economic activity in some of the world's most destitute and disadvantaged communities."[19]

By forming a global partnership with this organization, a corporation could directly raise millions of dollars which would be directed to grass roots projects identified by the Micro-Credit Summit Campaign members around the world. A donation could be made for every appliance sold by the company, with a sticker on each one informing customers about the brand's commitment to development and the practical contribution customers would be making by buying that brand's products. Further information could be provided which would enable customers to go beyond the donation they had made through their purchase, and join the campaign on an individual basis. Global advertising messages would promote not just the corporation's products, but the issue of development and the concept of micro-credit. It could start to change attitudes towards global poverty and our ability to tackle it. The corporation's employees could get involved: in every country where the company operates, local staff members could be linked with specific micro-businesses that had been started through the initiative, and free equipment and business expertise could be offered. The corporation could pioneer customer volunteering, using its contact with countless individuals around the world to mobilize action on poverty. And on a global level, the brand could become the lead sponsor of the Micro-Credit Summit Campaign, helping to spread the word about micro-finance and encouraging other companies and organizations to participate. At the same time, the company would be demonstrating its social credentials, and its brand strategy, to influential policy-makers and the media.

The key to making such a campaign a success would be for the corporation to embrace the idea enthusiastically, seeing it not as just another charity campaign, but as the primary means of articulating its corporate mission. There are plenty of similar, and similarly deserving charitable causes to which it could make a corporate donation, demonstrating an element of social responsibility. But corporate social leadership would come through using its various commercial levers, its marketing channels, its communications activity, its expertise, its employees, its customers, to turn this into a big idea and a big campaign. Leadership would mean getting consumers all over the world engaged in development issues. Addressing the issue in a traditional, quiet and small-scale way would have only a marginal effect. There would be little business or social benefit delivered if the company merely made the odd donation to a micro-credit fund. After all, there are plenty of companies already supporting micro-credit as part of their community investment or philanthropic activities – but who's ever heard of their support? And frankly, who in a mass market global audience has ever heard of micro-credit? Only by wholeheartedly adopting development as its social leadership campaign, and then focusing ruthlessly on this one cause, rather than dividing its attention on a range of worthy causes, would a corporation be able to make a notable difference – to its own business and to the world.

To be honest, if a corporation thought about an issue like this in conventional terms – donating some money, creating an internal staff volunteering campaign, issuing a few press releases in the hope of some "soft" media coverage, even running a one-off cause-related marketing promotion; the business benefit would be marginal, limited to a vague and intangible warm glow in certain parts of the organization. But if it decided to think differently and think big … if a corporation had the imagination and the courage to become the champion of development issues in general, and of micro-credit in particular, who knows what might happen? It could get the whole world talking about what it was doing. It could create a brand new platform for customer communications and loyalty programs. It could increase its market share. It could become the only company in its sector that bright graduates wanted to work for. It could show investors that it had a long-term vision and was a global force to be reckoned with. It could guarantee a fair hearing every time it wanted to talk about its many other activities in the social responsibility field. It could galvanize the entire workforce. It would be admired as an innovator. And it would increase the value of its most precious long-term asset, its reputation. The social benefit would be equally spectacular, bringing to the forefront of people's minds this practical and businesslike method of tackling poverty around the world. Imagine what could happen if every company thought like this when contemplating its corporate purpose and mission.

That's four ideas to get you going.

Now think of all the others: other social issues, other types of company, other ways in which business can be the ally of social progress. Think about a global diamond mining company that set itself the objective of clearing the world of landmines (thereby making its products more desirable and opening up new commercial exploration opportunities). Think about a restaurant chain that increased its sales by creating afternoon clubs for lonely senior citizens to meet, or for schoolchildren to do their homework. Think about a cell phone company that increased phone usage by linking customers to others in the local community who need company and conversation. Think about the airline that increased the desire to travel by helping people learn other languages, or by helping to restore the sight of people who can't see. The simple point is this: there are social and environmental issues that match the commercial strategies of every company. By approaching them from a social leadership perspective, rather than a philanthropic or social responsibility perspective, companies can make a more substantial difference to society, and achieve stronger business benefits in return. There's no need to invent new ideas for tackling social problems – the public and non-profit sectors are awash with creative thinking. What's needed is a revolution in the scale and type of corporate involvement, and the final chapter looks at some practical ways in which we could help bring that about.

7

Unity

Social responsibility. Socially responsible investing. Social leadership. Social marketing. Social reporting. Social auditing. It seems to be quite a thing, all this "social stuff." Lots of new socialists out there. And all of them capitalists.

But there aren't enough. Good business: your world needs you. And this is the section that readers who work in the marketing industry will recognize as the "next steps" chart in the Powerpoint presentation. In other words, the bit where you try to persuade the client to pay you some money to do something ... anything. We've tried to keep it short, and sweet, and simple (and we won't charge you extra). The aim is this: if you've been persuaded that business can profitably be a greater force for good in the world, we'd like to tell you what you can actually do about it. The suggestions are presented in four categories: what governments and policy-makers can do; what non-profit organizations can do; what citizens can do; and what company managers can do. We appreciate that everyone is a citizen, including government officials, charity workers and business leaders: but not every citizen falls into one of the other categories – and the truth is that all of you can play a part in promoting good business, whether or not you think you're in a position of organizational influence.

The good news for governments and policy-makers is that you don't have to do very much. Frankly, you've got enough to do:

running economies, providing local and national security, delivering welfare and public services, setting the rules for business ... you know the list. The real task for government is not to *do* much that is new or different, but to think in a new and different way. Various governments in the developed world are looking at "private–public partnerships" as a way of providing and improving public services. But the current debate is limited to the potential role of private corporations in building and running major infrastructure projects: railways, roads, schools, hospitals. This is not the place to debate the merits of this approach. The relevant point here is that there's an entirely different and additional dimension to the potential of private–public partnerships, and that is the ability of corporations to change social behavior, particularly through their trusted and ubiquitous consumer brands. As a policy-maker, when thinking about your various social challenges – how do we reduce teenage pregnancy? how do we increase volunteering? how do we encourage responsible car use? how do we promote healthy eating? how do we discourage criminal behavior? – think about working with corporations. You can tap into corporations' insights into the way people think and act, and harness corporations' ability to bring about change. Don't just see companies as an extra source of finance for public projects or an additional source of managerial expertise.

That's the general message: here are some practical observations.

First, in many countries, it's difficult for corporations, even those who want to help in this way, to determine exactly what they could do that would be most helpful. How about every government in the world creating a website that posted, in one sentence formats, each of the social behavior changes they wish to encourage? Corporations could take a look, and see which ones they could help with – and which ones fit their commercial strategy. There need be no formal and cumbersome connection; no need for contractual relationships. The process should be totally transparent. Just tell companies what you want done: with any luck, some of them will want to help do it. In addition, governments could follow the lead of the British Department for Education and Skills (which has established a Business Development Unit for this purpose) and set up specialist teams in each ministry to act as an interface with companies that want to help, simplifying the process and making sure that genuine social needs are met. Over time, we'll need to develop new rules for this new world; rules that assure the public that there's a level playing field, and that there's a strictly-enforced distinction between tackling social issues and corporate lobbying.

Second, how about every country that doesn't currently have one starting a version of the US Ad Council, an organization which brings together corporations, non-profits and media owners to create public service campaigns – for free? It's an immensely practical way of harnessing different sectoral talents in pursuit of social goals. (For more information, have a look at adcouncil.org.)

Third, it's important for local government to get in on this act. The model applies just as much on a small scale and at the local level with small, local businesses as it does on a grand scale with big, national and global businesses.

Finally, more needs to be done to highlight the fantastic work of social enterprise projects around the world. Many individual countries have individual award schemes, but they haven't created mass public awareness of the contribution social enterprise can make to tackling social problems. This suggestion isn't really one for governments, but since it doesn't fit anywhere else, it's going in here. Why isn't there a Nobel Prize for social entrepreneurs? After all, Alfred Nobel said in his will that his eponymous prizes should go to "those who, during the preceding year, shall have conferred the greatest benefit to mankind." If they can give one to an economist …

For the non-profit sector, there's even less that's new to do. Many of the best examples of innovative work in social policy are already being created by partnerships between non-profits and the private sector. For those non-profits that haven't got this message yet, it's a simple one: don't just ask corporations for money; ask them how they can help you achieve your mission. This applies with equal force to those non-profits and campaigners who specialize in anti-capitalism, who like to attack globalization. Keep

BISHOP BURTON COLLEGE
LIBRARY

up the pressure on exposing corporate wrong-doing, but be creative and open-minded about the potential for companies to help you change the world for the better.

Citizens: what can you do? Three things, actually.

As consumers, you can use your vote. Let's hear it for basket power. If you've got concerns about globalization, about corporate behavior, about the way that capitalism works, then don't just moan about it. Do something about it. Remember that capitalism is a good thing, that corporations create jobs and wealth; that they pay for public services and pay for pensions; that business is the only effective way to tackle world poverty. But equally, remember that without you, corporations are nothing. Ask questions, visit websites, take an interest in what you buy. And if you don't like the look of it, don't buy it. Why should companies change unless you tell them that you want them to change? If you keep on buying, how are they to interpret that, other than as a vote of approval? If you stop buying, they'll change soon enough. You can create a clamor for corporate social leadership. And support it when it happens. Take part in cause-related marketing campaigns, get involved in companies' social initiatives, write and tell them you support what they're doing.

As shareholders, you can use your vote too. You can invest in ethical funds. You can turn up to the annual meetings of companies you own shares in and ask about social and environmental performance. You can phone the investor relations people, send e-mails, write to the CEO. You can ask your pension company and your insurance company about where and how your money is invested. You can make a fuss. You can bring about change.

And citizens, listen to this. There's a third way you can change the world. As employees, you can change your company. It doesn't matter if you type the Annual Report or decide what goes in the Annual Report; it doesn't matter if you screw the pieces together or supervise the screwing – you can change your company, and help it to change the world. Ask to see a social audit, ask if someone can tell you about your company's social strategy, ask what social leadership activities are going on. Speak up and speak out, talk to your colleagues, challenge your boss. You won't be labeled a trouble-maker; these days, you'll be seen as smart. And when you get home at night and watch the news; when you come in every morning and read the paper, don't just shrug your shoulders at the state of the world. Think about ways you can use your work to do something about it. There's no need to leave your values at home. Be yourself. There's no job on the face of this earth that couldn't have a dual purpose, social as well as commercial.

So much for the workers. What about the bosses?

Business leaders have the most to do. The good news is, it'll be good for your business. You *can* help yourself by helping society. But you'll need to develop a new maturity in the way you operate in society: not afraid to take on a leadership role in those areas where you can bring about social change; comfortable in helping to tackle the serious issues that your customers and employees care about. Recognize the poverty of ambition in your current approach to corporate social responsibility. But please, don't take this as a criticism: take it as an inspiration to be more ambitious.

We know what you're thinking. "Never mind all this: show me the money." OK, let's cut to the chase. The simplest and quickest way of reaping financial rewards from all this "social stuff" is for Chief Executives to take it seriously. Really seriously. Not just saying it, but believing it. Not just signing up to it, but loving it.

For very good operational reasons, big corporations tend to be divided into functional units, with managers and budgets separated according to their specific tasks. The marketing director has a budget which needs to be spent on marketing; the production director has a budget that makes sure things are produced, and so on. Tucked away in there somewhere is usually a community affairs director or social responsibility director or some other similarly named executive, and they will have a budget which they spend on doing good things in the community, and checking up on everyone else's impact on society. The "social" budget is usually not a very large budget – at least not in comparison to the ones that are concerned with the company's main business activities – and very often, some or all of the budget is made over to a corporate foundation which in turn distributes the money to charities; alternatively, it's spent on social responsibility and community programs run in the corporation's name. As we've seen, many companies are making laudable attempts to ensure that their social responsibilities are more professionally managed; that their community budgets are spent better, that all this "social stuff" is more closely aligned with core business goals. But these attempts will ultimately be in vain without a new, holistic approach.

Here's what twenty-first century boards should do. First, understand what you're like. Find out what people like about you, as well as what they don't like. Don't commission bulging files of expensive research telling you what you suspected in the first place. The point is not to establish what people think of every aspect of your business, but how society feels about the whole. NGOs may criticize your production processes, but at the same time, your brands may be a trusted part of countless lives. What does this mean for a Chief Executive? Does it mean you should keep your head down till the NGOs are satisfied, or does it mean you should launch a new social campaign through your brands? It's inefficient to consider these questions in isolation. But that's exactly how they tend to be considered by big business. Most companies never aggregate the opinions that different groups hold; they separate them according to functional need. By assembling everyone's views in one place and at one time boards will be able to see what society thinks of their company, and how this affects their future ability to make money.

The next step is to think through what it means. There's a lesson to learn from the best political campaigns, which assess overall strengths and weaknesses and their impact on winning (or losing) votes. This type of analysis will tell boards what they need to do in order to win (and avoid losing) customers. Deal with the negatives? Emphasize the positives? When? In what order? In which places? On some issues, the answer will be to do nothing. On others, more action on social responsibility will be required. For others still, only a social leadership campaign will do the job.

The final step is to establish a clear plan of action. Everyone in the company plays a part in shaping society's view of the company, so everyone should be involved in the plan. It's no using leaving it to the marketing people, or the human resources people, or the corporate reputation people. All the people, all of the time, united by the company purpose which is based on the best thing society could think about you.

It's no use Chief Executives gnashing their teeth in the twelfth-floor office, bemoaning the fact that "we spend all this money on 'social stuff' but never seem to get any credit," while treating their company's social impact as just another department, with just another budget and just another executive in charge. That's like allocating a couple of hours a week, and an annual budget, to "love" in a marriage.

Chief Executives will need to have the guts to change the way they approach their company's impact on society. They'll need to simplify their corporate thinking in order to transform their social impact. Why? To avoid risks and to win support. Instead of having a social *department*, with a corresponding budget, the modern Chief Executive needs to have a social *strategy*, carried out by all departments. Then, two things will happen. First, social responsibility will be guaranteed: no more sleepless nights over unexploded bombs hidden in the corporate wiring; no more panic about potential boycotts and reputation risk. Second, social leadership will be achieved: delivered by the dual purpose that's found for everything the company does.

In parallel, corporations should develop a way to value their social contribution in financial terms. If it can be done for brands and included on balance sheets, it can be done for this. Such a valuation could cover everything from companies' direct economic impact: the taxes paid by their workers and the taxes corporations themselves pay; to the public sector costs saved by companies' social responsibility and social leadership programs.

Here's a simple test for every Chief Executive. Write down in one sentence your company's purpose. Does it capture your contribution to society? Do you have a social leadership program that uses every part of the corporate anatomy to bring that purpose alive? Could every employee and every customer tell you what it is?

Long ago, corporations learned the importance of focusing their visual identity and communications. The same logo, the same colors, the same type of messages. This type of consistency and single-minded focus is the only way to make an impact. The companies that succeed in the twenty-first century will be the ones that learn a similar lesson when it comes to corporate engagement in society. It's not really that radical. It's just putting into practice something that a great business leader said, many years ago. David Packard's words, the words with which we opened this book: "I want to discuss *why* a company exists in the first place. In other words, why are we here? I think many people assume, wrongly, that a company exists simply to make money. While this is an important result of a company's existence, we have to go deeper and find the real reasons for our being. As we investigate this, we inevitably come to the conclusion that a group of people get together and exist as an institution that we call a company so they are able to accomplish something collectively that they could not accomplish separately – they make a contribution to society, a phrase which sounds trite, but is fundamental."[1]

Social responsibility. Social leadership. Social marketing. Social reporting. Social auditing. All these social-ists; all of them capitalists.

This is why capitalism can become the anti-capitalist's ally.

Capitalists and anti-capitalists of the world, unite!

You have nothing to lose but your guilt.

"Risks"

(Origin unknown)

To laugh is to risk being a fool
To weep is to risk being sentimental
To reach out for another is to risk involvement
To show feelings is to risk showing yourself.

To place your ideas, your dreams
Before a crowd is to risk their loss
To love is to risk not being loved in return
To live is to risk dying
To hope is to risk despair
To try is to risk failure.

But risks must be taken because the greatest
hazard in life is to risk nothing
Those who risk nothing, do nothing, have nothing
and are nothing.

They may avoid suffering and sorrow
But they cannot learn, feel change,
Grow, love, live.

Chained by their certainties, they are slaves;
They have forfeited their freedom.
Only a person who risks ... is truly free.

Acknowledgements

Our agent, Tif Loehnis, was fantastic.

So was our editor, David Wilson.

Without Linda and Francis Whetstone, this book would never have been written.

Dom Loehnis and Maurice Saatchi provided invaluable comments on an early draft.

Dan Stilitz suggested the title for Chapter 1: thank you so much for your efforts.

Our colleagues at Good Business: thank you for helping to make our dream a reality.

Our Good Business clients: thank you for helping to make our dream a reality.

Maurice Saatchi gets a second mention. Without him and all the Saatchi people we would not only have no book, but no business.

Marjorie Thompson and the Commission for Racial Equality provided the inspiration for our ideas, and the motivation to put them into practice.

So many people have taught us about the potential for business to make the world a better place. In particular we'd like to thank Business in the Community, David Robinson at Community Links, and Andrew Mawson and Adele Blakebrough at the Community Action Network.

We apologize to anyone we've overlooked.

Notes

Orthodoxy

1. *Financial Times*, Special Report, 11th September, 2001
2. Klein, Naomi, *No Logo* (Flamingo, 2000), p.446
3. Monbiot, George, *Captive State* (Macmillan, 2000), p.17
4. Hertz, Noreena, *The Silent Takeover* (Heinemann, 2001), p.212
5. *The Observer*, 16th September, 2001
6. Frank, Thomas, *One Market Under God* (Secker & Warburg, 2001)
7. Klein, *No Logo*, p.266
8. *Financial Times*, Weekend, 20th/21st October, 2001
9. Coyle, Diane, *Paradoxes of Prosperity* (TEXERE, 2001), p.174
10. Frank, *One Market Under God*, p.49
11. Ibid
12. Tony Blair, speech to Labour Party Conference, 2nd October, 2001
13. *The Guardian*, 15th September, 2001

Heresy

1. Moore, Stephen and Simon, Julian Lincoln, *It's Getting Better All the Time* (Cato Institute, 2000), p.58
2. Ibid, p.62
3. Ibid, p.27
4. Norberg, Johan, *In Defence of Global Capitalism* (Timbro 2001), p.64 and 93

5. Ibid, p.26

6. Ibid, p.45

7. Ibid, pp.47–48

8. Ibid, p.28

9. Ibid, p.34

10. Ibid, p.43

11. Ibid, p.25

12. Ibid, p.26

13. Ibid, p.71

14. Ibid, p.25

15. Ibid, p.52

16. Ibid, p.146

17. Ibid, p.102

18. Ibid, p.102

19. Ibid, p.99

20. Ibid, p.103

21. Gwartney, James, Lawson, Robert and Block, Walter, *Economic Freedom of the World* (The Fraser Institute), p.xxviii

22. Norberg, *In Defence of Global Capitalism*, p.146

23. Newfarmer, Richard *et al.*, *Global Economic Prospects and the Developing Countries 2002: Making Trade Work for the World's Poor*, World Bank, October 2001

24. Norberg, *In Defence of Global Capitalism,* p.151

25. Ibid, p.37

26. *Index of Economic Freedom*, Heritage Foundation and the *Wall Street Journal* (2001), p.25

27. Norberg, *In Defence of Global Capitalism,* p.161

28. Coyle, Diane, *Paradoxes of Prosperity* (TEXERE, 2001), p.62

29. *New York Times*, 22nd June, 1997

30. Norberg, *In Defence of Global Capitalism*, p.187

31. Ibid, p.187

32. Baron Mitri, Liberty Institute Briefing Paper on Trade Development, New Delhi, November, 1999

33. Norberg, *In Defence of Global Capitalism*, p.181

34. *The Guardian*, 13th October, 2001

35. Moore and Simon, *It's Getting Better All the Time*, p.70

36. Hertz, Noreena, *The Silent Takeover* (Heinemann, 2001), p.7
37. Norberg, *In Defence of Global Capitalism*, p.200/201
38. *The Guardian*, 6th November, 2001
39. Ibid
40. *Financial Times*, 26th September, 2000

Responsibility

1. Roddick, Anita, *Take It Personally* (Thorsons, 2001), p.173
2. For a full picture of B&Q's corporate social responsibility visit diy.com and click on "About B&Q" or order B&Q publications such as *Being a Better Trading Neighbor*, and *How Green is My Patio?*
3. Quoted in *Ethical Corporation* magazine, Issue 1, December, 2001, p.7
4. Hertz, Noreena, *The Silent Takeover* (Heinemann, 2001), pp.193–194
5. Klein, Naomi, *No Logo*, (Flamingo, 2000), p.434
6. Both sides accept this version of events
7. *The Guardian*, 31st July, 2001
8. Friedman, Milton, *Capitalism and Freedom* (University of Chicago Press, 1962 and 1982) and "The Social Responsibility of Business Is To Increase Its Profits", reprinted in Beauchamp, T. and Bowie, N. (eds), *Ethical Theory and Business* (Prentice Hall, 1988)
9. *Financial Times*, 5th October, 2001, p.15
10. *People's Palace*, London, 28th February, 1998
11. UN Global compact website: unglobalcompact.org
12. *Ethical Performance*, Vol. 3, Issue 4, September 2001
13. Ibid
14. Net Impact Website: netimpact.org
15. *Ethical Performance*, Vol. 3, Issue 5, October 2001
16. Ethical Trading Initiative promotional leaflet
17. The World Commission on Environment and Development (Brundlandt Report): *Our Common Future* (Oxford University

Press, 1987)

18. UBS Warburg, Global Equity Research, report on Sustainability Investment, August, 2001

19. Ibid

20. *Financial Times*, letters, 14th July, 2001

21. For an up-to-date selection, see bitc.org; see also the Millennium Poll on Corporate Social Responsibility, available on pwcglobal.com and for a usefully skeptical review of such data, see Conversations with Disbelievers, available on zadek.net

22. Ibid

23. Ibid

24. Grayson, David and Hodges, Adrian, *Everybody's Business* (Dorling Kindersley, 2001), p.227

25. See mori.com, or To Whose Profit? – Building a Business Case for Sustainability (Cable & Wireless and the WWF, 2002)

26. de Geus, Arie, *The Living Company* (Nicholas Brealey, 1999)

27. Collins, James and Porras, Jerry, *Built to Last: Successful Habits of Visionary Companies* (Random House Business Books, 1994)

28. UBS Warburg, Global Equity Research, report on Sustainability Investment, August 2001; or for a good introduction to socially responsible investing visit socialinvest.org

29. Ibid

30. Ibid

31. Roddick, Anita, *Business as Unusual* (Thorsons, 2000), p.66

32. Pringle, Hamish and Thompson, Marjorie, *Brand Spirit* (John Wiley & Sons, 2001), p.237

33. Rockefeller Plaza, NYC

34. Roddick, *Business as Unusual*, p.66

35. Grayson, David and Hodges, Adrian, *Everybody's Business* (Dorling Kindersley, 2001)

36. Ibid, p.32

37. *The Guardian*, 27th August, 2001

38. *Corporate Spin: The Troubled Teenage Years of Corporate Social Reporting* (New Economics Foundation, 2000)

39. Grayson and Hodges, *Everybody's Business*, p.298

Leadership

1. bp "Helios Awards" promotional leaflet
2. *Marketing Magazine*, 22nd November, 2001
3. Good Business Ltd interview with BT executive
4. *The Guardian*, 31st July, 2001
5. Roddick, Anita, *Take It Personally* (Thorsons, 2001), p.56
6. Henderson, David, *Misguided Virtue: False Notions of Corporate Social Responsibility* (Institute of Economic Affairs, 2001) Hobart Paper No. 142, 5th November, p.150
7. *Ethical Performance*, November 2001
8. Schlosser, Eric, *Fast Food Nation* (Penguin, 2001), p.267
9. Roddick, *Take It Personally*, p.56
10. Ibid, p.89

Anatomy

1. Marx, Karl and Engels, Friedrich, *The Communist Manifesto* (Penguin, 1967), p.113
2. Ibid, p.69, (Engels, Friedrich, *Preface to the German Edition of 1890*)
3. *The Economist,* 8th September, 2001
4. *Marketing,* 13th September, 2001
5. See superbrands.org/research; The Henley Centre report, Planning for Social Change, and roar.org.uk
6. See coca-cola.co.uk/valuedyouth for more details
7. Young Voice/University of Oxford, *An Evaluation of Reach for the Sky*
8. National Foundation for Educational Research (1999), *The Impact of Careers Education and Guidance on Transition at 16*
9. Watson, D. and Bowden, R., *After Dearing: A Mid-term Report* (University of Brighton Education Research Centre, 2000)
10. The Industrial Society, *The Learning Agenda*, 1999
11. Good Business Ltd interview
12. Young Voice/University of Oxford, op.cit., using criteria from

Christophers, U., Stoney, S., Whetton, C., Lines, A. and Kendall, L., *Measurement of Guidance Impact* (NFER, 1993)

13. Good Business Ltd interview
14. Good Business Ltd interview
15. Good Business Ltd interview
16. For further information see laureus.com
17. Good Business Ltd interview
18. *The Guardian*, 1st December, 2001
19. Good Business Ltd interview
20. For further information see ericsson.com/ericssonresponse
21. The Giving List 2001, *The Guardian*, 5th November, 2001, p.20
22. See Blatchford, Peter, *Social Life in School – Pupils' Experiences of Breaktime and Recess from 7–16 years* (Falmer Press, 1998); Blatchford, Peter and Sharp, Sonia (eds), *Breaktime and the School: Understanding and Changing Playground Behaviour* (Routledge, 1994)
23. Carol Ross and Amanda Ryan in Blatchford and Sharp, op.cit.
24. Cullingford, Cedric, *The Causes of Exclusion – Home, School and the Development of Young Criminals* (Kogan Page, 1999)
25. *The Observer*, 4th November, 2001
26. Kelly, Elinor, *Racism and Sexism in the Playground* in Blatchford and Sharp, op.cit.
27. See Liza Featherstone and Doug Henwood, *Clothes Encounters: Activists and Economists Clash Over Sweatshops* (Lingua Franca, Vol.11, March, 2001)
28. See theglobalalliance.org for these and other surveys
29. Lukas, Aaron, *Globalisation and Developing Countries* (Cato Institute, 2000), WTO Report Card 3, Trade Briefing Paper
30. See youthsport.net for a full survey of its activities
31. Kelly, op.cit.
32. Interview on Channel 4 News, 18th July, 2001
33. Ibid
34. Andreasen, Alan R, *Marketing Social Change* (Jossey-Bass, 1995)
35. See bitc.org.uk for full case study

36. See peres-center.org for more information
37. For USA, see citycares.org; for UK see careinc.org
38. See timebank.org.uk
39. See mediatrust.org
40. Case study from *Accountability Quarterly*, Issue 16, Q2 2001, p.32; or visit cisco.com
41. See www.can-online.org
42. See percent.org.uk
43. The Giving List 2001, *The Guardian*, p.17
44. Ibid, p.6
45. Ibid, p.31
46. For example, venturephilanthropypartners.org
47. Charles Leadbeater, *The Rise of the Social Entrepreneur*, available from Demos
48. To see how this pioneering company puts social leadership into practice, see the Co-operative Bank's *Partnership Reports*, which can be accessed from the website co-operativebank.co.uk
49. For further information and to glimpse the broad range of Levi Strauss social programs see levistrauss.com/responsibility
50. Case study from *Ethical Performance* magazine, Volume 3, Issue 1, May, 2001
51. Ibid
52. See diageo.com, corporate citizenship section
53. To read the Taskforce report, and up-to-date progress reports, visit enterprising-communities.org.uk
54. These and other relevant research findings at crm.org.uk
55. *The Guardian*, 20th November, 2001, G2 p.11
56. See interfaceinc.com for an inspiring survey of the company's commitment to "doing well by doing good"
57. For an eye-opening insight into the depth of thinking Ford has put into this subject, visit ford.com and go to the pages on "environmental initiatives" and "corporate citizenship"
58. Contact the Chartered Institute of Marketing for more information at cim.co.uk
59. See Leonard-cheshire.org for a survey of the charity's work

Possibility

1. Reported in *Marketing Week*, 8th November, 2001
2. Ibid
3. Prince of Wales Business Leaders Forum, International Alert, Council on Economic Priorities, *The Business of Peace* (2000)
4. cnnsi.com/olympics/2002/11/27/bush_olympics_ap
5. From International Olympic Truce Foundation promotional materials; see olympictruce.org for more details
6. Prince of Wales Business Leaders Forum, International Alert, Council on Economic Priorities, *The Business of Peace* (2000), Executive Summary
7. Although the picture is a little more complex than this. For a comprehensive historical survey of global voter turnout, see idea.int/voter_turnout
8. *The Guardian*, 13th October, 2001
9. See who.int/whr/2001
10. Ibid
11. *The Observer*, Life, 21st October, 2001
12. Ibid
13. Ibid
14. Ibid
15. See grameen.com for a full history and overview of Grameen Bank's activities
16. Ibid
17. Micro-Credit Summit Campaign promotional brochure; see microcreditsummit.org for more information
18. Ibid
19. Ibid

Unity

1. David Packard, speech to employees (1960), Hewlett-Packard company archives, quoted in Collins, James and Porras, Jerry, *Built to Last: Successful Habits of Visionary Companies* (Random House Business Books, 1994)

Index

About TEXERE

TEXERE seeks to become the most progressive and authoritative voice in business publishing by cultivating and enhancing ideas that will illuminate the global business landscape. Our name defines the spirit of our vision: TEXERE is the ancient Latin verb "to weave." In an increasingly global business community, we seek to create an intersection where authors and readers can share the best thinking and the latest ideas. We want to leverage the expertise and insights of leading thinkers by weaving them with TEXERE's capability to deliver them to the marketplace.

To learn more and become a part of our community visit us at:

www.etexere.com

and

www.etexere.co.uk

About the Typeface

This book was set in 10.5/15 Stone Sans. Sumner Stone completed his designs for the Stone type family in 1987. The Stone family consists of three subfamilies, Serif, Sans, and Informal, each consisting of three weights plus matching italics. Unlike most type families – which often fail to work well together on the same page – the Stone types have been designed so that they can be mixed successfully with each other.